M

Night
Dawn
The Accident

by ELIE WIESEL

Night
Dawn
The Accident
The Town Beyond the Wall
The Gates of the Forest
The Jews of Silence
Legends of Our Time
A Beggar in Jerusalem
One Generation After
Souls on Fire

Night
Dawn
The Accident
THREE TALES

by ELIE WIESEL

HILL AND **WANG**   NEW YORK
A DIVISION OF FARRAR, STRAUS AND GIROUX

F
WIESEL

Night

Foreword by FRANÇOIS MAURIAC

Translated from the French
by STELLA RODWAY

*In memory of
my parents and of my little sister,
Tzipora*

Foreword

BY FRANÇOIS MAURIAC

Foreign journalists often come to see me. I dread their visits, being torn between a desire to reveal everything in my mind and a fear of putting weapons into the hands of an interviewer when I know nothing about his own attitude toward France. I am always careful during encounters of this kind.

That morning, the young Israeli who came to interview me for a Tel Aviv paper immediately won my sympathy, and our conversation very quickly took a personal turn. It led me to recall memories of the Occupation. It is not always the events we have been directly involved in that affect us the most. I confided to my young visitor that nothing I had seen during those somber years had left so deep a mark upon me as those trainloads of Jewish children standing at Austerlitz station. Yet I did not even see them myself! My wife described them to me, her voice still filled with horror. At that time we knew

7

nothing of Nazi methods of extermination. And who could have imagined them! Yet the way these lambs had been torn from their mothers in itself exceeded anything we had so far thought possible. I believe that on that day I touched for the first time upon the mystery of iniquity whose revelation was to mark the end of one era and the beginning of another. The dream which Western man conceived in the eighteenth century, whose dawn he thought he saw in 1789, and which, until August 2, 1914, had grown stronger with the progress of enlightenment and the discoveries of science—this dream vanished finally for me before those trainloads of little children. And yet I was still thousands of miles away from thinking that they were to be fuel for the gas chamber and the crematory.

This, then, was what I had to tell the young journalist. And when I said, with a sigh, "How often I've thought about those children!" he replied, "I was one of them." He was one of them. He had seen his mother, a beloved little sister, and all his family except his father disappear into an oven fed with living creatures. As for his father, the child was forced to be a spectator day after day to his martyrdom, his agony, and his death. And such a death! The circumstances of it are related in this book, and I will leave the discovery of them and of the miracle by which the child himself escaped to its readers, who should be as numerous as those of The Diary of Anne Frank.

What I maintain is that this personal record, coming after so many others and describing an outrage about which we might imagine we already know all that it is possible to know, is nevertheless different, distinct, unique. The fate of the Jews of the little Transylvanian town called Sighet, their blindness in the face of a destiny from which they would still have had time to flee; the inconceivable passivity with which

*they gave themselves up to it, deaf to the warnings and pleas
of a witness who had himself escaped the massacre, and who
brought them news of what he had seen with his own eyes;
their refusal to believe him, taking him for a madman—these
circumstances, it seems to me, would in themselves be sufficient
to inspire a book to which no other could be compared.*

*It is, however, another aspect of this extraordinary book
which has engaged me most deeply. The child who tells us
his story here was one of God's elect. From the time when his
conscience first awoke, he had lived only for God and had
been reared on the Talmud, aspiring to initiation into the
cabbala, dedicated to the Eternal. Have we ever thought
about the consequence of a horror that, though less apparent,
less striking than the other outrages, is yet the worst of all to
those of us who have faith: the death of God in the soul of a
child who suddenly discovers absolute evil?*

*Let us try to imagine what passed within him while his
eyes watched the coils of black smoke unfurling in the sky,
from the oven where his little sister and his mother were going
to be thrown with thousands of others: "Never shall I forget
that night, the first night in camp, which has turned my life
into one long night, seven times cursed and seven times sealed.
Never shall I forget that smoke. Never shall I forget the little
faces of the children, whose bodies I saw turned into wreaths
of smoke beneath a silent blue sky. Never shall I forget those
flames which consumed my Faith forever. Never shall I forget
that nocturnal silence which deprived me, for all eternity, of
the desire to live. Never shall I forget those moments which
murdered my God and my soul and turned my dreams to dust.
Never shall I forget these things, even if I am condemned to
live as long as God Himself. Never."*

It was then that I understood what had first drawn me to

the young Israeli: that look, as of a Lazarus risen from the dead, yet still a prisoner within the grim confines where he had strayed, stumbling among the shameful corpses. For him, Nietzsche's cry expressed an almost physical reality: God is dead, the God of love, of gentleness, of comfort, the God of Abraham, of Isaac, of Jacob, has vanished forevermore, beneath the gaze of this child, in the smoke of a human holocaust exacted by Race, the most voracious of all idols. And how many pious Jews have experienced this death! On that day, horrible even among those days of horror, when the child watched the hanging (yes!) of another child, who, he tells us, had the face of a sad angel, he heard someone behind him groan: " 'Where is God? Where is He? Where can He be now?' and a voice within me answered: 'Where? Here He is—He has been hanged here, on these gallows.' "

On the last day of the Jewish year, the child was present at the solemn ceremony of Rosh Hashanah. He heard thousands of these slaves cry with one voice: "Blessed be the name of the Eternal." Not so long before, he too would have prostrated himself, and with such adoration, such awe, such love! But on this day he did not kneel. The human creature, outraged and humiliated beyond all that heart and spirit can conceive of, defied a divinity who was blind and deaf. "That day, I had ceased to plead. I was no longer capable of lamentation. On the contrary, I felt very strong. I was the accuser, and God the accused. My eyes were open and I was alone— terribly alone in a world without God and without man. Without love or mercy. I had ceased to be anything but ashes, yet I felt myself to be stronger than the Almighty, to whom my life had been tied for so long. I stood amid that praying congregation, observing it like a stranger."

And I, who believe that God is love, what answer could I

give my young questioner, whose dark eyes still held the reflection of that angelic sadness which had appeared one day upon the face of the hanged child? What did I say to him? Did I speak of that other Israeli, his brother, who may have resembled him—the Crucified, whose Cross has conquered the world? Did I affirm that the stumbling block to his faith was the cornerstone of mine, and that the conformity between the Cross and the suffering of men was in my eyes the key to that impenetrable mystery whereon the faith of his childhood had perished? Zion, however, has risen up again from the crematories and the charnel houses. The Jewish nation has been resurrected from among its thousands of dead. It is through them that it lives again. We do not know the worth of one single drop of blood, one single tear. All is grace. If the Eternal is the Eternal, the last word for each one of us belongs to Him. This is what I should have told this Jewish child. But I could only embrace him, weeping.

They called him Moché the Beadle, as though he had never had a surname in his life. He was a man of all work at a Hasidic synagogue. The Jews of Sighet—that little town in Transylvania where I spent my childhood—were very fond of him. He was very poor and lived humbly. Generally my fellow townspeople, though they would help the poor, were not particularly fond of them. Moché the Beadle was the exception. Nobody ever felt embarrassed by him. Nobody ever felt encumbered by his presence. He was a past master in the art of making himself insignificant, of seeming invisible.

Physically he was as awkward as a clown. He made people smile, with his waiflike timidity. I loved his great, dreaming eyes, their gaze lost in the distance. He spoke little. He used to sing, or, rather, to chant. Such snatches as you could hear told of the suffering of the divinity, of the Exile of Providence, who, according to the cabbala, awaits his deliverance in that of man.

I got to know him toward the end of 1941. I was twelve. I believed profoundly. During the day I studied the Talmud, and at night I ran to the synagogue to weep over the destruction of the Temple.

One day I asked my father to find me a master to guide me in my studies of the cabbala.

"You're too young for that. Maimonides said it was only at thirty that one had the right to venture into the perilous world of mysticism. You must first study the basic subjects within your own understanding."

My father was a cultured, rather unsentimental man. There was never any display of emotion, even at home. He was more concerned with others than with his own family. The Jewish community in Sighet held him in the greatest esteem. They often used to consult him about public matters and even about private ones. There were four of us children: Hilda, the eldest; then Béa; I was the third, and the only son; the baby of the family was Tzipora.

My parents ran a shop. Hilda and Béa helped them with the work. As for me, they said my place was at school.

"There aren't any cabbalists at Sighet," my father would repeat.

He wanted to drive the notion out of my head. But it was in vain. I found a master for myself, Moché the Beadle.

He had noticed me one day at dusk, when I was praying.

"Why do you weep when you pray?" he asked me, as though he had known me a long time.

"I don't know why," I answered, greatly disturbed.

The question had never entered my head. I wept because—because of something inside me that felt the need for tears. That was all I knew.

"Why do you pray?" he asked me, after a moment.

Why did I pray? A strange question. Why did I live? Why did I breathe?

"I don't know why," I said, even more distrubed and ill at ease. "I don't know why."

After that day I saw him often. He explained to me

with great insistence that every question possessed a power that did not lie in the answer.

"Man raises himself toward God by the questions he asks Him," he was fond of repeating. "That is the true dialogue. Man questions God and God answers. But we don't understand His answers. We can't understand them. Because they come from the depths of the soul, and they stay there until death. You will find the true answers, Eliezer, only within yourself!"

"And why do you pray, Moché?" I asked him.

"I pray to the God within me that He will give me the strength to ask Him the right questions."

We talked like this nearly every evening. We used to stay in the synagogue after all the faithful had left, sitting in the gloom, where a few half-burned candles still gave a flickering light.

One evening I told him how unhappy I was because I could not find a master in Sighet to instruct me in the Zohar, the cabbalistic books, the secrets of Jewish mysticism. He smiled indulgently. After a long silence, he said:

"There are a thousand and one gates leading into the orchard of mystical truth. Every human being has his own gate. We must never make the mistake of wanting to enter the orchard by any gate but our own. To do this is dangerous for the one who enters and also for those who are already there."

And Moché the Beadle, the poor barefoot of Sighet, talked to me for long hours of the revelations and mysteries of the cabbala. It was with him that my initiation began. We would read together, ten times over, the same page of the Zohar. Not to learn it by heart, but to extract the divine essence from it.

And throughout those evenings a conviction grew in me that Moché the Beadle would draw me with him into eternity, into that time where question and answer would become *one*.

Then one day they expelled all the foreign Jews from Sighet. And Moché the Beadle was a foreigner.

Crammed into cattle trains by Hungarian police, they wept bitterly. We stood on the platform and wept too. The train disappeared on the horizon; it left nothing behind but its thick, dirty smoke.

I heard a Jew behind me heave a sigh.

"What can we expect?" he said. "It's war. . . ."

The deportees were soon forgotten. A few days after they had gone, people were saying that they had arrived in Galicia, were working there, and were even satisfied with their lot.

Several days passed. Several weeks. Several months. Life had returned to normal. A wind of calmness and reassurance blew through our houses. The traders were doing good business, the students lived buried in their books, and the children played in the streets.

One day, as I was just going into the synagogue, I saw, sitting on a bench near the door, Moché the Beadle.

He told his story and that of his companions. The train full of deportees had crossed the Hungarian frontier and on Polish territory had been taken in charge by the Gestapo. There it had stopped. The Jews had to get out and climb into lorries. The lorries drove toward a forest. The Jews were made to get out. They were made to dig huge graves. And when they had finished their work, the Gestapo began theirs. Without passion, without haste, they slaughtered their prisoners. Each one had to go up to the hole and present his neck. Babies were thrown into the air and the machine gunners used them as targets. This was in the forest of Galicia, near Kolomaye. How had Moché the Beadle escaped? Miraculously. He was wounded in the leg and taken for dead. . . .

Through long days and nights, he went from one Jewish house to another, telling the story of Malka, the young girl who had taken three days to die, and of Tobias, the tailor, who had begged to be killed before his sons. . . .

16

Moché had changed. There was no longer any joy in his eyes. He no longer sang. He no longer talked to me of God or the cabbala, but only of what he had seen. People refused not only to believe his stories, but even to listen to them.

"He's just trying to make us pity him. What an imagination he has!" they said. Or even: "Poor fellow. He's gone mad."

And as for Moché, he wept.

"Jews, listen to me. It's all I ask of you. I don't want money or pity. Only listen to me," he would cry between prayers at dusk and the evening prayers.

I did not believe him myself. I would often sit with him in the evening after the service, listening to his stories and trying my hardest to understand his grief. I felt only pity for him.

"They take me for a madman," he would whisper, and tears, like drops of wax, flowed from his eyes.

Once, I asked him this question:

"Why are you so anxious that people should believe what you say. In your place, I shouldn't care whether they believed me or not. . . ."

He closed his eyes, as though to escape time.

"You don't understand," he said in despair. "You can't understand. I have been saved miraculously. I managed to get back here. Where did I get the strength from? I wanted to come back to Sighet to tell you the story of my death. So that you could prepare yourselves while there was still time. To live? I don't attach my importance to my life any more. I'm alone. No, I wanted to come back, and to warn you. And see how it is, no one will listen to me. . . ."

That was toward the end of 1942. Afterward life returned to normal. The London radio, which we listened to every evening, gave us heartening news: the daily bombardment of Germany; Stalingrad; preparation for the second front. And we, the Jews of Sighet, were waiting for better days, which would not be long in coming now.

I continued to devote myself to my studies. By day, the Talmud, at night, the cabbala. My father was occupied with his business and the doings of the community. My grandfather had come to celebrate the New Year with us, so that he could attend the services of the famous rabbi of Borsche. My mother began to think that it was high time to find a suitable young man for Hilda.

Thus the year 1943 passed by.

Spring 1944. Good news from the Russian front. No doubt could remain now of Germany's defeat. It was only a question of time—of months or weeks perhaps.

The trees were in blossom. This was a year like any other, with its springtime, its betrothals, its weddings and births.

People said: "The Russian army's making gigantic strides forward . . . Hitler won't be able to do us any harm, even if he wants to."

Yes, we even doubted that he wanted to exterminate us.

Was he going to wipe out a whole people? Could he exterminate a population scattered throughout so many countries? So many millions! What methods could he use? And in the middle of the twentieth century!

Besides, people were interested in everything—in strategy, in diplomacy, in politics, in Zionism—but not in their own fate.

Even Moché the Beadle was silent. He was weary of speaking. He wandered in the synagogue or in the streets, with his eyes down, his back bent, avoiding people's eyes.

At that time, it was still possible to obtain emigration permits for Palestine. I had asked my father to sell out, liquidate his business, and leave.

"I'm too old, my son," he replied. "I'm too old to start a new life. I'm too old to start from scratch again in a country so far away. . . ."

The Budapest radio announced that the Fascist party had come into power. Horthy had been forced to ask one of the leaders of the Nyilas party to form a new government.

Still this was not enough to worry us. Of course we had heard about the Fascists, but they were still just an abstraction to us. This was only a change in the administration.

The following day, there was more disturbing news: with government permission, German troops had entered Hungarian territory.

Here and there, anxiety was aroused. One of our friends, Berkovitz, who had just returned from the capital, told us:

"The Jews in Budapest are living in an atmosphere of fear and terror. There are anti-Semitic incidents every day, in the streets, in the trains. The Fascists are attacking Jewish shops and synagogues. The situation is getting very serious."

This news spread like wildfire through Sighet. Soon it was on everyone's lips. But not for long. Optimism soon revived.

"The Germans won't get as far as this. They'll stay in Budapest. There are strategic and political reasons. . . ."

Before three days had passed, German army cars had appeared in our streets.

Anguish. German soldiers—with their steel helmets, and their emblem, the death's head.

However, our first impressions of the Germans were most reassuring. The officers were billeted in private houses, even in the homes of Jews. Their attitude toward their hosts was distant, but polite. They never demanded the impossible, made no unpleasant comments, and even smiled occasionally at the mistress of the house. One German officer lived in the house opposite ours. He had a room with the Kahn family. They said he was a charming man—calm, likable, polite, and sympathetic. Three days after he moved in he brought Madame Kahn a box of chocolates. The optimists rejoiced.

"Well, there you are, you see! What did we tell you? You wouldn't believe us. There they are *your* Germans! What do you think of them? Where is their famous cruelty?"

The Germans were already in the town, the Fascists were already in power, the verdict had already been pronounced, yet the Jews of Sighet continued to smile.

The week of Passover. The weather was wonderful. My mother bustled round her kitchen. There were no longer any synagogues open. We gathered in private houses: the Germans were not to be provoked. Practically every rabbi's flat became a house of prayer.

We drank, we ate, we sang. The Bible bade us rejoice during the seven days of the feast, to be happy. But our hearts were not in it. Our hearts had been beating more rapidly for some days. We wished the feast were over, so that we should not have to play this comedy any longer.

On the seventh day of Passover the curtain rose. The Germans arrested the leaders of the Jewish community.

From that moment, everything happened very quickly. The race toward death had begun.

The first step: Jews would not be allowed to leave their houses for three days—on pain of death.

Moché the Beadle came running to our house.

"I warned you," he cried to my father. And, without waiting for a reply, he fled.

That same day the Hungarian police burst into all the Jewish houses in the street. A Jew no longer had the right to keep in his house gold, jewels, or any objects of value. Everything had to be handed over to the authorities—on pain of death. My father went down into the cellar and buried our savings.

At home, my mother continued to busy herself with her usual tasks. At times she would pause and gaze at us, silent.

When the three days were up, there was a new decree: every Jew must wear the yellow star.

Some of the prominent members of the community came to see my father—who had highly placed connections in the Hungarian police—to ask him what he thought of the situation. My father did not consider it so grim—but perhaps he did not want to dishearten the others or rub salt in their wounds:

"The yellow star? Oh well, what of it? You don't die of it. . . ."

(Poor Father! Of what then did you die?)

But already they were issuing new decrees. We were no longer allowed to go into restaurants or cafés, to travel on the railway, to attend the synagogue, to go out into the street after six o'clock.

Then came the ghetto.

Two ghettos were set up in Sighet. A large one, in the center of the town, occupied four streets, and another smaller one extended over several small side streets in the outlying district. The street where we lived, Serpent Street, was inside the first ghetto. We still lived, therefore, in our own house. But as it was at the corner, the windows facing the outside street had to be blocked up. We gave up some of our rooms to relatives who had been driven out of their flats.

Little by little life returned to normal. The barbed wire which fenced us in did not cause us any real fear. We even thought ourselves rather well off; we were entirely self-contained. A little Jewish republic. . . . We appointed a Jewish Council, a Jewish police, an office for social assistance, a labor committee, a hygiene department—a whole government machinery.

Everyone marveled at it. We should no longer have before our eyes those hostile faces, those hate-laden stares. Our fear and anguish were at an end. We were living among Jews, among brothers. . . .

Of course, there were still some unpleasant moments. Every day the Germans came to fetch men to stoke coal on the military trains. There were not many volunteers for work of this kind. But apart from that the atmosphere was peaceful and reassuring.

The general opinion was that we were going to remain in the ghetto until the end of the war, until the arrival of the Red Army. Then everything would be as before. It was neither German nor Jew who ruled the ghetto—it was illusion.

On the Saturday before Pentecost, in the spring sunshine, people strolled, carefree and unheeding, through the swarming streets. They chatted happily. The children played games on the pavements. With some of my schoolmates, I sat in the Ezra Malik gardens, studying a treatise on the Talmud.

Night fell. There were twenty people gathered in our back yard. My father was telling them anecdotes and expounding his own views on the situation. He was a good story teller.

Suddenly the gate opened and Stern—a former tradesman who had become a policeman—came in and took my father aside. Despite the gathering dusk, I saw my father turn pale.

"What's the matter?" we all asked him.

"I don't know. I've been summoned to an extraordinary meeting of the council. Something must have happened."

The good story he had been in the middle of telling us was to remain unfinished.

"I'm going there," he went on. "I shall be back as soon as I can. I'll tell you all about it. Wait for me."

We were prepared to wait for some hours. The back yard became like the hall outside an operating room. We were only waiting for the door to open—to see the opening of the firmament itself. Other neighbors, having heard rumors, had come to join us. People looked at their watches. The time passed very slowly. What could such a long meeting mean?

"I've got a premonition of evil," said my mother. "This afternoon I noticed some new faces in the ghetto—two German officers, from the Gestapo, I believe. Since we've been here, not a single officer has ever shown himself. . . ."

It was nearly midnight. No one had wanted to go to bed. A few people had paid a flying visit to their homes to see that everything was all right. Others had returned home, but they left instructions that they were to be told as soon as my father came back.

At last the door opened and he appeared. He was pale. At once he was surrounded.

"What happened? Tell us what happened! Say something!"

How avid we were at that moment for one word of confidence, one sentence to say that there were no grounds for fear, that the meeting could not have been more commonplace, more routine, that it had only been a question of social welfare, of sanitary arrangements! But one glance at my father's haggard face was enough.

"I have terrible news," he said at last. "Deportation."

The ghetto was to be completely wiped out. We were to leave street by street, starting the following day.

We wanted to know everything, all the details. The news had stunned everyone, yet we wanted to drain the bitter draft to the dregs.

"Where are we being taken?"

This was a secret. A secret from all except one: the President of the Jewish Council. But he would not say; he *could* not say. The Gestapo had threatened to shoot him if he talked.

"There are rumors going around," said my father in a broken voice, "that we're going somewhere in Hungary, to work in the brick factories. Apparently, the reason is that the front is too close here. . . ."

And, after a moment's silence, he added:

"Each person will be allowed to take only his own personal belongings. A bag on our backs, some food, a few clothes. Nothing else."

Again a heavy silence.

"Go and wake the neighbors up," said my father. "So that they can get ready."

The shadows beside me awoke as from a long sleep. They fled, silently, in all directions.

For a moment we were alone. Then suddenly Batia Reich, a relative who was living with us, came into the room:

"There's someone knocking on the blocked-up window, the one that faces outside!"

It was not until after the war that I learned who it was that had knocked. It was an inspector in the Hungarian police, a friend of my father. Before we went into the ghetto, he had said to us: "Don't worry. If you're in any danger, I'll warn you." If he could have spoken to us that evening, we could perhaps have fled. . . . But by the time we had managed to open the window, it was too late. There was no one outside.

The ghetto awoke. One by one, lights came on in the windows.

I went into the house of one of my father's friends. I woke up the head of the household, an old man with a gray beard and the eyes of a dreamer. He was stooped from long nights of study.

"Get up, sir, get up! You've got to get ready for the journey! You're going to be expelled from here tomorrow with your whole family, and all the rest of the Jews. Where to? Don't ask me, sir. Don't ask me any questions. Only God could answer you. For heaven's sake, get up."

He had not understood a word of what I was saying. He probably thought I had gone out of my mind.

"What tale is this? Get ready for the journey? What journey? Why? What's going on? Have you gone mad?"

Still half asleep, he stared at me with terror-stricken eyes, as though he expected me to burst out laughing and say in the end, "Get back to bed. Go to sleep. Pleasant dreams. Nothing's happened at all. It was just a joke."

My throat was dry, the words choked in it, paralyzing my lips. I could not say any more.

Then he understood. He got out of bed and with automatic movements began to get dressed. Then he went up to the bed where his wife slept and touched her brow with infinite tenderness; she opened her eyes, and it seemed to me that her lips were brushed by a smile. Then he went to his children's beds and woke them swiftly, dragging them from their dreams. I fled.

Time passed very quickly. It was already four o'clock in the morning. My father ran to right and left, exhausted, comforting friends, running to the Jewish Council to see if the edict had not been revoked in the meantime. To the very last moment, a germ of hope stayed alive in our hearts.

The women were cooking eggs, roasting meat, baking cakes, and making knapsacks. The children wandered all over the place, hanging their heads, not knowing what to do with themselves, where to go, to keep from getting in the way of the grown-ups. Our back yard had become a real market place. Household treasures, valuable carpets, silver candelabra, prayer books, Bibles, and other religious articles littered the dusty ground beneath a wonderfully blue sky; pathetic objects which looked as though they had never belonged to anyone.

By eight o'clock in the morning, a weariness like molten lead began to settle in the veins, the limbs, the brain. I was in the midst of my prayers when suddenly there were shouts in the street. I tore myself from my phylacteries and ran to the window. Hungarian police had entered the ghetto and were shouting in the neighboring street:

"All Jews outside! Hurry!"

Some Jewish police went into the houses, saying in broken voices:

"The time's come now . . . you've got to leave all this. . . ."

The Hungarian police struck out with truncheons and rifle butts, to right and left, without reason, indiscriminately, their blows falling upon old men and women, children and invalids alike.

One by one the houses emptied, and the street filled with people and bundles. By ten o'clock, all the condemned were outside. The police took a roll call, once, twice, twenty times. The heat was intense. Sweat streamed from faces and bodies.

Children cried for water.

Water? There was plenty, close at hand, in the houses, in the yards, but they were forbidden to break the ranks.

"Water! Mummy! Water!"

The Jewish police from the ghetto were able to go and fill a few jugs secretly. Since my sisters and I were destined for the last convoy and we were still allowed to move about, we helped them as well as we could.

Then, at last, at one o'clock in the afternoon, came the signal to leave.

There was joy—yes, joy. Perhaps they thought that God could have devised no torment in hell worse than that of sitting there among the bundles, in the middle of the road, beneath a blazing sun; that anything would be preferable to that. They began their journey without a backward glance at the abandoned streets, the dead, empty houses, the gardens, the tombstones. . . . On everyone's back was a pack. In everyone's eyes was suffering drowned in tears. Slowly, heavily, the procession made its way to the gate of the ghetto.

And there was I, on the pavement, unable to make a move. Here came the Rabbi, his back bent, his face shaved, his pack on his back. His mere presence among the deportees added a touch of unreality to the scene. It was like a page torn from some story book, from some historical novel about the captivity of Babylon or the Spanish Inquisition.

One by one they passed in front of me, teachers, friends, others, all those I had been afraid of, all those I once could have laughed at, all those I had lived with over the years. They went by, fallen, dragging their packs, dragging their lives, deserting their homes, the years of their childhood, cringing like beaten dogs.

They passed without a glance in my direction. They must have envied me.

The procession disappeared round the corner of the street. A few paces farther on, and they would have passed beyond the ghetto walls.

The street was like a market place that had suddenly been abandoned. Everything could be found there: suitcases, portfolios, briefcases, knives, plates, banknotes, papers, faded portraits. All those things that people had thought of taking with them, and which in the end they had left behind. They had lost all value.

Everywhere rooms lay open. Doors and windows gaped onto the emptiness. Everything was free for anyone, belonging to nobody. It was simply a matter of helping oneself. An open tomb.

A hot summer sun.

We had spent the day fasting. But we were not very hungry. We were exhausted.

My father had accompanied the deportees as far as the entrance of the ghetto. They first had to go through the big synagogue, where they were minutely searched, to see that they were not taking away any gold, silver, or other objects of value. There were outbreaks of hysteria and blows with the truncheons.

"When is our turn coming?" I asked my father.

"The day after tomorrow. At least—at least, unless things turn out differently. A miracle, perhaps . . . ."

Where were the people being taken to? Didn't anyone know yet? No, the secret was well kept.

Night had fallen. That evening we went to bed early. My father said:

"Sleep well, children. It's not until the day after tomorrow, Tuesday."

Monday passed like a small summer cloud, like a dream in the first daylight hours.

Busy with getting our packs ready, with baking bread and cakes, we no longer thought of anything. The verdict had been delivered.

That evening, our mother made us go to bed very early, to conserve our strength, she said. It was our last night at home.

I was up at dawn. I wanted time to pray before we were expelled.

27

My father had got up earlier to go and seek information. He came back at about eight o'clock. Good news: it wasn't today that we were leaving the town. We were only to move into the little ghetto. There we would wait for the last transport. We should be the last to leave.

At nine o'clock, Sunday's scenes began all over again. Policemen with truncheons yelling:

"All Jews outside!"

We were ready. I was the first to leave. I did not want to see my parents' faces. I did not want to break into tears. We stayed sitting down in the middle of the road, as the others had done the day before yesterday. There was the same infernal heat. The same thirst. But there was no longer anyone left to bring us water.

I looked at our house, where I had spent so many years in my search for God; in fasting in order to hasten the coming of the Messiah; in imagining what my life would be like. Yet I felt little sorrow. I thought of nothing.

"Get up! Count off!"

Standing. Counting off. Sitting down. Standing up again. On the ground once more. Endlessly. We waited impatiently to be fetched. What were they waiting for? At last the order came:

"Forward march!"

My father wept. It was the first time I had ever seen him weep. I had never imagined that he could. As for my mother, she walked with a set expression on her face, without a word, deep in thought. I looked at my little sister Tzipora, her fair hair well combed, a red coat over her arm, a little girl of seven. The bundle on her back was too heavy for her. She gritted her teeth. She knew by now that it would be useless to complain. The police were striking out with their truncheons. "Faster!" I had no strength left. The journey had only just begun, and I felt so weak. . . .

"Faster! Faster! Get on with you, lazy swine!" yelled the Hungarian police.

It was from that moment that I began to hate them, and

my hate is still the only link between us today. They were our first oppressors. They were the first of the faces of hell and death.

We were ordered to run. We advanced in double time. Who would have thought we were so strong? Behind their windows, behind their shutters, our compatriots looked out at us as we passed.

At last we reached our destination. Throwing our bags to the ground, we sank down:

"Oh God, Lord of the Universe, take pity upon us in Thy great mercy. . . ."

The little ghetto. Three days before, people had still been living there—the people who owned the things we were using now. They had been expelled. Already we had completely forgotten them.

The disorder was greater than in the big ghetto. The people must have been driven out unexpectedly. I went to see the rooms where my uncle's family had lived. On the table there was a half-finished bowl of soup. There was a pie waiting to be put in the oven. Books were littered about on the floor. Perhaps my uncle had had dreams of taking them with him?

We settled in. (What a word!) I went to get some wood; my sisters lit the fire. Despite her own weariness, my mother began to prepare a meal.

"We must keep going, we must keep going," she kept on repeating.

The people's morale was not too bad; we were beginning to get used to the situation. In the street, they even went so far as to have optimistic conversations. The Boche would not have time to expel us, they were saying . . . as far as those who had already been deported were concerned, it was too bad; no more could be done. But they would probably allow us to live out our wretched little lives here, until the end of the war.

The ghetto was not guarded. Everyone could come and go as they pleased. Our old servant, Martha, came to see us. Weeping bitterly, she begged us to come to her village, where she could give us a safe refuge. My father did not want to hear of it.

"You can go if you want to," he said to me and to my older sisters. "I shall stay here with your mother and the child. . . ."

Naturally, we refused to be separated.

Night. No one prayed, so that the night would pass quickly. The stars were only sparks of the fire which devoured us. Should that fire die out one day, there would be nothing left in the sky but dead stars, dead eyes.

There was nothing else to do but to get into bed, into the beds of the absent ones; to rest, to gather one's strength.

At dawn, there was nothing left of this melancholy. We felt as though we were on holiday. People were saying:

"Who knows? Perhaps we are being deported for our own good. The front isn't very far off; we shall soon be able to hear the guns. And then the civilian population would be evacuated anyway. . . ."

"Perhaps they were afraid we might help the guer-rillas. . . ."

"If you ask me, the whole business of deportation is just a farce. Oh yes, don't laugh. The Boches just want to steal our jewelry. They know we've buried everything, and that they'll have to hunt for it: it's easier when the owners are on holiday. . . ."

On holiday!

These optimistic speeches, which no one believed, helped to pass the time. The few days we lived here went by pleasantly enough, in peace. People were better disposed toward one another. There were no longer any questions of wealth, of social distinction, and importance, only people all condemned to the same fate—still unknown.

Saturday, the day of rest, was chosen for our expulsion.

The night before, we had the traditional Friday evening meal. We said the customary grace for the bread and wine and swallowed our food without a word. We were, we felt, gathered for the last time round the family table. I spent the night turning over thoughts and memories in my mind, unable to find sleep.

At dawn, we were in the street, ready to leave. This time there were no Hungarian police. An agreement had been made with the Jewish Council that they should organize it all themselves.

Our convoy went toward the main synagogue. The town seemed deserted. Yet our friends of yesterday were probably waiting behind their shutters for the moment when they could pillage our houses.

The synagogue was like a huge station: luggage and tears. The altar was broken, the hangings torn down, the walls bare. There were so many of us that we could scarcely breathe. We spent a horrible twenty-four hours there. There were men downstairs; women on the first floor. It was Saturday; it was as though we had come to attend the service. Since no one could go out, people were relieving themselves in a corner.

The following morning, we marched to the station, where a convoy of cattle wagons was waiting. The Hungarian police made us get in—eighty people in each car. We were left a few loaves of bread and some buckets of water. The bars at the window were checked, to see that they were not loose. Then the cars were sealed. In each car one person was placed in charge. If anyone escaped, he would be shot.

Two Gestapo officers strolled about on the platform, smiling: all things considered, everything had gone off very well.

A prolonged whistle split the air. The wheels began to grind. We were on our way.

Lying down was out of the question, and we were only able to sit by deciding to take turns. There was very little air. The lucky ones who happened to be near a window could see the blossoming countryside roll by.

After two days of traveling, we began to be tortured by thirst. Then the heat became unbearable.

Free from all social constraint, the young people gave way openly to instinct, taking advantage of the darkness to copulate in our midst, without caring about anyone else, as though they were alone in the world. The rest pretended not to notice anything.

We still had a few provisions left. But we never ate enough to satisfy our hunger. To save was our rule; to save up for tomorrow. Tomorrow might be worse.

The train stopped at Kaschau, a little town on the Czechoslovak frontier. We realized then that we were not going to stay in Hungary. Our eyes were opened, but too late.

The door of the car slid open. A German officer, accompanied by a Hungarian lieutenant-interpreter, came up and introduced himself.

"From this moment, you come under the authority of the German army. Those of you who still have gold, silver, or watches in your possession must give them up now. Anyone who is later found to have kept anything will be shot on the spot. Secondly, anyone who feels ill may go to the hospital car. That's all."

The Hungarian lieutenant went among us with a basket and collected the last possessions from those who no longer wished to taste the bitterness of terror.

"There are eighty of you in the wagon," added the German officer. "If anyone is missing, you'll all be shot, like dogs...."

They disappeared. The doors were closed. We were caught in a trap, right up to our necks. The doors were nailed up; the way back was finally cut off. The world was a cattle wagon hermetically sealed.

We had a woman with us named Madame Schächter. She was about fifty; her ten-year-old son was with her, crouched in a corner. Her husband and two eldest sons had been deported with the first transport by mistake. The separation had completely broken her.

I knew her well. A quiet woman with tense, burning eyes, she had often been to our house. Her husband, who was a pious man, spent his days and nights in study, and it was she who worked to support the family.

Madame Schächter had gone out of her mind. On the first day of the journey she had already begun to moan and to keep asking why she had been separated from her family. As time went on, her cries grew hysterical.

On the third night, while we slept, some of us sitting one against the other and some standing, a piercing cry split the silence:

"Fire! I can see a fire! I can see a fire!"

There was a moment's panic. Who was it who had cried out? It was Madame Schächter. Standing in the middle of

33

the wagon, in the pale light from the windows, she looked like a withered tree in a cornfield. She pointed her arm toward the window, screaming:

"Look! Look at it! Fire! A terrible fire! Mercy! *Oh, that fire!*"

Some of the men pressed up against the bars. There was nothing there; only the darkness.

The shock of this terrible awakening stayed with us for a long time. We still trembled from it. With every groan of the wheels on the rail, we felt that an abyss was about to open beneath our bodies. Powerless to still our own anguish, we tried to console ourselves:

"She's mad, poor soul. . . ."

Someone had put a damp cloth on her brow, to calm her, but still her screams went on:

"Fire! Fire!"

Her little boy was crying, hanging onto her skirt, trying to take hold of her hands. "It's all right, Mummy! There's nothing there. . . . Sit down. . . ." This shook me even more than his mother's screams had done.

Some women tried to calm her. "You'll find your husband and your sons again . . . in a few days. . . ."

She continued to scream, breathless, her voice broken by sobs. "Jews, listen to me! I can see a fire! There are huge flames! It is a furnace!"

It was as though she were possessed by an evil spirit which spoke from the depths of her being.

We tried to explain it away, more to calm ourselves and to recover our own breath than to comfort her. "She must be very thirsty, poor thing! That's why she keeps talking about a fire devouring her."

But it was in vain. Our terror was about to burst the sides of the train. Our nerves were at breaking point. Our flesh was creeping. It was as though madness were taking possession of us all. We could stand it no longer. Some of the young men forced her to sit down, tied her up, and put a gag in her mouth.

Silence again. The little boy sat down by his mother, crying. I had begun to breathe normally again. We could hear the wheels churning out that monotonous rhythm of a train traveling through the night. We could begin to doze, to rest, to dream. . . .

An hour or two went by like this. Then another scream took our breath away. The woman had broken loose from her bonds and was crying out more loudly than ever:

"Look at the fire! Flames, flames everywhere. . . ."

Once more the young men tied her up and gagged her. They even struck her. People encouraged them:

"Make her be quiet! She's mad! Shut her up! She's not the only one. She can keep her mouth shut. . . ."

They struck her several times on the head—blows that might have killed her. Her little boy clung to her; he did not cry out; he did not say a word. He was not even weeping now.

An endless night. Toward dawn, Madame Schächter calmed down. Crouched in her corner, her bewildered gaze scouring the emptiness, she could no longer see us.

She stayed like that all through the day, dumb, absent, isolated among us. As soon as night fell, she began to scream: "There's a fire over there!" She would point at a spot in space, always the same one. They were tired of hitting her. The heat, the thirst, the pestilential stench, the suffocating lack of air—these were as nothing compared with these screams which tore us to shreds. A few days more and we should all have started to scream too.

But we had reached a station. Those who were next to the windows told us its name:

"Auschwitz."

No one had ever heard that name.

The train did not start up again. The afternoon passed slowly. Then the wagon doors slid open. Two men were allowed to get down to fetch water.

When they came back, they told us that, in exchange for a gold watch, they had discovered that this was the last stop. We would be getting out here. There was a labor camp. Conditions were good. Families would not be split up. Only the young people would go to work in the factories. The old men and invalids would be kept occupied in the fields.

The barometer of confidence soared. Here was a sudden release from the terrors of the previous nights. We gave thanks to God.

Madame Schächter stayed in her corner, wilted, dumb, indifferent to the general confidence. Her little boy stroked her hand.

As dusk fell, darkness gathered inside the wagon. We started to eat our last provisions. At ten in the evening, everyone was looking for a convenient position in which to sleep for a while, and soon we were all asleep. Suddenly:

"The fire! The furnace! Look, over there! . . ."

Waking with a start, we rushed to the window. Yet again we had believed her, even if only for a moment. But there was nothing outside save the darkness of night. With shame in our souls, we went back to our places, gnawed by fear, in spite of ourselves. As she continued to scream, they began to hit her again, and it was with the greatest difficulty that they silenced her.

The man in charge of our wagon called a German officer who was walking about on the platform, and asked him if Madame Schächter could be taken to the hospital car.

"You must be patient," the German replied. "She'll be taken there soon."

Toward eleven o'clock, the train began to move. We pressed against the windows. The convoy was moving slowly. A quarter of an hour later, it slowed down again. Through the windows we could see barbed wire; we realized that this must be the camp.

We had forgotten the existence of Madame Schächter. Suddenly, we heard terrible screams:

"Jews, look! Look through the window! Flames! Look!"

And as the train stopped, we saw this time that flames were gushing out of a tall chimney into the black sky.

Madame Schächter was silent herself. Once more she had become dumb, indifferent, absent, and had gone back to her corner.

We looked at the flames in the darkness. There was an abominable odor floating in the air. Suddenly, our doors opened. Some odd-looking characters, dressed in striped shirts and black trousers leapt into the wagon. They held electric torches and truncheons. They began to strike out to right and left, shouting:

"Everybody get out! Everyone out of the wagon! Quickly!"

We jumped out. I threw a last glance toward Madame Schächter. Her little boy was holding her hand.

In front of us flames. In the air that smell of burning flesh. It must have been about midnight. We had arrived —at Birkenau, reception center for Auschwitz.

The cherished objects we had brought with us thus far were left behind in the train, and with them, at last, our illusions.

Every two yards or so an SS man held his tommy gun trained on us. Hand in hand we followed the crowd.

An SS noncommissioned officer came to meet us, a truncheon in his hand. He gave the order:

"Men to the left! Women to the right!"

Eight words spoken quietly, indifferently, without emotion. Eight short, simple words. Yet that was the moment when I parted from my mother. I had not had time to think, but already I felt the pressure of my father's hand: we were alone. For a part of a second I glimpsed my mother and my sisters moving away to the right. Tzipora held Mother's hand. I saw them disappear into the distance; my mother was stroking my sister's fair hair, as though to protect her, while I walked on with my father and the other men. And I did not know that in that place, at that moment, I was parting from my mother and Tzipora forever. I went on walking. My father held onto my hand.

Behind me, an old man fell to the ground. Near him was an SS man, putting his revolver back in its holster.

My hand shifted on my father's arm. I had one thought —not to lose him. Not to be left alone.

The SS officers gave the order:

"Form fives!"

Commotion. At all costs we must keep together.

"Here, kid, how old are you?"

It was one of the prisoners who asked me this. I could not see his face, but his voice was tense and weary.

"I'm not quite fifteen yet."

"No. Eighteen."

"But I'm not," I said. "Fifteen."

"Fool. Listen to what *I* say."

Then he questioned my father, who replied:

"Fifty."

The other grew more furious than ever.

"No, not fifty. Forty. Do you understand? Eighteen and forty."

He disappeared into the night shadows. A second man came up, spitting oaths at us.

"What have you come here for, you sons of bitches? What are you doing here, eh?"

Someone dared to answer him.

"What do you think? Do you suppose we've come here for our own pleasure? Do you think we asked to come?"

A little more, and the man would have killed him.

"You shut your trap, you filthy swine, or I'll squash you right now! You'd have done better to have hanged yourselves where you were than to come here. Didn't you know what was in store for you at Auschwitz? Haven't you heard about it? In 1944?"

No, we had not heard. No one had told us. He could not believe his ears. His tone of voice became increasingly brutal.

39

"Do you see that chimney over there? See it? Do you see those flames? (Yes, we did see the flames.) Over there —that's where you're going to be taken. That's your grave, over there. Haven't you realized it yet? You dumb bastards, don't you understand anything? You're going to be burned. Frizzled away. Turned into ashes."

He was growing hysterical in his fury. We stayed motionless, petrified. Surely it was all a nightmare? An unimaginable nightmare?

I heard murmurs around me.

"We've got to do something. We can't let ourselves be killed. We can't go like beasts to the slaughter. We've got to revolt."

There were a few sturdy young fellows among us. They had knives on them, and they tried to incite the others to throw themselves on the armed guards.

One of the young men cried:

"Let the world learn of the existence of Auschwitz. Let everybody hear about it, while they can still escape. . . ."

But the older ones begged their children not to do anything foolish:

"You must never lose faith, even when the sword hangs over your head. That's the teaching of our sages. . . ."

The wind of revolt died down. We continued our march toward the square. In the middle stood the notorious Dr. Mengele (a typical SS officer: a cruel face, but not devoid of intelligence, and wearing a monocle); a conductor's baton in his hand, he was standing among the other officers. The baton moved unremittingly, sometimes to the right, sometimes to the left.

I was already in front of him:

"How old are you?" he asked, in an attempt at a paternal tone of voice.

"Eighteen." My voice was shaking.

"Are you in good health?"

"Yes."

"What's your occupation?"

Should I say that I was a student?

"Farmer," I heard myself say.

This conversation cannot have lasted more than a few seconds. It had seemed like an eternity to me.

The baton moved to the left. I took half a step forward. I wanted to see first where they were sending my father. If he went to the right, I would go after him.

The baton once again pointed to the left for him too. A weight was lifted from my heart.

We did not yet know which was the better side, right or left; which road led to prison and which to the crematory. But for the moment I was happy; I was near my father. Our procession continued to move slowly forward.

Another prisoner came up to us:

"Satisfied?"

"Yes," someone replied.

"Poor devils, you're going to the crematory."

He seemed to be telling the truth. Not far from us, flames were leaping up from a ditch, gigantic flames. They were burning something. A lorry drew up at the pit and delivered its load—little children. Babies! Yes, I saw it—saw it with my own eyes . . . those children in the flames. (Is it surprising that I could not sleep after that? Sleep had fled from my eyes.)

So this was where we were going. A little farther on was another and larger ditch for adults.

I pinched my face. Was I still alive? Was I awake? I could not believe it. How could it be possible for them to burn people, children, and for the world to keep silent? No, none of this could be true. It was a nightmare. . . . Soon I should wake with a start, my heart pounding, and find myself back in the bedroom of my childhood, among my books. . . .

My father's voice drew me from my thoughts:

"It's a shame . . . a shame that you couldn't have gone with your mother. . . . I saw several boys of your age going with their mothers. . . ."

His voice was terribly sad. I realized that he did not want to see what they were going to do to me. He did not want to see the burning of his only son.

My forehead was bathed in cold sweat. But I told him that I did not believe that they could burn people in our age, that humanity would never tolerate it. . . .

"Humanity? Humanity is not concerned with us. Today anything is allowed. Anything is possible, even these crematories. . . ."

His voice was choking.

"Father," I said, "if that is so, I don't want to wait here. I'm going to run to the electric wire. That would be better than slow agony in the flames."

He did not answer. He was weeping. His body was shaken convulsively. Around us, everyone was weeping. Someone began to recite the Kaddish, the prayer for the dead. I do not know if it has ever happened before, in the long history of the Jews, that people have ever recited the prayer for the dead for themselves.

"*Yitgadal veyitkadach shmé raba.* . . . May His Name be blessed and magnified. . . ." whispered my father.

For the first time, I felt revolt rise up in me. Why should I bless His name? The Eternal, Lord of the Universe, the All-Powerful and Terrible, was silent. What had I to thank Him for?

We continued our march. We were gradually drawing closer to the ditch, from which an infernal heat was rising. Still twenty steps to go. If I wanted to bring about my own death, this was the moment. Our line had now only fifteen paces to cover. I bit my lips so that my father would not hear my teeth chattering. Ten steps still. Eight. Seven. We marched slowly on, as though following a hearse at our own funeral. Four steps more. Three steps. There it was now, right in front of us, the pit and its flames. I gathered all that was left of my strength, so that I could break from the ranks and throw myself upon the barbed wire. In the depths of my heart, I bade farewell to my father, to the whole universe; and, in spite of myself, the words formed themselves and issued in a whisper from my lips: *Yitgadal veyitkadach shmé raba.* . . . May His name be blessed and magnified. . . . My heart was bursting. The moment had come. I was face to face with the Angel of Death. . . .

No. Two steps from the pit we were ordered to turn to the left and made to go into a barracks.

I pressed my father's hand. He said:

"Do you remember Madame Schächter, in the train?"

Never shall I forget that night, the first night in camp, which has turned my life into one long night, seven times cursed and seven times sealed. Never shall I forget that smoke. Never shall I forget the little faces of the children, whose bodies I saw turned into wreaths of smoke beneath a silent blue sky.

Never shall I forget those flames which consumed my faith forever.

Never shall I forget that nocturnal silence which deprived me, for all eternity, of the desire to live. Never shall I forget those moments which murdered my God and my soul and turned my dreams to dust. Never shall I forget these things, even if I am condemned to live as long as God Himself. Never.

The barracks we had been made to go into was very long. In the roof were some blue-tinged skylights. The antechamber of Hell must look like this. So many crazed men, so many cries, so much bestial brutality!

There were dozens of prisoners to receive us, truncheons in their hands, striking out anywhere, at anyone, without reason. Orders:

"Strip! Fast! *Los!* Keep only your belts and shoes in your hands. . . ."

We had to throw our clothes at one end of the barracks.

There was already a great heap there. New suits and old, torn coats, rags. For us, this was the true equality: nakedness. Shivering with the cold.

Some SS officers moved about in the room, looking for strong men. If they were so keen on strength, perhaps one should try and pass oneself off as sturdy? My father thought the reverse. It was better not to draw attention to oneself. Our fate would then be the same as the others. (Later, we were to learn that he was right. Those who were selected that day were enlisted in the *Sonder-Kommando*, the unit which worked in the crematories. Bela Katz—son of a big tradesman from our town—had arrived at Birkenau with the first transport, a week before us. When he heard of our arrival, he managed to get word to us that, having been chosen for his strength, he had himself put his father's body into the crematory oven.)

Blows continued to rain down.

"To the barber!"

Belt and shoes in hand, I let myself be dragged off to the barbers. They took our hair off with clippers, and shaved off all the hair on our bodies. The same thought buzzed all the time in my head—not to be separated from my father.

Freed from the hands of the barbers, we began to wander in the crowd, meeting friends and acquaintances. These meetings filled us with joy—yes, joy—"Thank God! You're still alive!"

But others were crying. They used all their remaining strength in weeping. Why had they let themselves be brought here? Why couldn't they have died in their beds? Sobs choked their voices.

Suddenly, someone threw his arms round my neck in an embrace: Yechiel, brother of the rabbi of Sighet. He was sobbing bitterly. I thought he was weeping with joy at still being alive.

"Don't cry, Yechiel," I said. "Don't waste your tears...."

44

"Not cry? We're on the threshold of death. . . . Soon we shall have crossed over. . . . Don't you understand? How could I not cry?"

Through the blue-tinged skylights I could see the darkness gradually fading. I had ceased to feel fear. And then I was overcome by an inhuman weariness.

Those absent no longer touched even the surface of our memories. We still spoke of them—"Who knows what may have become of them?"—but we had little concern for their fate. We were incapable of thinking of anything at all. Our senses were blunted; everything was blurred as in a fog. It was no longer possible to grasp anything. The instincts of self-preservation, of self-defense, of pride, had all deserted us. In one ultimate moment of lucidity it seemed to me that we were damned souls wandering in the half-world, souls condemned to wander through space till the generations of man came to an end, seeking their redemption, seeking oblivion—without hope of finding it.

Toward five o'clock in the morning, we were driven out of the barracks. The Kapos beat us once more, but I had ceased to feel any pain from their blows. An icy wind enveloped us. We were naked, our shoes and belts in our hands. The command: "Run!" And we ran. After a few minutes of racing, a new barracks.

A barrel of petrol at the entrance. Disinfection. Everyone was soaked in it. Then a hot shower. At high speed. As we came out from the water, we were driven outside. More running. Another barracks, the store. Very long tables. Mountains of prison clothes. On we ran. As we passed, trousers, tunic, shirt, and socks were thrown to us.

Within a few seconds, we had ceased to be men. If the situation had not been tragic, we should have roared with laughter. Such outfits! Meir Katz, a giant, had a child's trousers, and Stern, a thin little chap, a tunic which completely swamped him. We immediately began the necessary exchanges.

45

I glanced at my father. How he had changed! His eyes had grown dim. I would have liked to speak to him, but I did not know what to say.

The night was gone. The morning star was shining in the sky. I too had become a completely different person. The student of the Talmud, the child that I was, had been consumed in the flames. There remained only a shape that looked like me. A dark flame had entered into my soul and devoured it.

So much had happened within such a few hours that I had lost all sense of time. When had we left our houses? And the ghetto? And the train? Was it only a week? One night—*one single night?*

How long had we been standing like this in the icy wind? An hour? Simply an hour? Sixty minutes?

Surely it was a dream.

Not far from us there were some prisoners at work. Some were digging holes, others carrying sand. None of them so much as glanced at us. We were so many dried-up trees in the heart of a desert. Behind me, some people were talking. I had not the slightest desire to listen to what they were saying, to know who was talking or what they were talking about. No one dared to raise his voice, though there was no supervisor near us. People whispered. Perhaps it was because of the thick smoke which poisoned the air and took one by the throat. . . .

We were made to go into a new barracks, in the "gypsies' camp." In ranks of five.

"And now stay where you are!"

There was no floor. A roof and four walls. Our feet sank into the mud.

Another spell of waiting began. I went to sleep standing up. I dreamed of a bed, of my mother's caress. And I woke up: I was standing, my feet in the mud. Some people collapsed and lay where they were. Others cried:

"Are you mad? We've been told to stay standing. Do you want to bring trouble on us all?"

As if all the trouble in the world had not descended already upon our heads! Gradually, we all sat down in the mud. But we had to jump up constantly, every time a Kapo came in to see if anybody had a pair of new shoes. If so, they had to be given up to him. It was no use opposing this: blows rained down and in the final reckoning you had lost your shoes anyway.

I had new shoes myself. But as they were coated with a thick layer of mud, no one had noticed them. I thanked God, in an improvised prayer, for having created mud in His infinite and wonderful universe.

Suddenly the silence grew oppressive. An SS officer had come in and, with him, the odor of the Angel of Death. We stared fixedly at his fleshy lips. From the middle of the barracks, he harangued us:

"You're in a concentration camp. At Auschwitz. . . ."

A pause. He observed the effect his words had produced. His face has stayed in my memory to this day. A tall man, about thirty, with crime inscribed upon his brow and in the pupils of his eyes. He looked us over as if we were a pack of leprous dogs hanging onto our lives.

"Remember this," he went on. "Remember it forever, Engrave it into your minds. You are at Auschwitz. And Auschwitz is not a convalescent home. It's a concentration camp. Here, you have got to work. If not, you will go straight to the furnace. To the crematory. Work or the crematory—the choice is in your hands."

We had already lived through so much that night, we thought nothing could frighten us any more. But his clipped words made us tremble. Here the word "furnace" was not a word empty of meaning: it floated on the air, mingling with the smoke. It was perhaps the only word which did have any real meaning here. He left the barracks. Kapos appeared, crying:

47

"All skilled workers—locksmiths, electricians, watch-makers—one step forward!"

The rest of us were made to go to another barracks, a stone one this time. With permission to sit down. A gypsy deportee was in charge of us.

My father was suddenly seized with colic. He got up and went toward the gypsy, asking politely, in German:

"Excuse me, can you tell me where the lavatories are?"

The gypsy looked him up and down slowly, from head to foot. As if he wanted to convince himself that this man addressing him was really a creature of flesh and bone, a living being with a body and a belly. Then, as if he had suddenly woken up from a heavy doze, he dealt my father such a clout that he fell to the ground, crawling back to his place on all fours.

I did not move. What had happened to me? My father had just been struck, before my very eyes, and I had not flickered an eyelid. I had looked on and said nothing. Yesterday, I should have sunk my nails into the criminal's flesh. Had I changed so much, then? So quickly? Now remorse began to gnaw at me. I thought only: I shall never forgive them for that. My father must have guessed my feelings. He whispered in my ear, "It doesn't hurt." His cheek still bore the red mark of the man's hand.

"Everyone outside!"

Ten gypsies had come and joined our supervisor. Whips and truncheons cracked round me. My feet were running without my being aware of it. I tried to hide from the blows behind the others. The spring sunshine.

"Form fives!"

The prisoners whom I had noticed in the morning were working at the side. There was no guard near them, only the shadow of the chimney. . . . Dazed by the sunshine and by my reverie, I felt someone tugging at my sleeve. It was my father. "Come on, my boy."

48

We marched on. Doors opened and closed again. On we went between the electric wires. At each step, a white placard with a death's head on it stared us in the face. A caption: "Warning. Danger of death." Mockery: was there a single place here where you were not in danger of death?

The gypsies stopped near another barracks. They were replaced by SS, who surrounded us. Revolvers, machine guns, police dogs.

The march had lasted half an hour. Looking around me, I noticed that the barbed wires were behind us. We had left the camp.

It was a beautiful April day. The fragrance of spring was in the air. The sun was setting in the west.

But we had been marching for only a few moments when we saw the barbed wire of another camp. An iron door with this inscription over it:

"*Work is liberty!*"

Auschwitz.

First impression: this was better than Birkenau. There were two-storied buildings of concrete instead of wooden barracks. There were little gardens here and there. We were led to one of these prison blocks. Seated on the ground by the entrance, we began another session of waiting. Every now and then, someone was made to go in. These were the showers, a compulsory formality at the entrance to all these camps. Even if you were simply passing from one to the other several times a day, you still had to go through the baths every time.

After coming out from the hot water, we stayed shivering in the night air. Our clothes had been left behind in the other block, and we had been promised other outfits.

Toward midnight, we were told to run.

"Faster," shouted our guards. "The faster you run, the sooner you can go to bed."

After a few minutes of this mad race we arrived in front of another block. The prisoner in charge was waiting for us.

He was a young Pole, who smiled at us. He began to talk to us, and, despite our weariness, we listened patiently.

"Comrades, you're in the concentration camp of Auschwitz. There's a long road of suffering ahead of you. But don't lose courage. You've already escaped the gravest danger: selection. So now, muster your strength, and don't lose heart. We shall all see the day of liberation. Have faith in life. Above all else, have faith. Drive out despair, and you will keep death away from yourselves. Hell is not for eternity. And now, a prayer—or rather, a piece of advice: let there be comradeship among you. We are all brothers, and we are all suffering the same fate. The same smoke floats over all our heads. Help one another. It is the only way to survive. Enough said. You're tired. Listen. You're in Block 17. I am responsible for keeping order here. Anyone with a complaint against anyone else can come and see me. That's all. You can go to bed. Two people to a bunk. Good night." The first human words.

No sooner had we climbed into the bunks than we fell into a deep sleep.

The next morning, the "veteran" prisoners treated us without brutality. We went to the wash place. We were given new clothes. We were brought black coffee.

We left the block at about ten o'clock, so that it could be cleaned. Outside the sunshine warmed us. Our morale was much improved. We were feeling the benefit of a night's sleep. Friends met each other, exchanged a few sentences. We talked of everything, except those who had disappeared. The general opinion was that the war was about to end.

At about noon they brought us soup: a plate of thick soup for each person. Tormented though I was by hunger, I refused to touch it. I was still the spoiled child I had always been. My father swallowed my ration.

In the shade of the block, we then had a little siesta. He must have been lying, that SS officer in the muddy barracks. Auschwitz was in fact a rest home. . . .

In the afternoon we were made to line up. Three prisoners brought a table and some medical instruments. With the left sleeve rolled up, each person passed in front of the table. The three "veterans," with needles in their hands, engraved a number on our left arms. I became A-7713. After that I had no other name.

At dusk, roll call. The working units came back. Near the door, the band was playing military marches. Tens of thousands of prisoners stood in rows while the SS checked their numbers.

After roll call, the prisoners from all the blocks scattered to look for friends, relatives, and neighbors who had arrived in the last convoy.

Days passed. In the morning, black coffee. At noon, soup. (By the third day I was eating any kind of soup hungrily.) At six p.m., roll call. Then bread and something. At nine o'clock, bed.

We had already been eight days at Auschwitz. It was during roll call. We were not expecting anything except the sound of the bell which would announce the end of roll call. I suddenly heard someone passing between the rows asking, "Which of you is Wiesel of Sighet?"

The man looking for us was a bespectacled little fellow with a wrinkled, wizened face. My father answered him.

"I'm Wiesel of Sighet."

The little man looked at him for a long while, with his eyes narrowed.

"You don't recognize me—you don't recognize me. I'm a relative of yours. Stein. Have you forgotten me already? Stein! Stein of Antwerp. Reizel's husband. Your wife was Reizel's aunt. She often used to write to us . . . and such letters!"

My father had not recognized him. He must scarcely have known him, since my father was always up to his neck in the affairs of the Jewish community, and much less well versed in family matters. He was always elsewhere, lost in his thoughts. (Once a cousin came to see us at Sighet. She had been staying with us and eating at our table for over a fortnight before my father noticed her presence for the first time.) No, he could not have remembered Stein. As for me, I recognized him at once. I had known his wife Reizel before she left for Belgium.

He said, "I was deported in 1942. I heard that a transport had come in from your region, and I came to find you. I thought perhaps you might have news of Reizel and my little boys. They stayed behind in Antwerp. . . ."

I knew nothing about them. Since 1940, my mother had not had a single letter from them. But I lied.

"Yes, my mother's had news from your family. Reizel is very well. The children too. . . ."

He wept with joy. He would have liked to stay longer, to learn more details, to drink in the good news, but an SS came up, and he had to go, calling to us that he would be back the next day.

The bell gave us the signal to disperse. We went to get our evening meal of bread and margarine. I was dreadfully hungry and swallowed my ration on the spot.

My father said, "You don't want to eat it all at once. Tomorrow's another day. . . ."

And seeing that his advice had come too late and that there was nothing left of my ration, he did not even begin his own.

"Personally, I'm not hungry," he said.

We stayed at Auschwitz for three weeks. We had nothing to do. We slept a great deal in the afternoon and at night.

The only worry was to avoid moves, to stay here as long as possible. It was not difficult; it was simply a matter of never putting oneself down as a skilled worker. Laborers were being kept till the end.

At the beginning of the third week, the prisoner in charge of our block was deprived of his office, being considered too humane. Our new head was savage, and his assistants were real monsters. The good days were over.

We began to wonder if it would not be better to let oneself be chosen for the next move.

Stein, our relation from Antwerp, continued to visit us, and from time to time he would bring a half ration of bread.

"Here, this is for you, Eliezer."

Every time he came, there would be tears running down his face, congealing there, freezing. He would often say to my father:

"Take care of your son. He's very weak and dried up. Look after him well, to avoid the selection. Eat! It doesn't matter what or when. Eat everything you can. The weak don't hang about for long here. . . ."

And he was so thin himself, so dried up, so weak. . . .

"The only thing that keeps me alive," he used to say, "is that Reizel and the children are still alive. If it wasn't for them, I couldn't keep going."

He came toward us one evening, his face radiant.

"A transport's just come in from Antwerp. I'm going to see them tomorrow. They'll be sure to have news."

He went off.

We were not to see him again. He had had news. Real news.

In the evening, lying on our beds, we would try to sing some of the Hasidic melodies, and Akiba Drumer would break our hearts with his deep, solemn voice.

Some talked of God, of his mysterious ways, of the sins of the Jewish people, and of their future deliverance. But I had ceased to pray. How I sympathized with Job! I did not deny God's existence, but I doubted His absolute justice.

Akiba Drumer said: "God is testing us. He wants to find out whether we can dominate our base instincts and kill the Satan within us. We have no right to despair. And if he punishes us relentlessly, it's a sign that He loves us all the more."

Hersch Genud, well versed in the cabbala, spoke of the end of the world and the coming of Messiah.

Only occasionally during these conversations did the thought occur to me: "Where is my mother at this moment? And Tzipora . . . ?"

"Your mother is still a young woman," said my father on one occasion. "She must be in a labor camp. And Tzipora's a big girl now, isn't she? She must be in a camp, too."

How we should have liked to believe it. We pretended, for what if the other one should still be believing it?

All the skilled workers had already been sent to other camps. There were only about a hundred of us ordinary laborers left.

"It's your turn today," said the secretary of the block. "You're going with the next transport."

At ten o'clock we were given our daily ration of bread. We were surrounded by about ten SS. On the door the plaque: "*Work is liberty.*" We were counted. And then, there we were, right out in the country on the sunny road. In the sky a few little white clouds.

We walked slowly. The guards were in no hurry. We were glad of this. As we went through the villages, many of the Germans stared at us without surprise. They had probably already seen quite a few of these processions.

On the way, we met some young German girls. The guards began to tease them. The girls giggled, pleased. They let themselves be kissed and tickled, exploding with laughter. They were all laughing and joking and shouting blandishments at one another for a good part of the way. During this time, at least we did not have to endure either shouts or blows from the rifle butt.

At the end of four hours, we reached our new camp: Buna. The iron gate closed behind us.

The camp looked as though it had suffered an epidemic: empty and dead. There were just a few well-clad prisoners walking about between the blocks.

Of course, we had to go through the showers first. The head of our camp joined us there. He was a strong, well-built, broad-shouldered man: bull neck, thick lips, frizzled hair. He looked kind. A smile shone from time to time in his gray-blue eyes. Our convoy included a few children ten and twelve years old. The officer took an interest in them and gave orders for them to be brought food.

After we had been given new clothes, we were installed in two tents. We had to wait to be enlisted in the labor units, then we could pass into the block.

That evening, the labor units came back from the work yards. Roll call. We began to look for familiar faces, to seek information, to question the veteran prisoners about which labor unit was the best, which block one should try to get into. The prisoners all agreed, saying, "Buna's a very good camp. You can stand it. The important thing is not to get transferred to the building unit. . . ."

As if the choice were in our own hands.

The head of our tent was a German. An assassin's face, fleshy lips, hands like a wolf's paws. He was so fat he could hardly move. Like the leader of the camp, he loved children. As soon as we arrived, he had brought them bread, soup, and margarine. (Actually, this was not disinterested affection: there was a considerable traffic in children among homosexuals here, I learned later.)

The head told us: "You're staying here three days in quarantine. Then you're going to work. Tomorrow, medical inspection."

One of his assistants—a hard-faced boy, with hooligan's eyes—came up to me:

"Do you want to get into a good unit?"

"I certainly do. But on one condition: I want to stay with my father."

"All right," he said. "I can arrange that. For a small consideration: your shoes. I'll give you some others."

I refused to give him my shoes. They were all I had left.

"I'll give you an extra ration of bread and margarine."

He was very keen on my shoes; but I did not give them up to him. (Later on they were taken from me just the same. But in exchange for nothing this time.)

Medical examination in the open air in the early hours of the morning, before three doctors seated on a bench.

The first barely examined me at all. He was content merely to ask:

"Are you in good health?"

Who would have dared say anything to the contrary?

The dentist, on the other hand, seemed most conscientious: he would order us to open our mouths wide. Actually he was not looking for decayed teeth, but gold ones. Anyone who had gold in his mouth had his number added to a list. I myself had a gold crown.

The first three days passed by rapidly. On the fourth day, at dawn, when we were standing in front of the tent, the Kapos appeared. Then each began to choose the men who suited him:

"You ... you ... you and you...." They pointed a finger, as though choosing cattle or merchandise.

We followed our Kapo, a young man. He made us stop at the entrance to the first block, near the door of the camp. This was the orchestra block. "Go in," he ordered. We were surprised. What had we to do with music?

The band played a military march, always the same one. Dozens of units left for the workyards, in step. The Kapos beat time: "Left, right, left, right."

Some SS officers, pen and paper in hand, counted the men as they went out. The band went on playing the same march until the last unit had gone by. Then the conductor's baton was still. The band stopped dead, and the Kapos yelled:

"Form fives!"

We left the camp without music, but in step: we still had the sound of the march in our ears.

"Left, right! Left, right!"

We started talking to the musicians next to us.

We drew up in ranks of five, with the musicians. They were nearly all Jews: Juliek, a bespectacled Pole with a cynical smile on his pale face; Louis, a distinguished violinist who came from Holland—he complained that they would not let him play Beethoven: Jews were not allowed to play German music; Hans, a lively young Berliner. The foreman was a Pole, Franek, a former student from Warsaw.

Juliek explained to me: "We work in a warehouse for electrical equipment, not far from here. The work isn't in the least difficult or dangerous. But Idek, the Kapo, has bouts of madness now and then, when it's best to keep out of his way."

57

"You're lucky, son," smiled Hans. "You've landed in a good unit. . . ."

Ten minutes later, we were in front of the warehouse. A German employee, a civilian, the *meister*, came to meet us. He paid us about as much attention as a dealer might who was just receiving a delivery of old rags.

Our comrades had been right; the work was not difficult. Sitting on the ground, we had to count bolts, bulbs, and small electrical fittings. The Kapo explained to us at great length the vast importance of our work, warning us that anyone found slacking would have him to reckon with. My new comrades reassured me.

"There's nothing to be scared of. He has to say that because of the *meister*."

There were a number of Polish civilians there, and a few French women, who were casting friendly glances at the musicians.

Franek, the foreman, put me in a corner. "Don't kill yourself; there's no hurry. But mind an SS man doesn't catch you unawares."

"Please . . . I would have liked to be by my father."

"All right. Your father'll be working here by your side."

We were lucky.

There were two boys attached to our group: Yossi and Tibi, two brothers. They were Czechs whose parents had been exterminated at Birkenau. They lived, body and soul, for each other.

They and I very soon became friends. Having once belonged to a Zionist youth organization, they knew innumerable Hebrew chants. Thus we would often hum tunes evoking the calm waters of Jordan and the majestic sanctity of Jerusalem. And we would often talk of Palestine. Their parents, like mine, had lacked the courage to wind up their affairs and emigrate while there was still time. We decided that, if we were granted our lives until the liberation, we would not stay in Europe a day longer. We would take the first boat for Haifa.

58

Still lost in his cabbalistic dreams, Akiba Drumer had discovered a verse in the Bible which, interpreted in terms of numerology, enabled him to predict that the deliverance was due within the coming weeks.

We had left the tents for the musicians' block. We were entitled to a blanket, a wash bowl, and a bar of soap. The head of the block was a German Jew.

It was good to be under a Jew. He was called Alphonse. A young man with an extraordinarily aged face, he was entirely devoted to the cause of "his" block. Whenever he could, he would organize a cauldron of soup for the young ones, the weak, all those who were dreaming more about an extra plateful than of liberty.

One day when we had just come back from the warehouse, I was sent for by the secretary of the block.

"A-7713?"

"That's me."

"After eating, you're to go to the dentist."

"But I haven't got toothache."

"After eating. Without fail."

I went to the hospital block. There were about twenty prisoners waiting in a queue in front of the door. It did not take long to discover why we had been summoned: it was for the extraction of our gold teeth.

The dentist, a Jew from Czechoslovakia, had a face like a death mask. When he opened his mouth, there was a horrible sight of yellow, decaying teeth. I sat in the chair and asked him humbly: "Please, what are you going to do?"

"Simply take out your gold crown," he replied, indifferently.

I had the idea of pretending to be ill.

"You couldn't wait a few days, Doctor? I don't feel very well. I've got a temperature. . . ."

He wrinkled his brow, thought for a moment, and took my pulse.

"All right, son. When you feel better, come back and see me. But don't wait till I send for you!"

I went to see him a week later. With the same excuse: I still did not feel any better. He did not seem to show any surprise, and I do not know if he believed me. He was probably glad to see that I had come back of my own accord, as I had promised. He gave me another reprieve.

A few days after this visit of mine, they closed the dentist's surgery, and he was thrown into prison. He was going to be hanged. It was alleged that he had been running a private traffic of his own in the prisoners' gold teeth. I did not feel any pity for him. I was even pleased about what had happened. I had saved my gold crown. It might be useful to me one day to buy something—bread or life. I now took little interest in anything except my daily plate of soup and my crust of stale bread. Bread, soup—these were my whole life. I was a body. Perhaps less than that even: a starved stomach. The stomach alone was aware of the passage of time.

At the warehouse I often worked next to a young French girl. We did not speak to one another, since she knew no German and I did not understand French.

She seemed to me to be a Jewess, though here she passed as Aryan. She was a forced labor deportee.

One day when Idek was seized with one of his fits of frenzy, I got in his way. He leapt on me, like a wild animal, hitting me in the chest, on the head, throwing me down and pulling me up again, his blows growing more and more violent, until I was covered with blood. As I was biting my lips to stop myself from screaming with pain, he must have taken my silence for defiance, for he went on hitting me even harder.

Suddenly he calmed down. As if nothing had happened, he sent me back to work. It was as though we had been taking part together in some game where we each had our role to play.

I dragged myself to my corner. I ached all over. I felt

60

a cool hand wiping my blood-stained forehead. It was the French girl. She gave me her mournful smile and slipped a bit of bread into my hand. She looked into my eyes. I felt that she wanted to say something but was choked by fear. For a long moment she stayed like that, then her face cleared and she said to me in almost perfect German:

"Bite your lip, little brother. . . . Don't cry. Keep your anger and hatred for another day, for later on. The day will come, but not now. . . . Wait. Grit your teeth and wait. . . ."

Many years later, in Paris, I was reading my paper in the Metro. Facing me was a very beautiful woman with black hair and dreamy eyes. I had seen those eyes before somewhere. It was she.

"You don't recognize me?"

"I don't know you."

"In 1944 you were in Germany, at Buna, weren't you?"

"Yes. . . ."

"You used to work in the electrical warehouse. . . ."

"Yes," she said, somewhat disturbed. And then, after a moment's silence: "Wait a minute . . . I do remember. . . ."

"Idek, the Kapo . . . the little Jewish boy . . . your kind words. . . ."

We left the Metro together to sit down on the terrace of a café. We spent the whole evening reminiscing.

Before I parted from her, I asked her: "May I ask you a question?"

"I know what it will be—go on."

"What?"

"Am I Jewish . . . ? Yes, I am Jewish. From a religious family. During the occupation I obtained forged papers and passed myself off as an Aryan. That's how I was enlisted in the forced labor groups, and when I was deported to Germany, I escaped the concentration camp. At the warehouse, no one knew I could speak German. That would have aroused suspicions. Saying those few words to you was risky: but I knew you wouldn't give me away. . . ."

Another time we had to load Diesel engines onto trains supervised by German soldiers. Idek's nerves were on edge. He was restraining himself with great difficulty. Suddenly, his frenzy broke out. The victim was my father.

"You lazy old devil!" Idek began to yell. "Do you call that work?"

And he began to beat him with an iron bar. At first my father crouched under the blows, then he broke in two, like a dry tree struck by lightning, and collapsed.

I had watched the whole scene without moving. I kept quiet. In fact I was thinking of how to get farther away so that I would not be hit myself. What is more, any anger I felt at that moment was directed, not against the Kapo, but against my father. I was angry with him, for not knowing how to avoid Idek's outbreak. That is what concentration camp life had made of me.

Franek, the foreman, one day noticed the gold-crowned tooth in my mouth.

"Give me your crown, kid."

I told him it was impossible, that I could not eat without it.

"What do they give you to eat, anyway?"

I found another answer; the crown had been put down on a list after the medical inspection. This could bring trouble on us both.

"If you don't give me your crown, you'll pay for it even more."

This sympathetic, intelligent youth was suddenly no longer the same person. His eyes gleamed with desire. I told him I had to ask my father's advice.

"Ask your father, kid. But I want an answer by tomorrow."

When I spoke to my father about it, he turned pale, was silent a long while, and then said:

"No, son, you mustn't do it."

"He'll take it out on us!"

62

"He won't dare."

But alas, Franek knew where to touch me; he knew my weak point. My father had never done military service, and he never succeeded in marching in step. Here, every time we moved from one place to another in a body, we marched in strict rhythm. This was Franek's chance to torment my father and to thrash him savagely every day. Left, right: punch! Left, right: clout!

I decided to give my father lessons myself, to teach him to change step, and to keep to the rhythm. We began to do exercises in front of our block. I would give the commands: "Left, right!" and my father would practice. Some of the prisoners began to laugh at us.

"Look at this little officer teaching the old chap to march. . . . Hey, general, how many rations of bread does the old boy give you for this?"

But my father's progress was still inadequate, and blows continued to rain down on him.

"So you still can't march in step, you lazy old devil?"

These scenes were repeated for two weeks. We could not stand any more. We had to give in. When the day came, Franek burst into wild laughter.

"I knew it, I knew quite well I would win. Better late than never. And because you've made me wait, that's going to cost you a ration of bread. A ration of bread for one of my pals, a famous dentist from Warsaw, so that he can take your crown out."

"What? *My* ration of bread so that you can have *my* crown?"

Franek grinned.

"What would you like then? Shall I break your teeth with my fist?"

That same evening, in the lavatory the dentist from Warsaw pulled out my crowned tooth, with the aid of a rusty spoon.

Franek grew kinder. Occasionally, he even gave me

63

extra soup. But that did not last long. A fortnight later, all the Poles were transferred to another camp. I had lost my crown for nothing.

A few days before the Poles left, I had a new experience.

It was a Sunday morning. Our unit did not need to go to work that day. But all the same Idek would not hear of our staying in the camp. We had to go to the warehouse. This sudden enthusiasm for work left us stunned.

At the warehouse, Idek handed us over to Franek, saying, "Do what you like. But do something. If not, you'll hear from me. . . ."

And he disappeared.

We did not know what to do. Tired of squatting down, we each in turn went for a walk through the warehouse, looking for a bit of bread some civilian might have left behind.

When I came to the back of the building, I heard a noise coming from a little room next door. I went up and saw Idek with a young Polish girl, half-naked, on a mattress. Then I understood why Idek had refused to let us stay in the camp. Moving a hundred prisoners so that he could lie with a girl! It struck me as so funny that I burst out laughing.

Idek leapt up, turned around, and saw me, while the girl tried to cover up her breasts. I wanted to run away, but my legs were glued to the ground. Idek seized me by the throat.

Speaking in a low voice, he said, "You wait and see, kid. . . . You'll soon find out what leaving your work's going to cost you. . . . You're going to pay for this pretty soon. . . . And now, go back to your place."

Half an hour before work usually ended, the Kapo collected together the whole unit. Roll call. Nobody knew what had happened. Roll call at this time of day? Here? But I knew. The Kapo gave a short speech.

64

"An ordinary prisoner has no right to meddle in other people's affairs. One of you does not seem to have understood this. I'm obliged, therefore, to make it very clear to him once and for all."

I felt the sweat run down my back.

"A-7713!"

I came forward.

"A box!" he ordered.

They brought him a box.

"Lie down on it! On your stomach!"

I obeyed.

Then I was aware of nothing but the strokes of the whip.

"One . . . two . . .," he counted.

He took his time between each stroke. Only the first ones really hurt me. I could hear him counting:

"Ten . . . eleven . . ."

His voice was calm and reached me as through a thick wall.

"Twenty-three . . ."

Two more, I thought, half conscious. The Kapo waited.

"Twenty-four . . . twenty-five!"

It was over. But I did not realize it, for I had fainted. I felt myself come round as a bucket of cold water was thrown over me. I was still lying on the box. I could just vaguely make out the wet ground surrounding me. Then I heard someone cry out. It must have been the Kapo. I began to distinguish the words he was shouting.

"Get up!"

I probably made some movement to raise myself, because I felt myself falling back onto the box. How I longed to get up!

"Get up!" he yelled more loudly.

If only I could have answered him, at least; if only I could have told him that I could not move! But I could not manage to open my lips.

At Idek's command, two prisoners lifted me up and led me in front of him.

"Look me in the eye!"

I looked at him without seeing him. I was thinking of my father. He must have suffered more than I did.

"Listen to me, you bastard!" said Idek, coldly. "That's for your curiosity. You'll get five times more if you dare tell anyone what you saw! Understand?"

I nodded my head, once, ten times. I nodded ceaselessly. as if my head had decided to say yes without ever stopping.

One Sunday, when half of us—including my father—were at work, the rest—including myself—were in the block, taking advantage of the chance to stay in bed late in the morning.

At about ten o'clock, the air-raid sirens began to wail. An alert. The leaders of the block ran to assemble us inside, while the SS took refuge in the shelters. As it was relatively easy to escape during a warning—the guards left their lookout posts and the electric current was cut off in the barbed-wire fences—the SS had orders to kill anyone found outside the blocks.

Within a few minutes, the camp looked like an abandoned ship. Not a living soul on the paths. Near the kitchen, two cauldrons of steaming hot soup had been left, half full. Two cauldrons of soup, right in the middle of the path, with no one guarding them! A feast for kings, abandoned, supreme temptation! Hundreds of eyes looked at them, sparkling with desire. Two lambs, with a hundred wolves lying in wait for them. Two lambs without a shepherd—a gift. But who would dare?

Terror was stronger than hunger. Suddenly, we saw the door of Block 37 open imperceptibly. A man appeared, crawling like a worm in the direction of the cauldrons.

Hundreds of eyes followed his movements. Hundreds of men crawled with him, scraping their knees with his on the gravel. Every heart trembled, but with envy above all. This man had dared.

He reached the first cauldron. Hearts raced: he had

66

succeeded. Jealousy consumed us, burned us up like straw. We never thought for a moment of admiring him. Poor hero, committing suicide for a ration of soup! In our thoughts we were murdering him.

Stretched out by the cauldron, he was now trying to raise himself up to the edge. Either from weakness or fear he stayed there, trying, no doubt, to muster up the last of his strength. At last he succeeded in hoisting himself onto the edge of the pot. For a moment, he seemed to be looking at himself, seeking his ghostlike reflection in the soup. Then, for no apparent reason, he let out a terrible cry, a rattle such as I had never heard before, and, his mouth open, thrust his head toward the still steaming liquid. We jumped at the explosion. Falling back onto the ground, his face stained with soup, the man writhed for a few seconds at the foot of the cauldron, then he moved no more.

Then we began to hear the airplanes. Almost at once, the barracks began to shake.

"They're bombing Buna!" someone shouted.

I thought of my father. But I was glad all the same. To see the whole works go up in fire—what revenge! We had heard so much talk about the defeats of German troops on various fronts, but we did not know how much to believe. This, today, was real!

We were not afraid. And yet, if a bomb had fallen on the blocks, it alone would have claimed hundreds of victims on the spot. But we were no longer afraid of death; at any rate, not of that death. Every bomb that exploded filled us with joy and gave us new confidence in life.

The raid lasted over an hour. If it could only have lasted ten times ten hours! . . . Then silence fell once more. The last sound of an American plane was lost on the wind, and we found ourselves back again in the cemetery. A great trail of black smoke was rising up on the horizon. The sirens began to wail once more. It was the end of the alert.

Everyone came out of the blocks. We filled our lungs with the fire- and smoke-laden air, and our eyes shone with

67

hope. A bomb had fallen in the middle of the camp, near the assembly point, but it had not gone off. We had to take it outside the camp.

The head of the camp, accompanied by his assistant and the chief Kapo, made a tour of inspection along the paths. The raid had left traces of terror on his face.

Right in the middle of the camp lay the body of the man with the soup-stained face, the only victim. The cauldrons were taken back into the kitchen.

The SS had gone back to their lookout posts, behind their machine guns. The interlude was over.

At the end of an hour, we saw the units come back, in step, as usual. Joyfully, I caught sight of my father.

"Several buildings have been flattened right out," he said, "but the warehouse hasn't suffered."

In the afternoon we went cheerfully to clear away the ruins.

A week later, on the way back from work, we noticed in the center of the camp, at the assembly place, a black gallows.

We were told that soup would not be distributed until after roll call. This took longer than usual. The orders were given in a sharper manner than on other days, and in the air there were strange undertones.

"Bare your heads!" yelled the head of the camp, suddenly.

Ten thousand caps were simultaneously removed.

"Cover your heads!"

Ten thousand caps went back onto their skulls, as quick as lightning.

The gate to the camp opened. An SS section appeared and surrounded us: one SS at every three paces. On the lookout towers the machine guns were trained on the assembly place.

"They fear trouble," whispered Juliek.

Two SS men had gone to the cells. They came back with

68

the condemned man between them. He was a youth from Warsaw. He had three years of concentration camp life behind him. He was a strong, well-built boy, a giant in comparison with me.

His back to the gallows, his face turned toward his judge, who was the head of the camp, the boy was pale, but seemed more moved than afraid. His manacled hands did not tremble. His eyes gazed coldly at the hundreds of SS guards, the thousands of prisoners who surrounded him.

The head of the camp began to read his verdict, hammering out each phrase:

"In the name of Himmler . . . prisoner Number . . . stole during the alert. . . . According to the law . . . paragraph . . . prisoner Number . . . is condemned to death. May this be a warning and an example to all prisoners."

No one moved.

I could hear my heart beating. The thousands who had died daily at Auschwitz and at Birkenau in the crematory ovens no longer troubled me. But this one, leaning against his gallows—he overwhelmed me.

"Do you think this ceremony'll be over soon? I'm hungry. . . . " whispered Juliek.

At a sign from the head of the camp, the Lagerkapo advanced toward the condemned man. Two prisoners helped him in his task—for two plates of soup.

The Kapo wanted to bandage the victim's eyes, but he refused.

After a long moment of waiting, the executioner put the rope round his neck. He was on the point of motioning to his assistants to draw the chair away from the prisoner's feet, when the latter cried, in a calm, strong voice:

"Long live liberty! A curse upon Germany! A curse . . .! A cur—"

The executioners had completed their task.

A command cleft the air like a sword.

"Bare your heads."

Ten thousand prisoners paid their last respects.

"Cover your heads!"

Then the whole camp, block after block, had to march past the hanged man and stare at the dimmed eyes, the lolling tongue of death. The Kapos and heads of each block forced everyone to look him full in the face.

After the march, we were given permission to return to the blocks for our meal.

I remember that I found the soup excellent that evening. . . .

I witnessed other hangings. I never saw a single one of the victims weep. For a long time those dried-up bodies had forgotten the bitter taste of tears.

Except once. The Oberkapo of the fifty-second cable unit was a Dutchman, a giant, well over six feet. Seven hundred prisoners worked under his orders, and they all loved him like a brother. No one had ever received a blow at his hands, nor an insult from his lips.

He had a young boy under him, a *pipel*, as they were called—a child with a refined and beautiful face, unheard of in this camp.

(At Buna, the *pipel* were loathed; they were often crueller than adults. I once saw one of thirteen beating his father because the latter had not made his bed properly. The old man was crying softly while the boy shouted: "If you don't stop crying at once I shan't bring you any more bread. Do you understand?" But the Dutchman's little servant was loved by all. He had the face of a sad angel.)

One day, the electric power station at Buna was blown up. The Gestapo, summoned to the spot, suspected sabotage. They found a trail. It eventually led to the Dutch Oberkapo. And there, after a search, they found an important stock of arms.

The Oberkapo was arrested immediately. He was tortured for a period of weeks, but in vain. He would not give a single name. He was transferred to Auschwitz. We never heard of him again.

70

But his little servant had been left behind in the camp in prison. Also put to torture, he too would not speak. Then the SS sentenced him to death, with two other prisoners who had been discovered with arms.

One day when we came back from work, we saw three gallows rearing up in the assembly place, three black crows. Roll call. SS all round us, machine guns trained: the traditional ceremony. Three victims in chains—and one of them, the little servant, the sad-eyed angel.

The SS seemed more preoccupied, more disturbed than usual. To hang a young boy in front of thousands of spectators was no light matter. The head of the camp read the verdict. All eyes were on the child. He was lividly pale, almost calm, biting his lips. The gallows threw its shadow over him.

This time the Lagerkapo refused to act as executioner. Three SS replaced him.

The three victims mounted together onto the chairs.

The three necks were placed at the same moment within the nooses.

"Long live liberty!" cried the two adults.

But the child was silent.

"Where is God? Where is He?" someone behind me asked.

At a sign from the head of the camp, the three chairs tipped over.

Total silence throughout the camp. On the horizon, the sun was setting.

"Bare your heads!" yelled the head of the camp. His voice was raucous. We were weeping.

"Cover your heads!"

Then the march past began. The two adults were no longer alive. Their tongues hung swollen, blue-tinged. But the third rope was still moving; being so light, the child was still alive. . . .

For more than half an hour he stayed there, struggling between life and death, dying in slow agony under our eyes.

And we had to look him full in the face. He was still alive when I passed in front of him. His tongue was still red, his eyes were not yet glazed.

Behind me, I heard the same man asking:

"Where is God now?"

And I heard a voice within me answer him:

"Where is He? Here He is—He is hanging here on this gallows. . . ."

That night the soup tasted of corpses.

The summer was coming to an end. The Jewish year was nearly over.

On the eve of Rosh Hashanah, the last day of that accursed year, the whole camp was electric with the tension which was in all our hearts. In spite of everything, this day was different from any other. The last day of the year. The word "last" rang very strangely. What if it were indeed the last day?

They gave us our evening meal, a very thick soup, but no one touched it. We wanted to wait until after prayers. At the place of assembly, surrounded by the electrified barbed wire, thousands of silent Jews gathered, their faces stricken.

Night was falling. Other prisoners continued to crowd in, from every block, able suddenly to conquer time and space and submit both to their will.

"What are You, my God," I thought angrily, "compared to this afflicted crowd, proclaiming to You their faith, their anger, their revolt? What does Your greatness mean, Lord

73

of the Universe, in the face of all this weakness, this decomposition, and this decay? Why do You still trouble their sick minds, their crippled bodies?"

Ten thousand men had come to attend the solemn service, heads of the blocks, Kapos, functionaries of death.

"Bless the Eternal. . . ."

The voice of the officiant had just made itself heard. I thought at first it was the wind.

"Blessed be the Name of the Eternal!"

Thousands of voices repeated the benediction; thousands of men prostrated themselves like trees before a tempest.

"Blessed be the Name of the Eternal!"

Why, but why should I bless Him? In every fiber I rebelled. Because He had had thousands of children burned in His pits? Because He kept six crematories working night and day, on Sundays and feast days? Because in His great might He had created Auschwitz, Birkenau, Buna, and so many factories of death? How could I say to Him: "Blessed art Thou, Eternal, Master of the Universe, Who chose us from among the races to be tortured day and night, to see our fathers, our mothers, our brothers, end in the crematory? Praised be Thy Holy Name, Thou Who hast chosen us to be butchered on Thine altar?"

I heard the voice of the officiant rising up, powerful yet at the same time broken, amid the tears, the sobs, the sighs of the whole congregation:

"All the earth and the Universe are God's!"

He kept stopping every moment, as though he did not have the strength to find the meaning beneath the words. The melody choked in his throat.

And I, mystic that I had been, I thought:

"Yes, man is very strong, greater than God. When You were deceived by Adam and Eve, You drove them out of Paradise. When Noah's generation displeased You, You brought down the Flood. When Sodom no longer found

74

favor in Your eyes, You made the sky rain down fire and sulphur. But these men here, whom You have betrayed, whom You have allowed to be tortured, butchered, gassed, burned, what do they do? They pray before You! They praise Your name!"

"All creation bears witness to the Greatness of God!"

Once, New Year's Day had dominated my life. I knew that my sins grieved the Eternal; I implored his forgiveness. Once, I had believed profoundly that upon one solitary deed of mine, one solitary prayer, depended the salvation of the world.

This day I had ceased to plead. I was no longer capable of lamentation. On the contrary, I felt very strong. I was the accuser, God the accused. My eyes were open and I was alone—terribly alone in a world without God and without man. Without love or mercy. I had ceased to be anything but ashes, yet I felt myself to be stronger than the Almighty, to whom my life had been tied for so long. I stood amid that praying congregation, observing it like a stranger.

The service ended with the Kaddish. Everyone recited the Kaddish over his parents, over his children, over his brothers, and over himself.

We stayed for a long time at the assembly place. No one dared to drag himself away from this mirage. Then it was time to go to bed and slowly the prisoners made their way over to their blocks. I heard people wishing one another a Happy New Year!

I ran off to look for my father. And at the same time I was afraid of having to wish him a Happy New Year when I no longer believed in it.

He was standing near the wall, bowed down, his shoulders sagging as though beneath a heavy burden. I went up to him, took his hand and kissed it. A tear fell upon it. Whose was that tear? Mine? His? I said nothing. Nor did he. We had never understood one another so clearly.

The sound of the bell jolted us back to reality. We must go to bed. We came back from far away. I raised my eyes to look at my father's face leaning over mine, to try to discover a smile or something resembling one upon the aged, dried-up countenance. Nothing. Not the shadow of an expression. Beaten.

Yom Kippur. The Day of Atonement.

Should we fast? The question was hotly debated. To fast would mean a surer, swifter death. We fasted here the whole year round. The whole year was Yom Kippur. But others said that we should fast simply because it was dangerous to do so. We should show God that even here, in this enclosed hell, we were capable of singing His praises.

I did not fast, mainly to please my father, who had forbidden me to do so. But further, there was no longer any reason why I should fast. I no longer accepted God's silence. As I swallowed my bowl of soup, I saw in the gesture an act of rebellion and protest against Him.

And I nibbled my crust of bread.

In the depths of my heart, I felt a great void.

The SS gave us a fine New Year's gift.

We had just come back from work. As soon as we had passed through the door of the camp, we sensed something different in the air. Roll call did not take so long as usual. The evening soup was given out with great speed and swallowed down at once in anguish.

I was no longer in the same block as my father. I had been transferred to another unit, the building one, where, twelve hours a day, I had to drag heavy blocks of stone about. The head of my new block was a German Jew, small of stature, with piercing eyes. He told us that evening that no one would be allowed to go out after the evening soup. And soon a terrible word was circulating—selection.

We knew what that meant. An SS man would examine us. Whenever he found a weak one, a *musulman* as we called them, he would write his number down: good for the crematory.

76

After soup, we gathered together between the beds. The veterans said:

"You're lucky to have been brought here so late. This camp is paradise today, compared with what it was like two years ago. Buna was a real hell then. There was no water, no blankets, less soup and bread. At night we slept almost naked, and it was below thirty degrees. The corpses were collected in hundreds every day. The work was hard. Today, this is a little paradise. The Kapos had orders to kill a certain number of prisoners every day. And every week—selection. A merciless selection. . . . Yes, you're lucky."

"Stop it! Be quiet!" I begged. "You can tell your stories tomorrow or on some other day."

They burst out laughing. They were not veterans for nothing.

"Are you scared? So were we scared. And there was plenty to be scared of in those days."

The old men stayed in their corner, dumb, motionless, hunted. Some were praying.

An hour's delay. In an hour, we should know the verdict —death or a reprieve.

And my father? Suddenly I remembered him. How would he pass the selection? He had aged so much. . . .

The head of our block had never been outside concentration camps since 1933. He had already been through all the slaughterhouses, all the factories of death. At about nine o'clock, he took up his position in our midst:

"Achtung!"

There was instant silence.

"Listen carefully to what I am going to say." (For the first time, I heard his voice quiver.) "In a few moments the selection will begin. You must get completely undressed. Then one by one you go before the SS doctors. I hope you will all succeed in getting through. But you must help your own chances. Before you go into the next room, move about in some way so that you give yourselves a little color. Don't walk slowly, run! Run as if the devil were after you! Don't look at the SS. Run, straight in front of you!"

He broke off for a moment, then added:

"And, the essential thing, don't be afraid!"

Here was a piece of advice we should have liked very much to be able to follow.

I got undressed, leaving my clothes on the bed. There was no danger of anyone stealing them this evening.

Tibi and Yossi, who had changed their unit at the same time as I had, came up to me and said:

"Let's keep together. We shall be stronger."

Yossi was murmuring something between his teeth. He must have been praying. I had never realized that Yossi was a believer. I had even always thought the reverse. Tibi was silent, very pale. All the prisoners in the block stood naked between the beds. This must be how one stands at the last judgment.

"They're coming!"

There were three SS officers standing round the notorious Dr. Mengele, who had received us at Birkenau. The head of the block, with an attempt at a smile, asked us:

"Ready?"

Yes, we were ready. So were the SS doctors. Dr. Mengele was holding a list in his hand: our numbers. He made a sign to the head of the block: "We can begin!" As if this were a game!

The first to go by were the "officials" of the block: *Stubenaelteste*, Kapos, foremen, all in perfect physical condition of course! Then came the ordinary prisoners' turn. Dr. Mengele took stock of them from head to foot. Every now and then, he wrote a number down. One single thought filled my mind: not to let my number be taken; not to show my left arm.

There were only Tibi and Yossi in front of me. They passed. I had time to notice that Mengele had not written their numbers down. Someone pushed me. It was my turn.

78

I ran without looking back. My head was spinning: you're too thin, you're weak, you're too thin, you're good for the furnace. . . . The race seemed interminable. I thought I had been running for years. . . . You're too thin, you're too weak. . . . At last I had arrived exhausted. When I regained my breath, I questioned Yossi and Tibi:

"Was I written down?"

"No," said Yossi. He added, smiling: "In any case, he couldn't have written you down, you were running too fast. . . ."

I began to laugh. I was glad. I would have liked to kiss him. At that moment, what did the others matter! I hadn't been written down.

Those whose numbers had been noted stood apart, abandoned by the whole world. Some were weeping in silence.

The SS officers went away. The head of the block appeared, his face reflecting the general weariness.

"Everything went off all right. Don't worry. Nothing is going to happen to anyone. To anyone."

Again he tried to smile. A poor, emaciated, dried-up Jew questioned him avidly in a trembling voice:

"But . . . but, *Blockaelteste*, they did write me down!"

The head of the block let his anger break out. What! Did someone refuse to believe him!

"What's the matter now? Am I telling lies then? I tell you once and for all, nothing's going to happen to you! To anyone! You're wallowing in your own despair, you fool!"

The bell rang, a signal that the selection had been completed throughout the camp.

With all my might I began to run to Block 36. I met my father on the way. He came up to me:

"Well? So you passed?"

"Yes. And you?"

"Me too."

How we breathed again, now! My father had brought

me a present—half a ration of bread obtained in exchange for a piece of rubber, found at the warehouse, which would do to sole a shoe.

The bell. Already we must separate, go to bed. Everything was regulated by the bell. It gave me orders, and I automatically obeyed them. I hated it. Whenever I dreamed of a better world, I could only imagine a universe with no bells.

Several days had elapsed. We no longer thought about the selection. We went to work as usual, loading heavy stones into railway wagons. Rations had become more meager: this was the only change.

We had risen before dawn, as on every day. We had received the black coffee, the ration of bread. We were about to set out for the yard as usual. The head of the block arrived, running.

"Silence for a moment. I have a list of numbers here. I'm going to read them to you. Those whose numbers I call won't be going to work this morning; they'll stay behind in the camp."

And, in a soft voice, he read out about ten numbers. We had understood. These were numbers chosen at the selection. Dr. Mengele had not forgotten.

The head of the block went toward his room. Ten prisoners surrounded him, hanging onto his clothes:

"Save us! You promised . . .! We want to go to the yard. We're strong enough to work. We're good workers. We can . . . we will . . . ."

He tried to calm them, to reassure them about their fate, to explain to them that the fact that they were staying behind in the camp did not mean much, had no tragic significance.

"After all, I stay here myself every day," he added.

It was a somewhat feeble argument. He realized it, and without another word went and shut himself up in his room.

The bell had just rung.

"Form up!"

It scarcely mattered now that the work was hard. The essential thing was to be as far away as possible from the block, from the crucible of death, from the center of hell.

I saw my father running toward me. I became frightened all of a sudden.

"What's the matter?"

Out of breath, he could hardly open his mouth.

"Me, too . . . me, too . . . ! They told me to stay behind in the camp."

They had written down his number without his being aware of it.

"What will happen?" I asked in anguish.

But it was he who tried to reassure me.

"It isn't certain yet. There's still a chance of escape. They're going to do another selection today . . . a decisive selection."

I was silent.

He felt that his time was short. He spoke quickly. He would have liked to say so many things. His speech grew confused; his voice choked. He knew that I would have to go in a few moments. He would have to stay behind alone, so very alone.

"Look, take this knife," he said to me. "I don't need it any longer. It might be useful to you. And take this spoon as well. Don't sell them. Quickly! Go on. Take what I'm giving you!"

The inheritance.

"Don't talk like that, father." (I felt that I would break into sobs.) "I don't want you to say that. Keep the spoon and knife. You need them as much as I do. We shall see each other again this evening, after work."

He looked at me with his tired eyes, veiled with despair. He went on:

"I'm asking this of you. . . . Take them. Do as I ask, my son. We have no time. . . . Do as your father asks."

Our Kapo yelled that we should start.

The unit set out toward the camp gate. Left, right! I bit my lips. My father had stayed by the block, leaning against the wall. Then he began to run, to catch up with us. Perhaps he had forgotten something he wanted to say to me. . . . But we were marching too quicly. . . . Left, right!

We were already at the gate. They counted us, to the din of military music. We were outside.

The whole day, I wandered about as if sleepwalking. Now and then Tibi and Yossi would throw me a brotherly word. The Kapo, too, tried to reassure me. He had given me easier work today. I felt sick at heart. How well they were treating me! Like an orphan! I thought: even now, my father is still helping me.

I did not know myself what I wanted—for the day to pass quickly or not. I was afraid of finding myself alone that night. How good it would be to die here!

At last we began the return journey. How I longed for orders to run!

The military march. The gate. The camp.

I ran to Block 36.

Were there still miracles on this earth? He was alive. He had escaped the second selection. He had been able to prove that he was still useful. . . . I gave him back his knife and spoon.

Akiba Drumer left us, a victim of the selection. Lately, he had wandered among us, his eyes glazed, telling everyone of his weakness: "I can't go on . . . It's all over. . . ." It was impossible to raise his morale. He didn't listen to what we told him. He could only repeat that all was over for him, that he could no longer keep up the struggle, that he had no strength left, nor faith. Suddenly his eyes would become blank, nothing but two open wounds, two pits of terror.

He was not the only one to lose his faith during those selection days. I knew a rabbi from a little town in Poland, a bent old man, whose lips were always trembling. He used to pray all the time, in the block, in the yard, in the ranks. He would recite whole pages of the Talmud from memory, argue with himself, ask himself questions and answer himself. And one day he said to me: "It's the end. God is no longer with us."

And, as though he had repented of having spoken such words, so clipped, so cold, he added in his faint voice:

"I know. One has no right to say things like that. I know. Man is too small, too humble and inconsiderable to seek to understand the mysterious ways of God. But what can I do? I'm not a sage, one of the elect, nor a saint. I'm just an ordinary creature of flesh and blood. I've got eyes, too, and I can see what they're doing here. Where is the divine Mercy? Where is God? How can I believe, how could anyone believe, in this merciful God?"

Poor Akiba Drumer, if he could have gone on believing in God, if he could have seen a proof of God in this Calvary, he would not have been taken by the selection. But as soon as he felt the first cracks forming in his faith, he had lost his reason for struggling and had begun to die.

When the selection came, he was condemned in advance, offering his own neck to the executioner. All he asked of us was:

"In three days I shall no longer be here. . . . Say the Kaddish for me."

We promised him. In three days' time, when we saw the smoke rising from the chimney, we would think of him. Ten of us would gather together and hold a special service. All his friends would say the Kaddish.

Then he went off toward the hospital, his step steadier, not looking back. An ambulance was waiting to take him to Birkenau.

These were terrible days. We received more blows than food; we were crushed with work. And three days after he had gone we forgot to say the Kaddish.

Winter had come. The days were short, and the nights

had become almost unbearable. In the first hours of dawn, the icy wind cut us like a whip. We were given winter clothes—slightly thicker striped shirts. The veterans found in this a new source of derision.

"Now you'll really be getting a taste of the camp!"

We left for work as usual, our bodies frozen. The stones were so cold that it seemed as though our hands would be glued to them if we touched them. But you get used to anything.

On Christmas and New Year's Day, there was no work. We were allowed a slightly thicker soup.

Toward the middle of January, my right foot began to swell because of the cold. I was unable to put it on the ground. I went to have it examined. The doctor, a great Jewish doctor, a prisoner like ourselves, was quite definite: I must have an operation! If we waited, the toes—and perhaps the whole leg—would have to be amputated.

This was the last straw! But I had no choice. The doctor had decided on an operation, and there was no discussing it. I was even glad that it was he who had made the decision.

They put me into a bed with white sheets. I had forgotten that people slept in sheets.

The hospital was not bad at all. We were given good bread and thicker soup. No more bell. No more roll call. No more work. Now and then I was able to send a bit of bread to my father.

Near me lay a Hungarian Jew who had been struck down with dysentery—skin and bone, with dead eyes. I could only hear his voice; it was the sole indication that he was alive. Where did he get the strength to talk?

"You mustn't rejoice too soon, my boy. There's selection here too. More often than outside. Germany doesn't need sick Jews. Germany doesn't need me. When the next transport comes, you'll have a new neighbor. So listen to me, and take my advice: get out of the hospital before the next selection!"

These words which came from under the ground, from

84

a faceless shape, filled me with terror. It was indeed true that the hospital was very small and that if new invalids arrived in the next few days, room would have to be found for them.

But perhaps my faceless neighbor, fearing that he would be among the first victims, simply wanted to drive me away, to free my bed in order to give himself a chance to survive. Perhaps he just wanted to frighten me. Yet, what if he were telling the truth? I decided to await events.

The doctor came to tell me that the operation would be the next day.

"Don't be afraid," he added. "Everything will be all right."

At ten o'clock in the morning, they took me into the operating room. "My" doctor was there. I took comfort from this. I felt that nothing serious could happen while he was there. There was balm in every word he spoke, and every glance he gave me held a message of hope.

"It will hurt you a bit," he said, "but that will pass. Grit your teeth."

The operation lasted an hour. They had not put me to sleep. I kept my eyes fixed upon my doctor. Then I felt myself go under. . . .

When I came round, opening my eyes, I could see nothing at first but a great whiteness, my sheets; then I noticed the face of my doctor, bending over me:

"Everything went off well. You're brave, my boy. Now you're going to stay here for two weeks, rest comfortably, and it will be over. You'll eat well, and relax your body and your nerves."

I could only follow the movements of his lips. I scarcely understood what he was saying, but the murmur of his voice did me good. Suddenly a cold sweat broke out on my forehead. I could not feel my leg! Had they amputated it?

"Doctor," I stammered. "Doctor . . . ?"

"What's the matter, son?"

I lacked the courage to ask him the question.

"Doctor, I'm thirsty . . . ."

He had water brought to me. He was smiling. He was getting ready to go and visit the other patients.

"Doctor?"

"What?"

"Shall I still be able to use my leg?"

He was no longer smiling. I was very frightened. He said:

"Do you trust me, my boy?"

"I trust you absolutely, Doctor."

"Well then, listen to me. You'll be completely recovered in a fortnight. You'll be able to walk like anyone else. The sole of your foot was all full of pus. We just had to open the swelling. You haven't had your leg amputated. You'll see. In a fortnight's time you'll be walking about like everyone else."

I had only a fortnight to wait.

Two days after my operation, there was a rumor going round the camp that the front had suddenly drawn nearer. The Red Army, they said, was advancing on Buna; it was only a matter of hours now.

We were already accustomed to rumors of this kind. It was not the first time a false prophet had foretold to us peace-on-earth, negotiations-with-the-Red-Cross-for-our-release, or other false rumors. . . . And often we believed them. It was an injection of morphine.

But this time these prophecies seemed more solid. During these last few nights, we had heard the guns in the distance.

My neighbor, the faceless one, said:

"Don't let yourself be fooled with illusions. Hitler has made it very clear that he will annihilate all the Jews before the clock strikes twelve, before they can hear the last stroke."

86

I burst out:

"What does it matter to you? Do we have to regard Hitler as a prophet?"

His glazed, faded eyes looked at me. At last he said in a weary voice:

"I've got more faith in Hitler than in anyone else. He's the only one who's kept his promises, all his promises, to the Jewish people."

At four o'clock on the afternoon of the same day, as usual the bell summoned all the heads of the blocks to go and report.

They came back shattered. They could only just open their lips enough to say the word: evacuation. The camp was to be emptied, and we were to be sent farther back. Where to? To somewhere right in the depths of Germany, to other camps; there was no shortage of them.

"When?"

"Tomorrow evening."

"Perhaps the Russians will arrive first."

"Perhaps."

We knew perfectly well that they would not.

The camp had become a hive. People ran about, shouting at one another. In all the blocks, preparations for the journey were going on. I had forgotten about my bad foot. A doctor came into the room and announced:

"Tomorrow, immediately after nightfall, the camp will set out. Block after block. Patients will stay in the infirmary. They will not be evacuated."

This news made us think. Were the SS going to leave hundreds of prisoners to strut about in the hospital blocks, waiting for their liberators? Were they going to let the Jews hear the twelfth stroke sound? Obviously not.

"All the invalids will be summarily killed," said the faceless one. "And sent to the crematory in a final batch."

"The camp is certain to be mined," said another. "The moment the evacuation's over, it'll blow up."

As for me, I was not thinking about death, but I did not want to be separated from my father. We had already suffered so much, borne so much together; this was not the time to be separated.

I ran outside to look for him. The snow was thick, and the windows of the blocks were veiled with frost. One shoe in my hand, because it would not go onto my right foot, I ran on, feeling neither pain nor cold.

"What shall we do?"

My father did not answer.

"What shall we do, father?"

He was lost in thought. The choice was in our hands. For once we could decide our fate for ourselves. We could both stay in the hospital, where I could, thanks to my doctor, get him entered as a patient or a nurse. Or else we could follow the others.

"Well, what shall we do, father?"

He was silent.

"Let's be evacuated with the others," I said to him.

He did not answer. He looked at my foot.

"Do you think you can walk?"

"Yes, I think so."

"Let's hope that we shan't regret it, Eliezer."

I learned after the war the fate of those who had stayed behind in the hospital. They were quite simply liberated by the Russians two days after the evacuation.

I did not go back to the hospital again. I returned to my block. My wound was open and bleeding; the snow had grown red where I had trodden.

The head of the block gave out double rations of bread and margarine, for the journey. We could take as many shirts and other clothes as we liked from the store.

It was cold. We got into bed.

The last night in Buna. Yet another last night. The last night at home, the last night in the ghetto, the last night in the train, and, now, the last night in Buna. How much longer were our lives to be dragged out from one "last night" to another?

I did not sleep at all. Through the frosted panes bursts of red light could be seen. Cannon shots split the night-time silence. How close the Russians were! Between them and us—one night, our last night. There was whispering from one bed to another: with luck the Russians would be here before the evacuation. Hope revived again.

Someone shouted:

"Try and sleep. Gather your strength for the journey."

This reminded me of my mother's last words of advice in the ghetto.

But I could not sleep. My foot felt as if it were burning.

In the morning, the face of the camp had changed. Prisoners appeared in strange outfits: it was like a masquerade. Everyone had put on several garments, one on top of the other, in order to keep out the cold. Poor mountebanks, wider than they were tall, more dead than alive; poor clowns, their ghostlike faces emerging from piles of prison clothes! Buffoons!

I tried to find a shoe that was too large. In vain. I tore up a blanket and wrapped my wounded foot in it. Then I went wandering through the camp, looking for a little more bread and a few potatoes.

Some said we were being taken to Czechoslovakia. No, to Gros-Rosen. No, to Gleiwitz. No, to. . . .

Two o'clock in the afternoon. The snow was still coming down thickly.

The time was passing quickly now. Dusk had fallen. The day was disappearing in a monochrome of gray.

The head of the block suddenly remembered that he had forgotten to clean out the block. He ordered four prisoners to wash the wooden floor. . . . An hour before leaving the camp! Why? For whom?

"For the liberating army," he cried. "So that they'll realize there were men living here and not pigs."

Were we men then? The block was cleaned from top to bottom, washed in every corner.

At six o'clock the bell rang. The death knell. The burial. The procession was about to begin its march.

"Form up! Quickly!"

In a few moments we were all in rows, by blocks. Night had fallen. Everything was in order, according to the pre-arranged plan.

The searchlights came on. Hundreds of armed SS men rose up out of the darkness, accompanied by sheepdogs. The snow never ceased.

The gates of the camp opened. It seemed that an even darker night was waiting for us on the other side.

The first blocks began to march. We waited. We had to wait for the departure of the fifty-six blocks who came before us. It was very cold. In my pocket I had two pieces of bread. With how much pleasure could I have eaten them! But I was not allowed to. Not yet.

Our turn was coming: Block 53 . . . Block 55 . . .

Block 57, forward march!

It snowed relentlessly.

An icy wind blew in violent gusts. But we marched without faltering.

The SS made us increase our pace. "Faster, you swine, you filthy sons of bitches!" Why not? The movement warmed us up a little. The blood flowed more easily in our veins. One felt oneself reviving. . . .

"Faster, you filthy sons of bitches!" We were no longer marching; we were running. Like automatons. The SS were running too, their weapons in their hands. We looked as though we were fleeing before them.

Pitch darkness. Every now and then, an explosion in the night. They had orders to fire on any who could not keep up. Their fingers on the triggers, they did not deprive themselves of this pleasure. If one of us stopped for a second, a sharp shot finished off another filthy son of a bitch.

I was putting one foot in front of the other mechanically. I was dragging with me this skeletal body which weighed so much. If only I could have got rid of it! In spite of my efforts not to think about it, I could feel myself as two entities—my body and me. I hated it.

I repeated to myself: "Don't think. Don't stop. Run."

Near me, men were collapsing in the dirty snow. Shots.

At my side marched a young Polish lad called Zalman. He had been working in the electrical warehouse at Buna. They had laughed at him because he was always praying or meditating on some problem of the Talmud. It was his way of escaping from reality, of not feeling the blows. . . .

He was suddenly seized with cramp in the stomach. "I've got stomach ache," he whispered to me. He could not go on. He had to stop for a moment. I begged him:

"Wait a bit, Zalman. We shall all be stopping soon. We're not going to run like this till the end of the world."

But as he ran he began to undo his buttons, crying:

"I can't go on any longer. My stomach's bursting. . . ."

"Make an effort, Zalman. . . . Try. . . ."

"I can't. . . ." he groaned.

His trousers lowered, he let himself sink down.

That is the last picture I have of him. I do not think it can have been the SS who finished him, because no one had noticed. He must have been trampled to death beneath the feet of the thousands of men who followed us.

I quickly forgot him. I began to think of myself again. Because of my painful foot, a shudder went through me at each step. "A few more yards," I thought. "A few more yards, and that will be the end. I shall fall. A spurt of red flame. A shot." Death wrapped itself around me till I was stifled. It stuck to me. I felt that I could touch it. The idea of dying, of no longer being, began to fascinate me. Not to exist any longer. Not to feel the horrible pains in my foot. Not to feel anything, neither weariness, nor cold, nor anything. To break the ranks, to let oneself slide to the edge of the road. . . .

My father's presence was the only thing that stopped me. . . . He was running at my side, out of breath, at the end of his strength, at his wit's end. I had no right to let myself die. What would he do without me? I was his only support.

These thoughts had taken up a brief space of time, during which I had gone on running without feeling my throbbing foot, without realizing that I was running, without being conscious that I owned a body galloping there on the road in the midst of so many thousands of others.

When I came to myself again, I tried to slacken the pace. But there was no way. A great tidal wave of men came rolling onward and would have crushed me like an ant.

I was simply walking in my sleep. I managed to close my eyes and to run like that while asleep. Now and then, someone would push me violently from behind, and I would wake up. The other would shout: "Run faster. If you don't want to go on, let other people come past." All I had to do was to close my eyes for a second to see a whole world passing by, to dream a whole lifetime.

An endless road. Letting oneself be pushed by the mob; letting oneself be dragged along by a blind destiny. When the SS became tired, they were changed. But no one changed us. Our limbs numb with cold despite the running, our throats parched, famished, breathless, on we went.

We were masters of nature, masters of the world. We had forgotten everything—death, fatigue, our natural needs. Stronger than cold or hunger, stronger than the shots and the desire to die, condemned and wandering, mere numbers, we were the only men on earth.

At last, the morning star appeared in the gray sky. A trail of indeterminate light showed on the horizon. We were exhausted. We were without strength, without illusions.

The commandant announced that we had already covered forty-two miles since we left. It was a long time since we had passed beyond the limits of fatigue. Our legs were moving mechanically, in spite of us, without us.

We went through a deserted village. Not a living soul.

93

Not the bark of a dog. Houses with gaping windows. A few slipped out of the ranks to try and hide in some deserted building.

Still one hour's marching more, and at last came the order to rest.

We sank down as one man in the snow. My father shook me.

"Not here. . . . Get up. . . . A little farther on. There's a shed over there . . . come on."

I had neither the will nor the strength to get up. Nevertheless I obeyed. It was not a shed, but a brick factory with a caved-in roof, broken windows, walls filthy with soot. It was not easy to get in. Hundreds of prisoners were crowding at the door.

We at last succeeded in getting inside. There too the snow was thick. I let myself sink down. It was only then that I really felt my weariness. The snow was like a carpet, very gentle, very warm. I fell asleep.

I do not know how long I slept. A few moments or an hour. When I woke up, a frozen hand was patting my cheeks. I forced myself to open my eyes. It was my father.

How old he had grown since the night before! His body was completely twisted, shriveled up into itself. His eyes were petrified, his lips withered, decayed. Everything about him bore witness to extreme exhaustion. His voice was damp with tears and snow:

"Don't let yourself be overcome by sleep, Eliezer. It's dangerous to fall asleep in the snow. You might sleep for good. Come on, come on. Get up."

Get up? How could I? How could I get myself out of this fluffy bed? I could hear what my father said, but it seemed empty of meaning, as though he had told me to lift up the whole building in my arms. . . .

"Come on, son, come on. . . ."

I got up, gritting my teeth. Supporting me with his arm, he led me outside. It was far from easy. It was as difficult to go out as to get in. Under our feet were men crushed, trampled underfoot, dying. No one paid any attention.

We were outside. The icy wind stung my face. I bit my lips continually to prevent them from freezing. Around me everything was dancing a dance of death. It made my head reel. I was walking in a cemetery, among stiffened corpses, logs of wood. Not a cry of distress, not a groan, nothing but a mass agony, in silence. No one asked anyone else for help. You died because you had to die. There was no fuss.

In every stiffened corpse I saw myself. And soon I should not even see them; I should be one of them—a matter of hours.

"Come on, father, let's go back to the shed. . . ."

He did not answer. He was not looking at the dead.

"Come on, father, it's better over there. We can lie down a bit, one after the other. I'll watch over you, and then you can watch over me. We won't let each other fall asleep. We'll look after each other."

He agreed. Trampling over living bodies and corpses, we managed to re-enter the shed. Here we let ourselves sink down.

"Don't be afraid, son. Sleep—you can sleep. I'll look after you myself."

"No, you first, father. Go to sleep."

He refused. I lay down and tried to force myself to sleep, to doze a little, but in vain. God knows what I would not have given for a few moments of sleep. But, deep down, I felt that to sleep would mean to die. And something within me revolted against this death. All round me death was moving in, silently, without violence. It would seize upon some sleeping being, enter into him, and consume him bit by bit. Next to me there was someone trying to wake up his neighbor, his brother, perhaps, or a friend. In vain. Discouraged in the attempt, the man lay down in his turn, next to the corpse, and slept too. Who was there to wake him up? Stretching out an arm, I touched him:

"Wake up. You mustn't sleep here. . . ."

He half opened his eyes.

"No advice," he said in a faint voice. "I'm tired. Leave me alone. Leave me."

My father, too, was gently dozing. I could not see his eyes. His cap had fallen over his face.

"Wake up," I whispered in his ear.

He started up. He sat up and looked round him, bewildered, stupefied—a bereaved stare. He stared all round him in a circle as though he had suddenly decided to draw up an inventory of his universe, to find out exactly where he was, in what place, and why. Then he smiled.

I shall always remember that smile. From which world did it come?

The snow continued to fall in thick flakes over the corpses.

The door of the shed opened. An old man appeared, his moustache covered with frost, his lips blue with cold. It was Rabbi Eliahou, the rabbi of a small Polish community. He was a very good man, well loved by everyone in the camp, even by the Kapos and the heads of the blocks. Despite the trials and privations, his face still shone with his inner purity. He was the only rabbi who was always addressed as "Rabbi" at Buna. He was like one of the old prophets, always in the midst of his people to comfort them. And, strangely, his words of comfort never provoked rebellion; they really brought peace.

He came into the shed and his eyes, brighter than ever, seemed to be looking for someone:

"Perhaps someone has seen my son somewhere?"

He had lost his son in the crowd. He had looked in vain among the dying. Then he had scratched up the snow to find his corpse. Without result.

For three years they had stuck together. Always near each other, for suffering, for blows, for the ration of bread, for prayer. Three years, from camp to camp, from selection to selection. And now—when the end seemed near—fate had separated them. Finding himself near me, Rabbi Eliahou whispered:

"It happened on the road. We lost sight of one another during the journey. I had stayed a little to the rear of the column. I hadn't any strength left for running. And my son didn't notice. That's all I know. Where has he disappeared? Where can I find him? Perhaps you've seen him somewhere?"

"No, Rabbi Eliahou, I haven't seen him."

He left then as he had come: like a wind-swept shadow.

He had already passed through the door when I suddenly remembered seeing his son running by my side. I had forgotten that, and I didn't tell Rabbi Eliahou!

Then I remembered something else: his son had seen him losing ground, limping, staggering back to the rear of the column. He had seen him. And he had continued to run on in front, letting the distance between them grow greater.

A terrible thought loomed up in my mind: he had wanted to get rid of his father! He had felt that his father was growing weak, he had believed that the end was near and had sought this separation in order to get rid of the burden, to free himself from an encumbrance which could lessen his own chances of survival.

I had done well to forget that. And I was glad that Rabbi Eliahou should continue to look for his beloved son.

And, in spite of myself, a prayer rose in my heart, to that God in whom I no longer believed.

My God, Lord of the Universe, give me strength never to do what Rabbi Eliahou's son has done.

Shouts rose outside in the yard, where darkness had fallen. The SS ordered the ranks to form up.

The march began again. The dead stayed in the yard under the snow, like faithful guards assassinated, without burial. No one had said the prayer for the dead over them. Sons abandoned their fathers' remains without a tear.

On the way it snowed, snowed, snowed endlessly. We

were marching more slowly. The guards themselves seemed tired. My wounded foot no longer hurt me. It must have been completely frozen. The foot was lost to me. It had detached itself from my body like the wheel of a car. Too bad. I should have to resign myself; I could live with only one leg. The main thing was not to think about it. Above all, not at this moment. Leave thoughts for later.

Our march had lost all semblance of discipline. We went as we wanted, as we could. We heard no more shots. Our guards must have been tired.

But death scarcely needed any help from them. The cold was conscientiously doing its work. At every step someone fell and suffered no more.

From time to time, SS officers on motorcycles would go down the length of the column to try and shake us out of our growing apathy:

"Keep going! We are getting there!"

"Courage! Only a few more hours!"

"We're reaching Gleiwitz."

These words of encouragement, even though they came from the mouths of our assassins, did us a great deal of good. No one wanted to give up now, just before the end, so near to the goal. Our eyes searched the horizon for the barbed wire of Gleiwitz. Our only desire was to reach it as quickly as possible.

The night had now set in. The snow had ceased to fall. We walked for several more hours before arriving.

We did not notice the camp until we were just in front of the gate.

Some Kapos rapidly installed us in the barracks. We pushed and jostled one another as if this were the supreme refuge, the gateway to life. We walked over pain-racked bodies. We trod on wounded faces. No cries. A few groans. My father and I were ourselves thrown to the ground by this rolling tide. Beneath our feet someone let out a rattling cry:

"You're crushing me . . . mercy!"

A voice that was not unknown to me.

"You're crushing me . . . mercy! mercy!"

The same faint voice, the same rattle, heard somewhere before. That voice had spoken to me one day. Where? When? Years ago? No, it could only have been at the camp.

"Mercy!"

I felt that I was crushing him. I was stopping his breath. I wanted to get up. I struggled to disengage myself, so that he could breathe. But I was crushed myself beneath the weight of other bodies. I could hardly breathe. I dug my nails into unknown faces. I was biting all round me, in order to get air. No one cried out.

Suddenly I remembered. Juliek! The boy from Warsaw who played the violin in the band at Buna. . . .

"Juliek, is it you?"

"Eliezer . . . the twenty-five strokes of the whip. Yes . . . I remember."

He was silent. A long moment elapsed.

"Juliek! Can you hear me, Juliek?"

"Yes . . . ," he said, in a feeble voice. "What do you want?"

He was not dead.

"How do you feel, Juliek?" I asked, less to know the answer than to hear that he could speak, that he was alive.

"All right, Eliezer. . . . I'm getting on all right . . . hardly any air . . . worn out. My feet are swollen. It's good to rest, but my violin. . . ."

I thought he had gone out of his mind. What use was the violin here?

"What, your violin?"

He gasped.

"I'm afraid . . . I'm afraid . . . that they'll break my violin. . . . I've brought it with me."

I could not answer him. Someone was lying full length on top of me, covering my face. I was unable to breathe, through either mouth or nose. Sweat beaded my brow, ran down my spine. This was the end—the end of the road. A silent death, suffocation. No way of crying out, of calling for help.

I tried to get rid of my invisible assassin. My whole will to live was centered in my nails. I scratched. I battled for a mouthful of air. I tore at decaying flesh which did not respond. I could not free myself from this mass weighing down my chest. Was it a dead man I was struggling against? Who knows?

I shall never know. All I can say is that I won. I succeeded in digging a hole through this wall of dying people, a little hole through which I could drink in a small quantity of air.

"Father, how are you?" I asked, as soon as I could utter a word.

I knew he could not be far from me.

"Well!" answered a distant voice, which seemed to come from another world. I tried to sleep.

He tried to sleep. Was he right or wrong? Could one sleep here? Was it not dangerous to allow your vigilance to fail, even for a moment, when at any minute death could pounce upon you?

I was thinking of this when I heard the sound of a violin. The sound of a violin, in this dark shed, where the dead were heaped on the living. What madman could be playing the violin here, at the brink of his own grave? Or was it really an hallucination?

It must have been Juliek.

He played a fragment from Beethoven's concerto. I had never heard sounds so pure. In such a silence.

How had he managed to free himself? To draw his body from under mine without my being aware of it?

It was pitch dark. I could hear only the violin, and it was as though Juliek's soul were the bow. He was playing his life. The whole of his life was gliding on the strings—his lost hopes, his charred past, his extinguished future. He played as he would never play again.

I shall never forget Juliek. How could I forget that concert, given to an audience of dying and dead men! To this day, whenever I hear Beethoven played my eyes close and out of the dark rises the sad, pale face of my Polish friend, as he said farewell on his violin to an audience of dying men.

I do not know for how long he played. I was overcome by sleep. When I awoke, in the daylight, I could see Juliek, opposite me, slumped over, dead. Near him lay his violin, smashed, trampled, a strange overwhelming little corpse.

We stayed at Gleiwitz for three days. Three days without food or drink. We were not allowed to leave the barracks. SS men guarded the door.

I was hungry and thirsty. I must have been very dirty and exhausted, to judge from the appearance of the others. The bread we had brought from Buna had long since been devoured. And who knew when we would be given another ration?

The front was following us. We could hear new gun shots again, very close. But we had neither the strength nor the courage to believe that the Nazis would not have time to evacuate us, and that the Russians would soon be here.

We heard that we were going to be deported into the center of Germany.

On the third day, at dawn, we were driven out of the barracks. We all threw blankets over our shoulders, like prayer shawls. We were directed toward a gate which divided the camp into two. A group of SS officers were standing there. A rumor ran through our ranks—a selection!

The SS officers did the selecting. The weak, to the left; those who could walk well, to the right.

My father was sent to the left. I ran after him. An SS officer shouted at my back:

"Come back here!"

I slipped in among the others. Several SS rushed to bring me back, creating such confusion that many of the people from the left were able to come back to the right—and among them, my father and myself. However, there were some shots and some dead.

We were all made to leave the camp. After half an hour's marching we arrived right in the middle of a field divided by rails. We had to wait for the train to arrive.

The snow fell thickly. We were forbidden to sit down or even to move.

The snow began to form a thick layer over our blankets. They brought us bread—the usual ration. We threw ourselves upon it. Someone had the idea of appeasing his thirst by eating the snow. Soon the others were imitating him. As we were not allowed to bend down, everyone took out his spoon and ate the accumulated snow off his neighbor's back. A mouthful of bread and a spoonful of snow. The SS who were watching laughed at this spectacle.

Hours went by. Our eyes grew weary of scouring the horizon for the liberating train. It did not arrive until much later in the evening. An infinitely long train, composed of cattle wagons, with no roofs. The SS pushed us in, a hundred to a carriage, we were so thin! Our embarkation completed, the convoy set out.

Pressed up against the others in an effort to keep out the cold, head empty and heavy at the same time, brain a whirlpool of decaying memories. Indifference deadened the spirit. Here or elsewhere—what difference did it make? To die today or tomorrow, or later? The night was long and never ending.

When at last a gray glimmer of light appeared on the horizon, it revealed a tangle of human shapes, heads sunk upon shoulders, crouched, piled one on top of the other, like a field of dust-covered tombstones in the first light of the dawn. I tried to distinguish those who were still alive from those who had gone. But there was no difference. My gaze was held for a long time by one who lay with his eyes open, staring into the void. His livid face was covered with a layer of frost and snow.

My father was huddled near me, wrapped in his blanket, his shoulders covered with snow. And was he dead, too? I called him. No answer. I would have cried out if I could have done so. He did not move.

My mind was invaded suddenly by this realization—there was no more reason to live, no more reason to struggle.

The train stopped in the middle of a deserted field. The suddenness of the halt woke some of those who were asleep. They straightened themselves up, throwing startled looks around them.

Outside, the SS went by, shouting:

"Throw out all the dead! All corpses outside!"

The living rejoiced. There would be more room. Volunteers set to work. They felt those who were still crouching.

"Here's one! Take him!"

They undressed him, the survivors avidly sharing out his clothes, then two "gravediggers" took him, one by the head and one by the feet, and threw him out of the wagon like a sack of flour.

From all directions came cries:

"Come on! Here's one! This man next to me. He doesn't move."

I woke from my apathy just at the moment when two men came up to my father. I threw myself on top of his body. He was cold. I slapped him. I rubbed his hands, crying:

"Father! Father! Wake up. They're trying to throw you out of the carriage. . . ."

His body remained inert.

The two gravediggers seized me by the collar.

"Leave him. You can see perfectly well that he's dead."

"No!" I cried. "He isn't dead! Not yet!"

I set to work to slap him as hard as I could. After a moment my father's eyelids moved slightly over his glazed eyes. He was breathing weakly.

"You see," I cried.

The two men moved away.

Twenty bodies were thrown out of our wagon. Then the train resumed its journey, leaving behind it a few hundred naked dead, deprived of burial, in the deep snow of a field in Poland.

We were given no food. We lived on snow; it took the place of bread. The days were like nights, and the nights left the dregs of their darkness in our souls. The train was traveling slowly, often stopping for several hours and then setting off again. It never ceased snowing. All through these days and nights we stayed crouching, one on top of the other, never speaking a word. We were no more than frozen bodies. Our eyes closed, we waited merely for the next stop, so that we could unload our dead.

Ten days, ten nights of traveling. Sometimes we would pass through German townships. Very early in the morning, usually. The workmen were going to work. They stopped and stared after us, but otherwise showed no surprise.

One day when we had stopped, a workman took a piece of bread out of his bag and threw it into a wagon. There was a stampede. Dozens of starving men fought each other to the death for a few crumbs. The German workmen took a lively interest in this spectacle.

Some years later, I watched the same kind of scene at Aden. The passengers on our boat were amusing themselves by throwing coins to the "natives," who were diving in to get them. An attractive, aristocratic Parisienne was deriving special pleasure from the game. I suddenly noticed that two children were engaged in a death struggle, trying to strangle each other. I turned to the lady.

"Please," I begged, "don't throw any more money in!"

"Why not?" she said. "I like to give charity. . . ."

In the wagon where the bread had fallen, a real battle had broken out. Men threw themselves on top of each other, stamping on each other, tearing at each other, biting each other. Wild beasts of prey, with animal hatred in their eyes; an extraordinary vitality had seized them, sharpening their teeth and nails.

A crowd of workmen and curious spectators had collected along the train. They had probably never seen a train with such a cargo. Soon, nearly everywhere, pieces of bread were being dropped into the wagons. The audience stared at these skeletons of men, fighting one another to the death for a mouthful.

A piece fell into our wagon. I decided that I would not move. Anyway, I knew that I would never have the strength to fight with a dozen savage men! Not far away I noticed an old man dragging himself along on all fours. He was trying to disengage himself from the struggle. He held one hand to his heart. I thought at first he had received a blow in the chest. Then I understood; he had a bit of bread under his shirt. With remarkable speed he drew it out and put it to his mouth. His eyes gleamed; a smile, like a grimace, lit up his dead face. And was immediately extinguished. A shadow had just loomed up near him. The shadow threw itself upon him. Felled to the ground, stunned with blows, the old man cried:

"Meir. Meir, my boy! Don't you recognize me? I'm your father . . . you're hurting me . . . you're killing your father! I've got some bread . . . for you too . . . for you too. . . ."

He collapsed. His fist was still clenched around a small piece. He tried to carry it to his mouth. But the other one threw himself upon him and snatched it. The old man again whispered something, let out a rattle, and died amid the general indifference. His son searched him, took the bread, and began to devour it. He was not able to get very far. Two men had seen and hurled themselves upon him. Others joined in. When they withdrew, next to me were two corpses, side by side, the father and the son.

I was fifteen years old.

In our wagon, there was a friend of my father's called Meir Katz. He had worked as a gardener at Buna and used to bring us a few green vegetables occasionally. Being less undernourished than the rest of us, he had stood up to imprisonment better. Because he was relatively more vigorous, he had been put in charge of the wagon.

On the third night of our journey I woke up suddenly and felt two hands on my throat, trying to strangle me. I just had the time to shout, "Father!"

Nothing but this word. I felt myself suffocating. But my father had woken up and seized my attacker. Too weak to overcome him, he had the idea of calling Meir Katz.

"Come here! Come quickly! There's someone strangling my son."

A few moments later I was free. I still do not know why the man wanted to strangle me.

After a few days, Meir Katz spoke to my father:

"Chlomo, I'm getting weak. I'm losing my strength. I can't hold on. . . ."

"Don't let yourself go under," my father said, trying to encourage him. "You must resist. Don't lose faith in yourself."

But Meir Katz groaned heavily in reply.

"I can't go on any longer, Chlomo! What can I do? I can't carry on. . . ."

My father took his arm. And Meir Katz, the strong man, the most robust of us all, wept. His son had been taken from him at the time of the first selection, but it was now that he wept. It was now that he cracked up. He was finished, at the end of his tether.

On the last day of our journey a terrible wind arose; it snowed without ceasing. We felt that the end was near— the real end. We could never hold out in this icy wind, in these gusts.

Someone got up and shouted:

"We mustn't stay sitting down at a time like this. We shall freeze to death! Let's all get up and move a bit. . . ."

We all got up. We held our damp blankets more tightly around us. And we forced ourselves to move a few steps, to turn around where we were.

Suddenly a cry rose up from the wagon, the cry of a wounded animal. Someone had just died.

Others, feeling that they too were about to die, imitated his cry. And their cries seemed to come from beyond the grave. Soon everyone was crying out. Wailing, groaning, cries of distress hurled into the wind and the snow.

The contagion spread to the other carriages. Hundreds of cries rose up simultaneously. Not knowing against whom we cried. Not knowing why. The death rattle of a whole convoy who felt the end upon them. We were all going to die here. All limits had been passed. No one had any strength left. And again the night would be long.

Meir Katz groaned:

"Why don't they shoot us all right away?"

That same evening, we reached our destination.

It was late at night. The guards came to unload us. The dead were abandoned in the train. Only those who could still stand were able to get out.

Meir Katz stayed in the train. The last day had been the most murderous. A hundred of us had got into the wagon. A dozen of us got out—among them, my father and I.

We had arrived at Buchenwald.

At the gate of the camp, SS officers were waiting for us. They counted us. Then we were directed to the assembly place. Orders were given us through loudspeakers:

"Form fives!" "Form groups of a hundred!" "Five paces forward!"

I held onto my father's hand—the old, familiar fear: not to lose him.

Right next to us the high chimney of the crematory oven rose up. It no longer made any impression on us. It scarcely attracted our attention.

An established inmate of Buchenwald told us that we should have a shower and then we could go into the blocks. The idea of having a hot bath fascinated me. My father was silent. He was breathing heavily beside me.

"Father," I said. "Only another moment more. Soon we can lie down—in a bed. You can rest. . . ."

He did not answer. I was so exhausted myself that his

silence left me indifferent. My only wish was to take a bath as quickly as possible and lie down in a bed.

But it was not easy to reach the showers. Hundreds of prisoners were crowding there. The guards were unable to keep any order. They struck out right and left with no apparent result. Others, without the strength to push or even to stand up, had sat down in the snow. My father wanted to do the same. He groaned.

"I can't go on. . . . This is the end. . . . I'm going to die here. . . ."

He dragged me toward a hillock of snow from which emerged human shapes and ragged pieces of blanket.

"Leave me," he said to me. "I can't go on. . . . Have mercy on me. . . . I'll wait here until we can get into the baths. . . . You can come and find me."

I could have wept with rage. Having lived through so much, suffered so much, could I leave my father to die now? Now, when we could have a good hot bath and lie down?

"Father!" I screamed. "Father! Get up from here! Immediately! You're killing yourself. . . ."

I seized him by the arm. He continued to groan.

"Don't shout, son. . . . Take pity on your old father. . . . Leave me to rest here. . . . Just for a bit, I'm so tired . . . at the end of my strength. . . ."

He had become like a child, weak, timid, vulnerable.

"Father," I said. "You can't stay here."

I showed him the corpses all around him; they too had wanted to rest here.

"I can see them, son. I can see them all right. Let them sleep. It's so long since they closed their eyes. . . . They are exhausted . . . exhausted. . . ."

His voice was tender.

I yelled against the wind:

"They'll never wake again! Never! Don't you understand?"

For a long time this argument went on. I felt that I was

not arguing with him, but with death itself, with the death that he had already chosen.

The sirens began to wail. An alert. The lights went out throughout the camp. The guards drove us toward the blocks. In a flash, there was no one left on the assembly place. We were only too glad not to have had to stay outside longer in the icy wind. We let ourselves sink down onto the planks. The beds were in several tiers. The cauldrons of soup at the entrance attracted no one. To sleep, that was all that mattered.

It was daytime when I awoke. And then I remembered that I had a father. Since the alert, I had followed the crowd without troubling about him. I had known that he was at the end, on the brink of death, and yet I had abandoned him.

I went to look for him.

But at the same moment this thought came into my mind: "Don't let me find him! If only I could get rid of this dead weight, so that I could use all my strength to struggle for my own survival, and only worry about myself." Immediately I felt ashamed of myself, ashamed forever.

I walked for hours without finding him. Then I came to the block where they were giving out black "coffee." The men were lining up and fighting.

A plaintive, beseeching voice caught me in the spine: "Eliezer . . . my son . . . bring me . . . a drop of coffee. . . ."

I ran to him.

"Father! I've been looking for you for so long. . . . Where were you? Did you sleep? . . . How do you feel?"

He was burning with fever. Like a wild beast, I cleared a way for myself to the coffee cauldron. And I managed to carry back a cupful. I had a sip. The rest was for him. I can't forget the light of thankfulness in his eyes while he gulped it down—an animal gratitude. With those few gulps of hot water, I probably brought him more satisfaction than I had done during my whole childhood.

He was lying on a plank, livid, his lips pale and dried

up, shaken by tremors. I could not stay by him for long. Orders had been given to clear the place for cleaning. Only the sick could stay.

We stayed outside for five hours. Soup was given out. As soon as we were allowed to go back to the blocks, I ran to my father.

"Have you had anything to eat?"

"No."

"Why not?"

"They didn't give us anything ... they said that if we were ill we should die soon anyway and it would be a pity to waste the food. I can't go on any more. . . ."

I gave him what was left of my soup. But it was with a heavy heart. I felt that I was giving it up to him against my will. No better than Rabbi Eliahou's son had I withstood the test.

He grew weaker day by day, his gaze veiled, his face the color of dead leaves. On the third day after our arrival at Buchenwald, everyone had to go to the showers. Even the sick, who had to go through last.

On the way back from the baths, we had to wait outside for a long time. They had not yet finished cleaning the blocks.

Seeing my father in the distance, I ran to meet him. He went by me like a ghost, passed me without stopping, without looking at me. I called to him. He did not come back. I ran after him:

"Father, where are you running to?"

He looked at me for a moment, and his gaze was distant, visionary; it was the face of someone else. A moment only and on he ran again.

Struck down with dysentery, my father lay in his bunk, five other invalids with him. I sat by his side, watching him, not daring to believe that he could escape death again. Nevertheless, I did all I could to give him hope.

Suddenly, he raised himself on his bunk and put his feverish lips to my ear:

"Eliezer . . . I must tell you where to find the gold and the money I buried . . . in the cellar. . . . You know. . . ."

He began to talk faster and faster, as though he were afraid he would not have time to tell me. I tried to explain to him that this was not the end, that we would go back to the house together, but he would not listen to me. He could no longer listen to me. He was exhausted. A trickle of saliva, mingled with blood, was running from between his lips. He had closed his eyes. His breath was coming in gasps.

For a ration of bread, I managed to change beds with a prisoner in my father's bunk. In the afternoon the doctor came. I went and told him that my father was very ill.

"Bring him here!"

I explained that he could not stand up. But the doctor refused to listen to anything. Somehow, I brought my father to him. He stared at him, then questioned him in a clipped voice:

"What do you want?"

"My father's ill," I answered for him. "Dysentery. . ."

"Dysentery? That's not my business. I'm a surgeon. Go on! Make room for the others."

Protests did no good.

"I can't go on, son. . . . Take me back to my bunk. . . ."

I took him back and helped him to lie down. He was shivering.

"Try and sleep a bit, father. Try to go to sleep. . . ."

His breathing was labored, thick. He kept his eyes shut. Yet I was convinced that he could see everything, that now he could see the truth in all things.

Another doctor came to the block. But my father would not get up. He knew that it was useless.

Besides, this doctor had only come to finish off the sick. I could hear him shouting at them that they were lazy and just wanted to stay in bed. I felt like leaping at his throat, strangling him. But I no longer had the courage or the

113

strength. I was riveted to my father's deathbed. My hands hurt, I was clenching them so hard. Oh, to strangle the doctor and the others! To burn the whole world! My father's murderers! But the cry stayed in my throat.

When I came back from the bread distribution, I found my father weeping like a child:

"Son, they keep hitting me!"

"Who?"

I thought he was delirious.

"Him, the Frenchman . . . and the Pole . . . they were hitting me."

Another wound to the heart, another hate, another reason for living lost.

"Eliezer . . . Eliezer . . . tell them not to hit me. . . . I haven't done anything. . . . Why do they keep hitting me?"

I began to abuse his neighbors. They laughed at me. I promised them bread, soup. They laughed. Then they got angry; they could not stand my father any longer, they said, because he was now unable to drag himself outside to relieve himself.

The following day he complained that they had taken his ration of bread.

"While you were asleep?"

"No. I wasn't asleep. They jumped on top of me. They snatched my bread . . . and they hit me . . . again. . . . I can't stand any more, son . . . a drop of water . . . ."

I knew that he must not drink. But he pleaded with me for so long that I gave in. Water was the worst poison he could have, but what else could I do for him? With water, without water, it would all be over soon anyway. . . .

"You, at least, have some mercy on me. . . ."

Have mercy on him! I, his only son!

A week went by like this.

"This is your father, isn't it?" asked the head of the block.

"Yes."

"He's very ill."

"The doctor won't do anything for him."

"The doctor *can't* do anything for him, now. And neither can you."

He put his great hairy hand on my shoulder and added:

"Listen to me, boy. Don't forget that you're in a concentration camp. Here, every man has to fight for himself and not think of anyone else. Even of his father. Here, there are no fathers, no brothers, no friends. Everyone lives and dies for himself alone. I'll give you a sound piece of advice— don't give your ration of bread and soup to your old father. There's nothing you can do for him. And you're killing yourself. Instead, you ought to be having his ration."

I listened to him without interrupting. He was right, I thought in the most secret region of my heart, but I dared not admit it. It's too late to save your old father, I said to myself. You ought to be having two rations of bread, two rations of soup. . . .

Only a fraction of a second, but I felt guilty. I ran to find a little soup to give my father. But he did not want it. All he wanted was water.

"Don't drink water . . . have some soup. . . ."

"I'm burning . . . why are you being so unkind to me, my son? Some water. . . ."

I brought him some water. Then I left the block for roll call. But I turned around and came back again. I lay down on the top bunk. Invalids were allowed to stay in the block. So I would be an invalid myself. I would not leave my father.

There was silence all round now, broken only by groans. In front of the block, the SS were giving orders. An officer passed by the beds. My father begged me:

"My son, some water. . . . I'm burning. . . . My stomach. . . ."

"Quiet, over there!" yelled the officer.

"Eliezer," went on my father, "some water. . . ."

The officer came up to him and shouted at him to be quiet. But my father did not hear him. He went on calling me. The officer dealt him a violent blow on the head with his truncheon.

I did not move. I was afraid. My body was afraid of also receiving a blow.

Then my father made a rattling noise and it was my name: "Eliezer."

I could see that he was still breathing—spasmodically.

I did not move.

When I got down after roll call, I could see his lips trembling as he murmured something. Bending over him, I stayed gazing at him for over an hour, engraving into myself the picture of his blood-stained face, his shattered skull.

Then I had to go to bed. I climbed into my bunk, above my father, who was still alive. It was January 28, 1945.

I awoke on January 29 at dawn. In my father's place lay another invalid. They must have taken him away before dawn and carried him to the crematory. He may still have been breathing.

There were no prayers at his grave. No candles were lit to his memory. His last word was my name. A summons, to which I did not respond.

I did not weep, and it pained me that I could not weep. But I had no more tears. And, in the depths of my being, in the recesses of my weakened conscience, could I have searched it, I might perhaps have found something like— free at last!

I had to stay at Buchenwald until April eleventh. I have nothing to say of my life during this period. It no longer mattered. After my father's death, nothing could touch me any more.

I was transferred to the children's block, where there were six hundred of us.

The front was drawing nearer.

I spent my days in a state of total idleness. And I had but one desire—to eat. I no longer thought of my father or of my mother.

From time to time I would dream of a drop of soup, of an extra ration of soup. . . .

On April fifth, the wheel of history turned.

It was late in the afternoon. We were standing in the block, waiting for an SS man to come and count us. He was late in coming. Such a delay was unknown till then in the history of Buchenwald. Something must have happened.

Two hours later the loudspeakers sent out an order from the head of the camp: all the Jews must come to the assembly place.

This was the end! Hitler was going to keep his promise.

The children in our block went toward the place. There was nothing else we could do. Gustav, the head of the block, made this clear to us with his truncheon. But on the way we met some prisoners who whispered to us:

"Go back to your block. The Germans are going to shoot you. Go back to your block, and don't move."

We went back to our block. We learned on the way that the camp resistance organization had decided not to abandon the Jews and was going to prevent their being liquidated.

As it was late and there was great upheaval—innumerable Jews had passed themselves off as non-Jews—the head of the camp decided that a general roll call would take place the following day. Everybody would have to be present.

The roll call took place. The head of the camp announced that Buchenwald was to be liquidated. Ten blocks of deportees would be evacuated each day. From this moment, there would be no further distribution of bread and soup. And the evacuation began. Every day, several thousand prisoners went through the camp gate and never came back.

On April tenth, there were still about twenty thousand of us in the camp, including several hundred children. They decided to evacuate us all at once, right on until the evening. Afterward, they were going to blow up the camp.

So we were massed in the huge assembly square, in rows of five, waiting to see the gate open. Suddenly, the sirens began to wail. An alert! We went back to the blocks. It was too late to evacuate us that evening. The evacuation was postponed again to the following day.

We were tormented with hunger. We had eaten nothing

for six days, except a bit of grass or some potato peelings found near the kitchens.

At ten o'clock in the morning the SS scattered through the camp, moving the last victims toward the assembly place.

Then the resistance movement decided to act. Armed men suddenly rose up everywhere. Bursts of firing. Grenades exploding. We children stayed flat on the ground in the block.

The battle did not last long. Toward noon everything was quiet again. The SS had fled and the resistance had taken charge of the running of the camp.

At about six o'clock in the evening, the first American tank stood at the gates of Buchenwald.

Our first act as free men was to throw ourselves onto the provisions. We thought only of that. Not of revenge, not of our families. Nothing but bread.

And even when we were no longer hungry, there was still no one who thought of revenge. On the following day, some of the young men went to Weimar to get some potatoes and clothes—and to sleep with girls. But of revenge, not a sign.

Three days after the liberation of Buchenwald I became very ill with food poisoning. I was transferred to the hospital and spent two weeks between life and death.

One day I was able to get up, after gathering all my strength. I wanted to see myself in the mirror hanging on the opposite wall. I had not seen myself since the ghetto.

From the depths of the mirror, a corpse gazed back at me.

The look in his eyes, as they stared into mine, has never left me.

Dawn

Translated from the French

by FRANCES FRENAYE

to François Mauriac

Somewhere a child began to cry. In the house across the way an old woman closed the shutters. It was hot with all the heat of an autumn evening in Palestine.

Standing near the window I looked out at the transparent twilight whose descent made the city seem silent, motionless, unreal, and very far away. Tomorrow, I thought for the hundredth time, I shall kill a man, and I wondered if the crying child and the woman across the way knew.

I did not know the man. To my eyes he had no face; he did not even exist, for I knew nothing about him. I did not know whether he scratched his nose when he ate, whether he talked or kept quiet when he was making love, whether he gloried in his hate, whether he betrayed his wife or his God or his own future. All I knew was that he was an Englishman and my enemy. The two terms were synonymous.

"Don't torture yourself," said Gad in a low voice. "This is war."

His words were scarcely audible, and I was tempted to tell him to speak louder, because no one could possibly hear. The child's crying covered all other sounds. But I could not open my mouth, because I was thinking of the man who was doomed to die. Tomorrow, I said to myself, we shall be bound together for all eternity by the tie that binds a victim and his executioner.

"It's getting dark," said Gad. "Shall I put on the light?"

I shook my head. The darkness was not yet complete. As yet there was no face at the window to mark the exact moment when day changed into night.

A beggar had taught me, a long time ago, how to distinguish night from day. I met him one evening in my home town when I was saying my prayers in the overheated synagogue, a gaunt, shadowy fellow, dressed in shabby black clothes, with a look in his eyes that was not of this world. It was at the beginning of the war. I was twelve years old, my parents were still alive, and God still dwelt in our town.

"Are you a stranger?" I asked him.

"I'm not from around here," he said in a voice that seemed to listen rather than speak.

Beggars inspired me with mingled feelings of love and fear. I knew that I ought to be kind to them, for they might not be what they seemed. Hassidic literature tells us that a beggar may be the prophet Elijah in disguise, come to visit the earth and the hearts of men and to offer the reward of eternal life to those that treat him well. Nor is the prophet Elijah the only one to put on the garb of a beggar. The Angel of Death delights in frightening men in the same way. To do him wrong is more dangerous; he may take a man's life or his soul in return.

And so the stranger in the synagogue inspired me with fear. I asked him if he was hungry and he said no. I tried to find out if there was anything he wanted, but without success. I had an urge to do something for him, but did not know what.

The synagogue was empty and the candles had begun to burn low. We were quite alone, and I was overcome by increasing anxiety. I knew that I shouldn't be there with him at midnight, for that is the hour when the dead rise up from their graves and come to say their prayers. Anyone they find in the synagogue risks being carried away, for fear he betray their secret.

"Come to my house," I said to the beggar. "There you can find food to eat and a bed in which to sleep."

"I never sleep," he replied.

I was quite sure then that he was not a real beggar. I told him that I had to go home and he offered to keep me company. As we walked along the snow-covered streets he asked me if I was ever afraid of the dark.

"Yes, I am," I said. I wanted to add that I was afraid of him, too, but I felt he knew that already.

"You mustn't be afraid of the dark," he said, gently grasping my arm and making me shudder. "Night is purer than day; it is better for thinking and loving and dreaming. At night everything is more intense, more true. The echo of words that have been spoken during the day takes on a new and deeper meaning. The tragedy of man is that he doesn't know how to distinguish between day and night. He says things at night that should only be said by day."

He came to a halt in front of my house. I asked him again if he didn't want to come in, but he said no, he must be on his way. That's it, I thought; he's going back to the synagogue to welcome the dead.

"Listen," he said, digging his fingers into my arm. "I'm going to teach you the art of distinguishing between day and night. Always look at a window, and failing that look into the eyes of a man. If you see a face, any face, then you can be sure that night has succeeded day. For, believe me, night has a face."

Then, without giving me time to answer, he said good-by and disappeared into the snow.

Every evening since then I had made a point of standing near a window to witness the arrival of night. And every evening I saw a face outside. It was not always the same face, for no one night was like another. In the beginning I saw the face of the beggar. Then, after my father's death, I saw his face, with the eyes grown large with death and memory. Sometimes total strangers lent the night their tearful face or their forgotten smile. I knew nothing about them except that they were dead.

"Don't torture yourself in the dark," said Gad. "This is war."

I thought of the man I was to kill at dawn, and of the beggar. Suddenly I had an absurd thought: what if the beggar were the man I was to kill?

Outside, the twilight faded abruptly away as it so often does in the Middle East. The child was still crying, it seemed to me more plaintively than before. The city was like a ghost ship, noiselessly swallowed up by the darkness.

I looked out the window, where a shadowy face was taking shape out of the deep of the night. A sharp pain caught my throat. I could not take my eyes off the face. It was my own.

An hour earlier Gad had told me the Old Man's decision. The execution was to take place, as executions always do, at dawn. His message was no surprise; like everyone else

I was expecting it. Everyone in Palestine knew that the Movement always kept its word. And the English knew it too.

A month earlier one of our fighters, wounded during a terrorist operation, had been hauled in by the police and weapons had been found on him. A military tribunal had chosen to exact the penalty stipulated by martial law: death by hanging. This was the tenth death sentence the mandatory power in Palestine had imposed upon us. The Old Man decided that things had gone far enough; he was not going to allow the English to transform the Holy Land into a scaffold. And so he announced a new line of action —reprisals.

By means of posters and underground-radio broadcasts he issued a solemn warning: Do not hang David ben Moshe; his death will cost you dear. From now on, for the hanging of every Jewish fighter an English mother will mourn the death of her son. To add weight to his words the Old Man ordered us to take a hostage, preferably an army officer. Fate willed that our victim should be Captain John Dawson. He was out walking alone one night, and this made him an easy prey for our men were on the lookout for English officers who walked alone in the night.

John Dawson's kidnaping plunged the whole country into a state of nervous tension. The English army proclaimed a forty-eight-hour curfew, every house was searched, and hundreds of suspects were arrested. Tanks were stationed at the crossroads, machine guns set up on the rooftops, and barbed-wire barricades erected at the street corners. The whole of Palestine was one great prison, and within it there was another, smaller prison where the hostage was successfully hidden.

In a brief, horrifying proclamation the High Commissioner of Palestine announced that the entire population would be held responsible if His Majesty's Captain John Dawson were to be killed by the terrorists. Fear reigned, and the ugly word *pogrom* was on everyone's lips.

"Do you really think they'd do it?"

"Why not?"

"The English? Could the *English* ever organize a pogrom?"

"Why not?"

"They wouldn't dare."

"Why not?"

"World opinion wouldn't tolerate it."

"Why not? Just remember Hitler; world opinion tolerated him for quite some time."

The situation was grave. The Zionist leaders recommended prudence; they got in touch with the Old Man and begged him, for the sake of the nation, not to go too far: there was talk of vengeance, of a pogrom, and this meant that innocent men and women would have to pay.

The Old Man answered: If David ben Moshe is hanged, John Dawson must die. If the Movement were to give in the English would score a triumph. They would take it for a sign of weakness and impotence on our part, as if we were saying to them: Go ahead and hang all the young Jews who are holding out against you. No, the Movement cannot give in. Violence is the only language the English can understand. Man for man. Death for death.

Soon the whole world was alerted. The major newspapers of London, Paris, and New York headlined the story, with David ben Moshe sharing the honors, and a dozen special correspondents flew into Lydda. Once more Jerusalem was the center of the universe.

In London, John Dawson's mother paid a visit to the Colonial Office and requested a pardon for David ben

Moshe, whose life was bound up with that of her son. With a grave smile the Secretary of State for Colonial Affairs told her: Have no fear. The Jews will never do it. You know how they are; they shout and cry and make a big fuss, but they are frightened by the meaning of their own words. Don't worry; your son isn't going to die.

The High Commissioner was less optimistic. He sent a cable to the Colonial Office, recommending clemency. Such a gesture, he said, would dispose world-wide public opinion in England's favor.

The Secretary personally telephoned his reply. The recommendation had been studied at a Cabinet meeting. Two members of the Cabinet had approved it, but the others said no. They alleged not only political reasons but the prestige of the Crown as well. A pardon would be interpreted as a sign of weakness; it might give ideas to young, self-styled idealists in other parts of the Empire. People would say: "In Palestine a group of terrorists has told Great Britain where to get off." And the Secretary added, on his own behalf: "We should be the laughingstock of the world. And think of the repercussions in the House of Commons. The opposition are waiting for just such a chance to sweep us away."

"So the answer is no?" asked the High Commissioner.
"It is."
"And what about John Dawson, sir?"
"They won't go through with it."
"Sir, I beg to disagree."
"You're entitled to your opinion."
A few hours later the official Jerusalem radio announced that David ben Moshe's execution would take place in the prison at Acre at dawn the next day. The condemned man's family had been authorized to pay him a farewell visit and the population was enjoined to remain calm.

After this came the other news of the day. At the United Nations a debate on Palestine was in the offing. In the Mediterranean two ships carrying illegal immigrants had been detained and the passengers taken to internment on Cyprus. An automobile accident at Natanya: one man dead, two injured. The weather forecast for the following day: warm, clear, visibility unlimited. . . . We repeat the first bulletin: David ben Moshe, condemned to death for terroristic activities, will be hanged. . . .

The announcer made no mention of John Dawson. But his anguished listeners knew. John Dawson, as well as David ben Moshe, would die. The Movement would keep its word.

"Who is to kill him?" I asked Gad.

"You are," he replied.

"Me?" I said, unable to believe my own ears.

"You," Gad repeated. "Those are the Old Man's orders."

I felt as if a fist had been thrust into my face. The earth yawned beneath my feet and I seemed to be falling into a bottomless pit, where existence was a nightmare.

"This is war," Gad was saying.

His voice sounded as if it came from very far away; I could barely hear it.

"This is war. Don't torture yourself."

"Tomorrow I shall kill a man," I said to myself, reeling in my fall. "I shall kill a man, tomorrow."

Elisha is my name. At the time of this story I was eighteen years old. Gad had recruited me for the Movement and brought me to Palestine. He had made me into a terrorist.

I had met Gad in Paris, where I went, straight from Buchenwald, immediately after the war. When the Americans liberated Buchenwald they offered to send me home, but I rejected the offer. I didn't want to relive my childhood, to see our house in foreign hands. I knew that my parents were dead and my native town was occupied by the Russians. What was the use of going back? "No thanks," I said; "I don't want to go home."

"Then where do you want to go?"

I said I didn't know; it didn't really matter.

After staying on for five weeks in Buchenwald I was put aboard a train for Paris. France had offered me asylum, and as soon as I reached Paris a rescue committee sent me for a month to a youth camp in Normandy.

When I came back from Normandy the same organization got me a furnished room on the rue de Marois and gave me a grant which covered my living expenses and the cost of the French lessons which I took every day of the week except Saturday and Sunday from a gentleman with a mustache whose name I have forgotten. I wanted to master the language sufficiently to sign up for a philosophy course at the Sorbonne.

The study of philosophy attracted me because I wanted to understand the meaning of the events of which I had been the victim. In the concentration camp I had cried out in sorrow and anger against God and also against man, who seemed to have inherited only the cruelty of his creator. I was anxious to re-evaluate my revolt in an atmosphere of detachment, to view it in terms of the present.

So many questions obsessed me. Where is God to be found? In suffering or in rebellion? When is a man most truly a man? When he submits or when he refuses? Where does suffering lead him? To purification or to bestiality? Philosophy, I hoped, would give me an answer. It would free me from my memories, my doubts, my feeling of guilt. It would drive them away or at least bring them out in concrete form into the light of day. My purpose was to enroll at the Sorbonne and devote myself to this endeavor.

But I did nothing of the sort, and Gad was the one who caused me to abandon my original aim. If today I am only a question mark, he is responsible.

One evening there was a knock at my door. I went to open it, wondering who it could be. I had no friends or acquaintances in Paris and spent most of the time in my room, reading a book or sitting with my hand over my eyes, thinking about the past.

"I would like to talk with you."

The man who stood in the doorway was young, tall, and slender. Wearing a raincoat, he had the appearance of a detective or an adventurer.

"Come in," I said after he had already entered.

He didn't take off his coat. Silently he walked over to the table, picked up the few books that were there, riffled their pages, and then put them down. Then he turned to me.

"I know who you are," he said. "I know everything about you."

His face was tanned, expressive. His hair was unruly, one strand perpetually on his forehead. His mouth was hard, almost cruel; thus accentuating the kindness, the intensity, and warm intelligence in his eyes.

"You are more fortunate than I, for I know very little about myself."

A smile came to his lips. "I didn't come to talk about your past."

"The future," I answered, "is of limited interest to me."

He continued to smile.

"The future," he asked, "are you attached to it?"

I felt uneasy. I didn't understand him. The meaning of his questions escaped me. Something in him set me on edge. Perhaps it was the advantage of his superior knowledge, for he knew who I was, although I didn't even know his name. He looked at me with such familiarity, such expectation, that for a moment I thought he had mistaken me for someone else, that it wasn't me he had come to see.

"Who are you?" I asked. "What do you want with me?"

"I am Gad," he said in a resonant voice, as if he were uttering some cabalistic sentence which contained an answer to every question. He said "I am Gad" in the same way that Jehovah said "I am that I am."

"Very good," I said with mingled curiosity and fear.

"Your name is Gad. Happy to know you. And now that you've introduced yourself, may I ask the purpose of your call? What do you want of me?"

His piercing eyes seemed to look straight through me. After several moments of this penetrating stare he said in a quite matter-of-fact way:

"I want you to give me your future."

Having been brought up in the Hassidic tradition I had heard strange stories about the Meshulah, the mysterious messenger of fate to whom nothing is impossible. His voice is such as to make a man tremble, for the message it brings is more powerful than either the bearer or the recipient. His every word seems to come from the absolute, the infinite, and its significance is at the same time fearful and fascinating. Gad is a Meshulah, I said to myself. It was not his physical appearance that gave me this impression, but rather what he said and the way he said it.

"Who are you?" I asked again, in terror.

Something told me that at the end of the road we were to travel together I should find another man, very much like myself, whom I should hate.

"I am a messenger," he said.

I felt myself grow pale. My premonition was correct. He was a messenger, a man sent by fate, to whom I could refuse nothing. I must sacrifice everything to him, even hope, if he asked it.

"You want my future?" I asked. "What will you do with it?"

He smiled again, but in a cold, distant manner, as one who possesses a power over men.

"I'll make it into an outcry," he said, and there was a strange light in his dark eyes. "An outcry first of despair and then of hope. And finally a shout of triumph."

I sat down on my bed, offering him the only chair in the

room, but he remained standing. In the Hassidic legends the messenger is always portrayed standing, as if his body must at all times serve as a connecting link between heaven and earth. Standing thus, in a trench coat which seemed as if it had never been taken off and were an integral part of his body, with his head inclined toward his right shoulder and a fiery expression in his eyes, he proceeded to tell me about the Movement.

He smoked incessantly. But even when he paused to light a cigarette he continued to stare obliquely at me and never stopped talking. He talked until dawn, and I listened with my eyes and mind wide open. Just so I had listened as a child to the grizzled master who revealed to me the mysterious universe of the Cabala, where every idea is a story and every story, even one concerned with the life of a ghost, is a spark from eternity.

That night Gad told me about Palestine and the age-old Jewish dream of recreating an independent homeland, one where every human act would be free. He told me also of the Movement's desperate struggle with the English.

"The English government has sent a hundred thousand soldiers to maintain so-called order. We of the Movement are no more than a hundred strong, but we strike fear into their hearts. Do you understand what I am saying? We cause the English—yes, the English—to tremble!" The sparks in his dark eyes lit up the fear of a hundred thousand uniformed men.

This was the first story I had ever heard in which the Jews were not the ones to be afraid. Until this moment I had believed that the mission of the Jews was to represent the trembling of history rather than the wind which made it tremble.

"The paratroopers, the police dogs, the tanks, the planes, the tommy guns, the executioners—they are all afraid. The

Holy Land has become, for them, a land of fear. They don't dare walk out on the streets at night, or look a young girl in the eye for fear that she may shoot them in the belly, or stroke the head of a child for fear that he may throw a hand grenade in their face. They dare neither to speak nor to be silent. They are afraid."

Hour after hour Gad spoke to me of the blue nights of Palestine, of their calm and serene beauty. You walk out in the evening with a woman, you tell her that she is beautiful and you love her, and twenty centuries hear what you are saying. But for the English the night holds no beauty. For them every night opens and shuts like a tomb. Every night two, three, a dozen soldiers are swallowed up by the darkness and never seen again.

Then Gad told me the part he expected me to play. I was to give up everything and go with him to join the struggle. The Movement needed fresh recruits and reinforcements. It needed young men who were willing to offer it their future. The sum of their futures would be the freedom of Israel, the future of Palestine.

It was the first time that I had heard of any of these things. My parents had not been Zionists. To me Zion was a sacred ideal, a Messianic hope, a prayer, a heartbeat, but not a place on the map or a political slogan, a cause for which men killed and died.

Gad's stories were utterly fascinating. I saw in him a prince of Jewish history, a legendary messenger sent by fate to awaken my imagination, to tell the people whose past was now their religion: Come, come; the future is waiting for you with open arms. From now on you will no longer be humiliated, persecuted, or even pitied. You will not be strangers encamped in an age and a place that are not yours. Come, brothers, come!

Gad stopped talking and went to look out the window at

the approaching dawn. The shadows melted away and a pale, prematurely weary light the color of stagnant water invaded my small room.

"I accept your offer," I said.

I said it so softly that Gad seemed not to hear. He remained standing by the window and after a moment of silence turned around to say:

"Here is the dawn. In our land it is very different. Here the dawn is gray; in Palestine it is red like fire."

"I accept, Gad," I repeated.

"I heard you," he said, with a smile the color of the Paris dawn. "You'll be leaving in three weeks."

The autumn breeze blowing in through the window made me shiver. Three weeks, I reflected, before I plunge into the unknown. Perhaps my shiver was caused not so much by the breeze as by this reflection. I believe that even then unconsciously I knew that at the end of the road I was to travel with Gad, a man was waiting, a man who would be called upon to kill another man, myself.

Radio Jerusalem. . . . Last-minute news flashes. David ben Moshe's execution will take place at dawn tomorrow. The High Commissioner has issued an appeal for calm. Curfew at nine o'clock. No one will be allowed on the streets. I repeat, no one will be allowed on the streets. The army has orders to shoot at sight. . . .

The announcer's voice betrayed his emotion. As he said the name David ben Moshe there must have been tears in his eyes.

All over the world the young Jewish fighter was the hero of the day. All the wartime resistance movements of Europe held rallies in front of the British embassies; the chief rabbis of the capital cities sent a joint petition to His

Majesty the King. Their telegram—with some thirty signatures at the bottom—ran: "Do not hang a young man whose only crime is fidelity to his ideal." A Jewish delegation was received at the White House and the President promised to intercede. That day the heart of humanity was one with that of David ben Moshe.

It was eight o'clock in the evening and completely dark. Gad switched on the light. Outside the child was still crying.

"The dirty dogs," said Gad; "they're going to hang him."

His face and hands were red and perspiring. He paced up and down the room, lighting one cigarette after another, only to throw each one away.

"They're going to hang him," he repeated. "The bastards!"

The news broadcast came to an end and a program of choral singing followed. I started to turn the radio off but Gad held me back.

"It's a quarter past eight," he said. "See if you can get our station."

I was too nervous to turn the dial.

"I'll find it," said Gad.

The broadcast had just begun. The announcer was a girl with a resonant, grave voice familiar to every one of us. Every evening at this hour men, women, and children paused in their work or play to listen to the vibrant, mysterious voice which always began with the same eight words: *You are listening to the Voice of Freedom.* . . .

The Jews of Palestine loved this girl or young woman without knowing who she was. The English would have given anything to lay hands upon her. In their eyes she was as dangerous as the Old Man; she too was a part of the Legend. Only a very few people, no more than five, knew her identity, and Gad and I were among them. Her name was Ilana; she and Gad were in love and I was a friend to both of them. Their love was an essential part of my life. I needed to know that there was such a thing as love and that it brought smiles and joy in its wake.

You are listening to the Voice of Freedom, Ilana repeated.

Gad's dark face quivered. He was bent almost double over the radio, as if he wanted to touch with his hands and eyes the clear, deeply moving voice of Ilana, which tonight was his voice and mine and that of the whole country.

"Two men are preparing to meet death at dawn tomorrow," said Ilana, as if she were reading a passage from the Bible. "One of them deserves our admiration, the other our pity. Our brother and guide, David ben Moshe, knows why he is dying; John Dawson does not know. Both of them are vigorous and intelligent, on the threshold of life and happiness. They might have been friends, but now this can never be. At dawn tomorrow at the same hour, the same minute, they will die—but not together, for there is an abyss between them. David ben Moshe's death is meaningful; John Dawson's is not. David is a hero, John a victim. . . ."

For twenty minutes Ilana went on talking. The last part of her broadcast was dedicated exclusively to John Dawson, because he had the greater need of comfort and consolation.

I knew neither David nor John, but I felt bound to them and their fates. It flashed across my mind that in speaking of John Dawson's imminent death Ilana was speaking of me also, since I was his killer. Who was to kill David ben Moshe? For a moment I had the impression that I was to kill both of them and all the other Johns and Davids on earth. I was the executioner. And I was eighteen years old.

Eighteen years of searching and suffering, of study and rebellion, and they all added up to this. I wanted to understand the pure, unadulterated essence of human nature, the path to the understanding of man. I had sought after the truth, and here I was about to become a killer, a participant in the work of death and God. I went over to the mirror hanging on the wall and looked into my face. I almost cried out, for everywhere I saw my own eyes.

As a child I was afraid of death. I was not afraid to die, but every time I thought of death I shuddered.

"Death," Kalman, the grizzled master, told me, "is a being without arms or legs or mouth or head; it is all eyes. If ever you meet a creature with eyes everywhere, you can be sure that it is death."

Gad was still leaning over the radio.

"Look at me," I said, but he did not hear.

"John Dawson, you have a mother," Ilana was saying. "At this hour she must be crying, or eating her heart out in silent despair. She will not go to bed tonight. She will sit in a chair near the window, watch in hand, waiting for dawn. Her heart will skip a beat when yours stops beating forever. 'They've killed my son,' she will say. 'Those murderers!' But we are not murderers, Mrs. Dawson. . . ."

"Look at me, Gad," I repeated.

He raised his eyes, shot me a glance, shrugged his shoulders, and went back to the voice of Ilana. Gad doesn't know that I am death, I thought to myself. But John Dawson's mother, sitting near the window of her London flat, must surely know. She is gazing out into the night, and the night has a thousand eyes, which are mine.

"No, Mrs. Dawson, we are not murderers. Your Cabinet ministers are murderers; they are responsible for the death of your son. We should have preferred to receive him as a brother, to offer him bread and milk and show him the beauties of our country. But your government made him our enemy and by the same token signed his death warrant. No, we are not murderers."

I buried my head in my hands. The child outside had stopped crying.

In all probability I had killed before, but under entirely different circumstances. The act had other dimensions, other witnesses. Since my arrival in Palestine several months before, I had taken part in various tangles with the police, in sabotage operations, in attacks on military convoys making their way across the green fields of Galilee or the white desert. There had been casualties on both sides, but the odds were in our favor because the night was our ally. Under cover of darkness we took the enemy by surprise; we set fire to an army encampment, killed a dozen soldiers, and disappeared without leaving any traces behind us. The Movement's objective was to kill the greatest number of soldiers possible. It was that simple.

Ever since the day of my arrival, my first steps on the soil of Palestine, this idea had been imprinted upon my brain. As I stepped off the ship at Haifa two comrades picked me up in their car and took me to a two-storey house some-where between Ramat-Gan and Tel Aviv. This house was ostensibly occupied by a professor of languages, to justify the comings and goings of a large number of young people who were actually, like myself, apprentices of a school of terrorist techniques. The cellar served as a dungeon where we kept prisoners, hostages, and those of our comrades who were wanted by the police. Here it was that John Dawson was awaiting execution. The hiding place was absolutely secure. Several times English soldiers had searched the house from top to bottom; their police dogs had come within a few inches of John Dawson, but there was a wall between them.

Gad directed our terrorist instruction. Other masked teachers taught us the use of a revolver, a machine gun, a hand grenade. We learned also to wield a dagger, to strangle a man from behind without making a sound, and to get out of practically any prison. The course lasted for six weeks. For two hours every day Gad indoctrinated us with the Movement's ideology. The goal was simply to get the English out; the method, intimidation, terror, and sudden death.

"On the day when the English understand that their occupation will cost them blood they won't want to stay," Gad told us. "It's cruel—inhuman, if you like. But we have no other choice. For generations we've wanted to be better, more pure in heart than those who persecuted us. You've all seen the result: Hitler and the extermination camps in Germany. We've had enough of trying to be more just than those who claim to speak in the name of justice. When the Nazis killed a third of our people just men found nothing to say. If ever it's a question of killing off Jews, everyone is silent; there are twenty centuries of history to prove it.

We can rely only on ourselves. If we must become more unjust and inhuman than those who have been unjust and inhuman to us, then we shall do so. We don't like to be bearers of death; heretofore we've chosen to be victims rather than executioners. The commandment *Thou shalt not kill* was given from the summit of one of the mountains here in Palestine, and we were the only ones to obey it. But that's all over; we must be like everybody else. Murder will be not our profession but our duty. In the days and weeks and months to come you will have only one purpose: to kill those who have made us killers. We shall kill in order that once more we may be men. . . ."

On the last day of the course a masked stranger addressed us. He spoke of what our leaders called the eleventh commandment: *Hate your enemy*. He had a soft, timid, romantic voice, and I think he was the Old Man. I'm not quite sure, but his words fired our enthusiasm and made us tremble with emotion. Long after he had gone away I felt them vibrate within me. Thanks to him I became part of a Messianic world where destiny had the face of a masked beggar, where not a single act was lost or a single glance wasted.

I remembered how the grizzled master had explained the sixth commandment to me. Why has a man no right to commit murder? Because in so doing he takes upon himself the function of God. And this must not be done too easily. Well, I said to myself, if in order to change the course of our history we have to become God, we shall become Him. How easy that is we shall see. No, it was not easy.

The first time I took part in a terrorist operation I had to make a superhuman effort not be sick at my stomach. I found myself utterly hateful. Seeing myself with the eyes of the past I imagined that I was in the dark gray uniform of an SS officer. The first time . . .

They ran like rabbits, like drunken rabbits, looking for the shelter of a tree. They seemed to have neither heads nor hands, but only legs. And these legs ran like rabbits sotted with wine and sorrow. But we were all around them, forming a circle of fire from which there was no escape. We were there with our tommy guns, and our bullets were a flaming wall on which their lives were shattered to the accompaniment of agonized cries which I shall hear until the last day of my life.

There were six of us. I don't remember the names of the five others, but Gad was not among them. That day he stayed at the school, as if to show that he had complete confidence in us, as if he were saying: "Go to it; you can get along without me." My five comrades and I set out either to kill or to be killed.

"Good luck!" said Gad as he shook hands with us before we went away. "I'll wait here for your return."

This was the first time that I had been assigned to any operation, and I knew that when I came back—if I came back—I should be another man. I should have undergone my baptism of fire, my baptism of blood. I knew that I should feel very differently, but I had no idea that I should be ready to vomit.

Our mission was to attack a military convoy on the road between Haifa and Tel Aviv. The exact spot was the curve near the village of Hedera; the time late afternoon. In the disguise of workmen coming home from their job we arrived at the chosen place thirty minutes before H-hour. If we had come any earlier our presence might have attracted attention. We set mines on either side of the curve and moved into planned positions. A car was waiting fifty yards away to take us to Petach Tivka, where we were to split up and be driven in three other cars back to our base at the school.

The convoy arrived punctually upon the scene: three open trucks carrying about twenty soldiers. The wind ruffled their hair and the sun shone upon their faces. At the curve the first truck was exploded by one of our mines and the others came to an abrupt halt with screeching brakes. The soldiers leaped to the ground and were caught in the cross-fire of our guns. They ran with lowered heads in every direction, but their legs were cut by our bullets, as if by an immense scythe, and they fell shrieking to the ground.

The whole episode lasted no more than a single minute. We withdrew in good order and everything went according to plan. Our mission was accomplished. Gad was waiting at the school and we made our report to him. His face glowed with pride.

"Good work," he said. "The Old Man won't believe it."

It was then that nausea overcame me. I saw the legs running like frightened rabbits and I found myself utterly hateful. I remembered the dreaded SS guards in the Polish ghettos. Day after day, night after night, they slaughtered the Jews in just the same way. Tommy guns were scattered here and there, and an officer, laughing or distractedly eating, barked out the order: *Fire!* Then the scythe went to work. A few Jews tried to break through the circle of fire, but they only rammed their heads against its insurmountable wall. They too ran like rabbits, like rabbits sotted with wine and sorrow, and death mowed them down.

No, it was not easy to play the part of God, especially when it meant putting on the field-gray uniform of the SS. But it was easier than killing a hostage.

In the first operation and those that followed I was not alone. I killed, to be sure, but I was one of a group. With John Dawson I would be on my own. I would look into his face and he would look into mine and see that I was all eyes.

"Don't torture yourself, Elisha," said Gad. He had turned off the radio and was scrutinizing me intently. "This is war."

I wanted to ask him whether God, the God of war, wore a uniform. But I chose to keep silent. God doesn't wear a uniform, I said to myself. God is a member of the Resistance movement, a terrorist.

Ilana arrived a few minutes before the curfew with her two bodyguards, Gideon and Joab. She was restless and somber, more beautiful than ever. Her delicate features seemed chiseled out of brown marble and there was an expression of heartrending melancholy on her face. She was wearing a gray skirt and a white blouse and her lips were very pale.

"Unforgettable . . . that broadcast of yours," murmured Gad.

"The Old Man wrote it," said Ilana.

"But your voice. . . ."

"That's the Old Man's creation, too," said Ilana, sinking exhausted into a chair. And after a moment of complete silence she added: "Today I saw him crying. I have an idea that he cries more often than we know."

The lucky fellow, I thought to myself. At least he can cry. When a man weeps he knows that one day he will stop.

Joab gave us the latest news of Tel Aviv, of its atmosphere of anxiety and watchful waiting. People were afraid of mass reprisals, and all the newspapers had appealed to the Old Man to call off John Dawson's execution.

The name of John Dawson rather than that of David ben Moshe was on everyone's lips.

"That's why the Old Man was crying," said Gad, brushing a stubborn lock of hair back from his forehead. "The Jews are not yet free of their persecution reflex. They haven't the guts to strike back."

"In London the Cabinet is in session," Joab went on. "In New York the Zionists are holding a huge demonstration in Madison Square Garden. The UN is deeply concerned."

"I hope David knows," said Ilana. Her face had paled to a bronze hue.

"No doubt the hangman will tell him," said Gad.

I understood the bitterness in his voice. David was a childhood friend and they had entered the Movement together. Gad had told me this only after David's arrest, for it would have been unsafe before. The less any one of us knew about his comrades the better; this is one of the basic principles of any underground organization.

Gad had been present when David was wounded; in fact, he was in command of the operation. It was supposed to be what we called a "soft job," but the courageous stupidity of a sentry had spoiled it. His was the fault if David was to be hanged on the morrow. Although wounded and in convulsions he had continued to crawl along the ground with a bullet in his belly and even to shoot off his gun. The mischief that a courageous, diehard fool can do!

It was night. An army truck came to a halt at the entrance of the red-capped paratroopers' camp near Gedera, in the south. In it were a major and three soldiers.

"We've come to get some arms," the major said to the

sentry. "A terrorist attack is supposed to take place this evening."

"Those goddamned terrorists," the sentry mumbled from under his mustache, handing back the major's identification papers.

"Very good, major," he said, opening the gate. "You can come in."

"Thanks," said the major. "Where are the stores?"

"Straight ahead and then two left turns."

The car drove through, followed these directions and stopped in front of a stone building.

"Here we are," said the major.

They got out, and a sergeant saluted the major and opened the door. The major returned his salute and handed him an order with a colonel's signature at the bottom, an order to consign to the bearer five tommy guns, twenty rifles, twenty revolvers, and the necessary ammunition.

"We're expecting a terrorist attack," the major explained condescendingly.

"Goddamned terrorists," muttered the sergeant.

"We've no time to lose," the major added. "Can you hurry?"

"Of course, sir," said the sergeant. "I quite understand."

He pointed out the arms and ammunition to the three soldiers, who silently and quickly loaded them onto the truck. In a very few minutes it was all done.

"I'll just keep this order, sir," said the sergeant as the visitors started to go away.

"Right you are, Sergeant," said the major, climbing into the truck.

The sentry was just about to open the gate when in his sentry box the telephone rang. With a hasty apology he went to answer. The major and his men waited impatiently.

"Sorry, sir," said the sentry as he emerged from the box. "The sergeant wants to see you. He says the order you brought him is not satisfactory."

The major got down from the truck.

"I'll clear it up with him on the telephone," he said.

As the sentry turned around to re-enter the box the major brought his fist down on the back of his neck. The sentry fell noiselessly to the ground. Gad went over to the gate, opened it, and signaled to the driver to go through. Just then the sentry came to and started shooting. Dan put a bullet into his belly while Gad jumped onto the truck and called out:

"Let's go! And hurry!"

The wounded sentry continued to shoot and one of his bullets punctured a tire. Gad retained his self-possession and decided that the tire must be changed.

"David and Dan, keep us covered," he said in a quiet, assured voice.

David and Dan grabbed two of the recently received tommy guns and stood by.

By now the whole camp was alerted. Orders rang out and gunfire followed. Every second was precious. Covered by David and Dan, Gad changed the tire. But the paratroopers were drawing near. Gad knew that the important thing was to make off with the weapons.

"David and Dan," he said, "stay where you are. We're leaving. See if you can hold them back for three minutes longer while we get away. After that you can make a dash for it. Try to get to Gedera, where friends will give you shelter. You know where to find them."

"Yes, I know," said David, continuing to shoot. "Go on, and hurry!"

The arms and ammunition were saved, but David and Dan had to pay. Dan was killed and David wounded. All on account of a stubbornly courageous sentry with a bullet in his belly!

"He was a wonderful fellow, David," said Ilana. Already she spoke of him as if he belonged to the past.

"I hope the hangman knows it," retorted Gad.

I understood his bitterness; indeed I envied it. He was losing a friend, and it hurt. But when you lose a friend every day it doesn't hurt so much. And I'd lost plenty of friends in my time; sometimes I thought of myself as a living graveyard. That was the real reason I followed Gad to Palestine and became a terrorist: I had no more friends to lose.

"They say that the hangman always wears a mask," said Joab, who had been standing silently in front of the kitchen door. "I wonder if it's true."

"I think it is," I said. "The hangman wears a mask. You can't see anything but his eyes."

Ilana went over to Gad, stroked his hair, and said in a sad voice:

"Don't torture yourself, Gad. This is war."

During the hour
that followed nobody said a word. They were all thinking
of David ben Moshe. David was not alone in his death
cell; his friends were with him. All except me. I did not
think of David except when they pronounced his name.
When they were silent my thoughts went out to someone else, to a man I did not yet know, any more than I
knew David, but whom I was fated to know. My David
ben Moshe had the name and face of an Englishman,
Captain John Dawson.

We sat around the table and Ilana served us some
steaming tea. For some time we sipped it without speaking.
We looked into the golden liquid in our cups as if we
were searching in it for the next step after our silence
and the meaning of the events which had brought it about.
Then, in order to kill time, we spoke of our memories,
of such of them that centered on death.

"Death saved my life," Joab began.

He had a young, innocent, tormented face; dark, confused eyes, and hair as white as that of an old man. He wore a perpetually sleepy expression and yawned from one end of the day to the other.

"A neighbor who was against us because of his pacifist convictions reported me to the police," he went on. "I took shelter in an insane asylum whose superintendent was an old school friend. I stayed there for two weeks, until the police found my traces. 'Is he here?' they asked the superintendent. 'Yes,' he admitted. 'He's here; he's a very sick man.' 'What's the matter with him?' they asked. 'He imagines he's dead,' the superintendent told them. But they insisted on seeing me. I was brought to the superintendent's office, where two police officials assigned to the antiterrorist campaign were waiting. They spoke to me but I did not answer. They asked me questions but I pretended not to hear. Even so, they were not convinced that I was crazy. Overriding the superintendent's protest, they took me away and submitted me to forty-eight hours of interrogation. I played dead, and played it successfully. I refused to eat or drink; when they slapped my hands and face I did not react. Dead men feel no pain and so they do not cry. After forty-eight hours I was taken back to the asylum."

As I listened to Joab various thoughts floated to the surface of my mind. I remembered hearing some of my comrades refer to Joab as the Madman.

"Funny, isn't it?" he said. "Death actually saved my life."

We kept silence for several minutes, as if to pay homage to death for saving his life and giving the name of Madman to a fellow with an innocent, tormented face.

"Several days later, when I left the asylum, I saw that my hair had turned white," Joab concluded.

"That's one of death's little jokes," I put in. "Death loves to change the color of people's hair. Death has no hair; it has only eyes. God, on the other hand, has no eyes at all."

"God saved me from death," said Gideon.

We called Gideon the Saint. First because he *was* a saint, and second because he looked like one. He was a husky, inarticulate fellow some twenty years old, who took pains to make himself inconspicuous and was always mumbling prayers. He wore a beard and side curls, went nowhere without a prayer book in his pocket. His father was a rabbi, and when he learned that his son meant to become a terrorist he gave him his blessing. There are times, his father said, when words and prayers are not enough. The God of grace is also the God of war. And war is not a matter of mere words.

"God saved me from death," Gideon repeated. "His eyes saved me. I too was arrested and tortured. They pulled my beard, lit matches under my fingernails, and spat in my face, all in order to make me confess that I had taken part in an attempt against the life of the High Commissioner. But in spite of the pain I did not talk. More than once I was tempted to cry out, but I kept quiet because I felt that God's eyes were upon me. God is looking at me, I said to myself, and I must not disappoint Him. My torturers never stopped shouting, but I kept my thoughts on God and on His eyes, which are drawn to human pain. For lack of evidence they finally had to set me free. If I had admitted my guilt I should be dead."

"And then," I put in, "God would have closed His eyes."

Ilana refilled our cups.

"What about you, Ilana?" I asked. "What saved your life?"

"A cold in the head," she replied.

I burst out laughing, but no one else joined in. My laugh was raucous and artificial.

"A cold in the head?" I repeated.

"Yes," said Ilana, quite seriously. "The English have no description of me; they know only my voice. One day they hauled in a whole group of women, myself among them. At the police station a sound engineer compared each one of our voices to that of the mysterious announcer of the Voice of Freedom. Thanks to the fact that I had a heavy cold I was quickly eliminated and four other women were detained for further questioning."

Once more I was tempted to laugh, but the others were glum and silent. A cold, I thought to myself. And in this case it turned out to have more practical use than either faith or courage. Next we all looked at Gad, who was almost crushing his teacup between his fingers.

"I owe my life to three Englishmen," he said. With his head almost on his right shoulder and his eyes fixed on the cup, he seemed to be addressing the rapidly cooling tea. "It was very early in the game," he went on. "For reasons that no longer matter the Old Man had ordered three hostages taken. They were all sergeants, and I was assigned to kill one of them, any one; the choice was up to me. I was young then, about the age of Elisha, and suffered great mental agony from having this unwanted role thrust upon me. I was willing to play the executioner, but not the judge. Unfortunately, during the night I lost contact with the Old Man and could not explain my reluctance. The sentence had to be carried out at dawn, and how was I to choose the victim? Finally I had an idea. I went down to the cellar and told the three seargeants that the choice was up to them. If you don't make it, I said, then all three of you will be shot. They decided to draw lots, and when dawn came I put a bullet in the unlucky fellow's neck."

Involuntarily I looked at Gad's hands and face, the familiar hands and face of my friend, who had put a bullet in the neck of a fellow human being and now talked coldly, almost indifferently, about it. Was the sergeant's face gazing up at him from his cup of golden cool tea?

"What if the sergeants had refused to settle it among themselves?" I asked. "What then?"

Gad squeezed the cup harder than ever, almost as if he were trying to break it.

"I think I'd have killed myself instead," he said in a flat voice. And after a moment of heavy silence he added: "I tell you I was young and very weak."

All eyes turned toward me, in expectation of my story. I gulped down a mouthful of bitter tea and wiped the perspiration off my forehead.

"I owe my life to a laugh," I said. "It was during one winter at Buchenwald. We were clothed in rags and hundreds of people died of cold every day. In the morning we had to leave our barracks and wait outside in the snow for as long as two hours until they had been cleaned. One day I felt so sick that I was sure the exposure would kill me, and so I stayed behind, in hiding. Quite naturally I was discovered and the cleaning squad dragged me before one of the many assistant barracks leaders. Without stopping to question me he caught hold of my throat and said dispassionately: 'I'm going to choke you.' His powerful hands closed in on my throat and in my enfeebled condition I did not even try to put up a fight. Very well, I said to myself; it's all over. I felt the blood gather in my head and my head swell to several times its normal size, so that

I must have looked like a caricature, a miserable clown. I was sure from one minute to the next that it would burst into a thousand shreds like a child's toy balloon. At this moment the assistant leader took a good look at me and found the sight so comical that he released his grip and burst out laughing. He laughed so long that he forgot his intention to kill. And that's how I got out of it unharmed. It's funny, isn't it, that I should owe my life to an assassin's sense of humor?"

I expected my listeners to scrutinize my head to see if it had really returned to its normal size, but they did nothing of the sort. They continued to stare into their stone-cold tea. In the next few minutes nobody opened his mouth. We had no more desire to call up the past or to listen to our fellows tell their troubled life stories. We sat in restless silence around the table. Every one of us, I am sure, was asking himself to what he *really* owed his life. Gideon was the first to speak.

"We ought to take the Englishman something to eat," he said.

Yes, I said to myself, Gideon is sad, too. He's thinking of John Dawson. He must be; it's inevitable.

"I don't imagine he's hungry," I said aloud. "You can't expect a man condemned to die to have an appetite." And to myself I added: "Or a man condemned to kill, either."

There must have been a strange tone in my voice, for the others raised their heads and I felt the puzzled quality of their penetrating stares.

"No," I said stubbornly; "a man condemned to die can't be hungry."

They did not stir, but sat petrified as the seconds dragged interminably by.

"The condemned man's traditional last meal is a joke,"

I said loudly, "a joke in the worst possible taste, an insult to the corpse that he is about to be. What does a man care if he dies with an empty stomach?"

The expression of astonishment lingered in Gad's eyes, but Ilana looked at me with compassion and Gideon with friendliness. Joab did not look at me at all. His eyes were lowered, but perhaps that was his way of looking out of them.

"He doesn't know," remarked Gideon.

"He doesn't know what?" I asked, without any conscious reason for raising my voice. Perhaps I wanted to hear myself shout, to arouse my anger and see it reflected in the motionless shadows in the mirror and on the wall. Or perhaps out of sheer weakness. I felt powerless to change anything, least of all myself, in spite of the fact that I wanted to introduce a transformation into the room, to reorder the whole of creation. I would have made the Saint into a madman, have given John Dawson's name to Gad and his fate to David. But I knew there was nothing I could do. To have such power I should have had to take the place of death, not just of the individual death of John Dawson, the English captain who had no more appetite than I.

"What doesn't he know?" I repeated stridently.

"He doesn't know he's going to die," said Gideon in a sorrowfully dreamy voice.

"His stomach knows," I retorted. "A man about to die listens only to his stomach. He pays no attention to his heart or to his past, or to yours for that matter. He doesn't even hear the voice of the storm. He listens to his stomach and his stomach tells him that he is going to die and that he isn't hungry."

I had talked too fast and too loud and I was left panting. I should have liked to run away, but my friends' stares transfixed me. Death sealed off every exit, and everywhere there were eyes.

"I'm going down to the cellar," said Gideon. "I'll ask him if he wants something to eat."

"Don't ask him anything," I said. "Simply tell him that tomorrow, when the sun rises above the blood-red horizon, he, John Dawson, will say good-by to life, good-by to his stomach. Tell him that he's going to die."

Gideon got up, with his eyes still on me, and started toward the kitchen and the entrance to the cellar. At the door he paused.

"I'll tell him," he said, with a quickly fading smile. Then he turned on his heels and I heard him going down the stairs.

I was grateful for his consent. He and not I would warn John Dawson of his approaching end. I could never have done it. It's easier to kill a man than to break the news that he is going to die.

"Midnight," said Joab.

Midnight, I reflected, the hour when the dead rise out of their graves and come to say their prayers in the synagogue, the hour when God Himself weeps over the destruction of the Temple, the hour when a man should be able to plumb the depths of his being and to discover the Temple in ruins. A God that weeps and dead men that pray.

"Poor boy!" murmured Ilana.

She did not look at me, but her tears scrutinized my face. Her tears rather than her eyes caressed me.

"Don't say that, Ilana. Don't call me 'poor boy.'"

There were tears in her eyes, or rather there were tears in the place of her eyes, tears which with every passing second grew heavier and more opaque and threatened to overflow. . . . I was afraid that suddenly the worst would happen: the dusky Ilana would no longer be there; she would have drowned in her tears. I wanted to touch her arm and say *Don't cry.* Say what you like, but don't cry.

But she wasn't crying. It takes eyes to cry, and she had no eyes, only tears where her eyes should have been.

"Poor boy!" she repeated.

Then what I had foreseen came true. Ilana disappeared, and Catherine was there instead. I wondered why Catherine had come, but her apparition did not particularly surprise me. She liked the opposite sex, and particularly she liked little boys who were thinking of death. She liked to speak of love to little boys, and since men going to their death are little boys she liked to speak to them of love. For this reason her presence in the magical room—magical because it transcended the differences, the boundary lines between the victim and the executioner, between the present and the past—was not surprising.

I had met Catherine in Paris in 1945, when I had just come from Buchenwald, that other magical spot, where the living were transformed into dead and their future into darkness. I was weakened and half starved. One of the many rescue committees sent me to a camp where a hundred boys and girls were spending their summer vacation. The camp was in Normandy, where the early morning breeze rustled the same way it did in Palestine.

Because I knew no French I could not communicate with the other boys and girls. I ate and sunbathed with them, but I had no way of talking. Catherine was the only person who seemed to know any German and occasionally we exchanged a few words. Sometimes she came up to me at the dining-room table and asked me whether I had slept well, enjoyed my meal, or had a good time during the day.

She was twenty-six or -seven years old; small, frail, and almost transparent, with silky blonde, sunlit hair and blue, dreamy eyes which never cried. Her face was thin but saved from being bony by the delicacy of the features. She was the first woman I had seen from nearby. Before this—that is, before the war—I did not look at women. On my way to school or the synagogue I walked close to the walls, with my eyes cast down on the ground. I knew that women existed, and why, but I did not appreciate the fact that they had a body, breasts, legs, hands, and lips whose touch sets a man's heart to beating. Catherine revealed this to me.

The camp was at the edge of a wood, and after supper I went walking there all by myself, talking to the murmuring breeze and watching the sky turn a deeper and deeper blue. I liked to be alone.

One evening Catherine asked if she might go with me, and I was too timid to say anything but yes. For half an hour, an hour, we walked in complete silence. At first I found the silence embarrassing, then to my surprise I began to enjoy it. The silence of two people is deeper than the silence of one. Involuntarily I began to talk.

"Look how the sky is opening up," I said.

She threw back her head and looked above her. Just as I had said, the sky was opening up. Slowly at first, as if swept by an invisible wind, the stars drew away from the zenith, some moving to the right, others to the left, until the center of the sky was an empty space, dazzlingly blue and gradually acquiring depth and outline.

"Look hard," I said. "There's nothing there."

From behind me Catherine looked up and said not a word.

"That's enough," I said; "let's go on walking."

As we walked on I told her the legend of the open

sky. When I was a child the old master told me that there were nights when the sky opened up in order to make way for the prayers of unhappy children. On one such night a little boy whose father was dying said to God: "Father, I am too small to know how to pray. But I ask you to heal my sick father." God did what the boy asked, but the boy himself was turned into a prayer and carried up into Heaven. From that day on, the master told me, God has from time to time shown Himself to us in the face of a child.

"That is why I like to look at the sky at this particular moment," I told Catherine. "I hope to see the child. But you are a witness to the truth. There's nothing there. The child is only a story."

It was then for the first time during the evening that Catherine spoke.

"Poor boy!" she exclaimed. "Poor boy!"

She's thinking of the boy in the story, I said to myself. And I loved her for her compassion.

After this Catherine often went walking with me. She questioned me about my childhood and my more recent past, but I did not always answer. One evening she asked me why I kept apart from the other boys and girls in the camp.

"Because they speak a language I can't understand," I told her.

"Some of the girls know German," she said.

"But I have nothing to say to them."

"You don't have to say anything," she said slowly, with a smile. "All you have to do is love them."

I didn't see what she was driving at and said so. Her smile widened and she began to speak to me of love. She spoke easily and well. Love is this and love is that; man is born to love; he is only alive when he is in the presence of a woman he loves or should love. I told her that I knew nothing of love, that I didn't know it existed or had a right to exist.

"I'll prove it to you," she said.

The next evening, as she walked at my left side over the leaf-covered path, she took hold of my arm. At first I thought she needed my support, but actually it was because she wanted to make me feel the warmth of her body. Then she claimed to be tired and said it would be pleasant to sit down on the grass under a tree. Once we had sat down she began to stroke my face and hair. Then she kissed me several times; first her lips touched mine and then her tongue burned the inside of my mouth. For several nights running we returned to the same place, and she spoke to me of love and desire and the mysteries of the heart. She took my hand and guided it over her breasts and thighs, and I realized that women had breasts and thighs and hands that could set a man's heart to beating and turn his blood to fire.

Then came the last evening. The month of vacation was over and I was to go back to Paris the next day. As soon as we had finished supper we went to sit for the last time under the tree. I felt sad and lonely, and Catherine held my hand in hers without speaking. The night was fair and calm. At intervals, like a warm breath, the wind played over our faces. It must have been one or two o'clock in the morning when Catherine broke the silence, turned her melancholy face toward me, and said:

"Now we're going to make love."

These words made me tremble. I was going to make love for the first time. Before her there had been no woman upon earth. I didn't know what to say or do; I was afraid of saying the wrong thing or making some inappropriate gesture. Awkwardly I waited for her to take the initiative. With a suddenly serious look on her face she began to get undressed. She took off her blouse and in the starlight I saw her ivory-white breasts. Then she took off the rest of her clothes and was completely naked before me.

"Take off your shirt," she ordered.

I was paralyzed; there was iron in my throat and lead in my veins; my arms and hands would not obey me. I could only look at her from head to foot and follow the rise and fall of her breasts. I was hypnotized by the call of her outstretched, naked body.

"Take off your shirt," she repeated.

Then, as I did not move, she began to undress me. Deliberately she took off my shirt and shorts. Then she lay back on the grass and said:

"Take me."

I got down on my knees. I stared at her for a long time and then I covered her body with kisses. Absently and without saying a word she stroked my hair.

"Catherine," I said, "first there is something I must tell you."

Her face took on a blank and anguished expression, and there was anguish in the rustle of the breeze among the trees.

"No, no!" she cried. "Don't tell me anything. Take me, but don't talk."

Heedless of her objection I went on:

"First, Catherine, I must tell you. . . ."

Her lips twisted with pain, and there was pain in the rustle of the breeze.

"No, no, no!" she implored. "Don't tell me. Be quiet. Take me quickly, but don't talk."

"What I have to tell you is this," I insisted: "You've won the game. I love you, Catherine. . . . I love you."

She burst into sobs and repeated over and over again: "Poor boy! You poor boy!"

I picked up my shirt and shorts and ran away. Now I understood. She was referring not to the little boy in the sky but to me. She had spoken to me of love because she knew that I was the little boy who had been turned into a prayer and carried up into Heaven. She knew that I had died and come back to earth, dead. This was why she had spoken to me of love and wanted to make love with me. I saw it all quite clearly. She liked making love with little boys who were going to die; she enjoyed the company of those who were obsessed with death. No wonder that her presence this night in Palestine was not surprising.

"Poor boy!" said Ilana, in a very quiet voice, for the last time. And a deep sigh escaped from her breast, which made her tears free to flow, to flow on and on until the end of time.

Suddenly I became aware that the room was stuffy, so stuffy that I was almost stifled.

No wonder. The room was small, far too small to receive so many visitors at one time. Ever since midnight the visitors had been pouring in. Among them were people I had known, people I had hated, admired, forgotten. As I let my eyes wander about the room I realized that all of those who had contributed to my formation, to the formation of my permanent identity, were there. Some of them were familiar, but I could not pin a label upon them; they were names without faces or faces without names. And yet I knew that at some point my life had crossed theirs.

My father was there, of course, and my mother, and the beggar. And the grizzled master. The English soldiers of the convoy we had ambushed at Gedera were there also. And around them friends and brothers and comrades, some of them out of my childhood, others that I had seen live

166

and suffer, hope and curse at Buchenwald and Auschwitz. Alongside my father there was a boy who looked strangely like myself as I had been before the concentration camps, before the war, before everything. My father smiled at him, and the child picked up the smile and sent it to me over the multitude of heads which separated us.

Now I understood why the room was so stuffy. It was too small to hold so many people at a time. I forced a passage through the crowd until I came to the little boy and thanked him for the smile. I wanted to ask him what all these people were doing in the room, but on second thought I saw that this would be discourteous toward my father. Since he was present I should address my question to him.

"Father, why are all these people here?"

My mother stood beside him, looking very pale, and her lips tirelessly murmured: "Poor little boy, poor little boy! . . ."

"Father," I repeated, "answer me. What are you all doing here?"

His large eyes, in which I had so often seen the sky open up, were looking at me, but he did not reply. I turned around and found myself face to face with the rabbi, whose beard was more grizzled than ever.

"Master," I said, "what has brought all these people here tonight?"

Behind me I heard my mother whisper, "Poor little boy, my poor little boy."

"Well, Master," I repeated, "answer me, I implore you."

But he did not answer either; indeed, he seemed not even to have heard my question, and his silence made me afraid. As I had known him before, he was always present in my hour of need. Then his silence had been reassuring. Now I tried to look into his eyes, but they were two globes

167

of fire, two suns that burned my face. I turned away and went from one visitor to another, seeking an answer to my question, but my presence struck them dumb. Finally I came to the beggar, who stood head and shoulders above them all. And he spoke to me, quite spontaneously.

"This is a night of many faces," he said.

I was sad and tired.

"Yes," I said wearily, "this is a night of many faces, and I should like to know the reason why. If you are the one I think you are, enlighten and comfort me. Tell me the meaning of these looks, this muteness, these presences. Tell me, I beseech you, for I can endure them no longer."

He took my arm, gently pressed it, and said:

"Do you see that little boy over there?" and he pointed to the boy who looked like myself as I had been.

"Yes, I see him," I replied.

"He will answer all your questions," said the beggar. "Go talk to him."

Now I was quite sure that he was not a beggar. Once more I elbowed my way through the crowd of ghosts and arrived, panting with exhaustion, at the young boy's side.

"Tell me," I said beseechingly, "what you are doing here? And all the others?"

He opened his eyes wide in astonishment.

"Don't you know?" he asked.

I confessed that I did not know.

"Tomorrow a man is to die, isn't he?"

"Yes," I said, "at dawn tomorrow."

"And you are to kill him, aren't you?"

"Yes, that's true; I have been charged with his execution."

"And you don't understand, do you?"

"No."

"But it's all quite simple," he exclaimed. "We are here to be present at the execution. We want to see you carry it out. We want to see you turn into a murderer. That's natural enough, isn't it?"

"How is it natural? Of what concern is the killing of John Dawson to you?"

"You are the sum total of all that we have been," said the youngster who looked like my former self. "In a way we are the ones to execute John Dawson. Because you can't do it without us. Now, do you see?"

I was beginning to understand. An act so absolute as that of killing involves not only the killer but, as well, those who have formed him. In murdering a man I was making them murderers.

"Well," said the boy, "do you see?"

"Yes, I see," I said.

"Poor boy, poor boy!" murmured my mother, whose lips were now as gray as the old master's hair.

"He's hungry," said Gideon's voice, unexpectedly.

I had not heard him come back up the stairs. Saints have a disconcertingly noiseless way. They walk, laugh, eat, and pray, all without making a sound.

"Impossible," I protested.

He can't be hungry, I was thinking. He's going to die, and a man who's going to die can't be hungry.

"He said so himself," Gideon insisted, with a shade of emotion in his voice.

Everyone was staring at me. Ilana had stopped crying, Joab was no longer examining his nails, and Gad looked weary. All the ghosts, too, seemed to be expecting something of me, a sign perhaps, or a cry.

"Does he know?" I asked Gideon.

169

"Yes, he knows." And after a moment he added: "I told him."

"How did he react?"

It was important for me to know the man's reaction. Was the news a shock? Had he stayed calm, or protested his innocence?

"He smiled," said Gideon. "He said that he already knew. His stomach had told him."

"And he said he was hungry?"

Gideon hid his twitching hands behind his back.

"Yes, that's what he said. He said he was hungry and he had a right to a good last meal."

Gad laughed, but the tone of his laugh was hollow.

"Typically English," he remarked. "The stiff upper lip."

His remark hung over our heads in midair; no one opened up to receive it. My father shot me a hard glance, as if to say *A man is going to die, and he's hungry.*

"Might as well admit it," said Gad. "The English have iron digestions."

No one paid any attention to this remark either. I felt a sudden stab of pain in my stomach. I had not eaten all day. Ilana got up and went into the kitchen.

"I'll fix him something to eat," she declared.

I heard her moving about, slicing a loaf of bread, opening the icebox, starting to make coffee. In a few minutes she came back with a cup of coffee in one hand and a plate in the other.

"This is all I can find," she said. "A cheese sandwich and some black coffee. There's no sugar. . . . Not much of a meal, but it's the best I can do." And after several seconds of silence she asked: "Who's going to take it down?"

The boy standing beside my father stared hard at me. His stare had a voice, which said:

"Go on. Take him something to eat. He's hungry, you know."

"No," I responded. "Not I. I don't want to see him. Above all, I don't want to see him eat. I want to think of him, later on, as a man who never ate."

I wanted to add that I had cramps in my stomach, but I realized that this was unimportant. Instead I said: "I don't want to be alone with him. Not now."

"We'll go with you," said the little boy. "It's wrong to hold back food from a man who's hungry. You know that."

Yes, I knew. I had always given food to the hungry. You, beggar, you remember. Didn't I offer you bread? But tonight is different. Tonight I can't do it.

"That's true," said the little boy, picking up the train of my reflections. "Tonight is different, and you are different also, or at least you're going to be. But that has nothing to do with the fact that a man's hungry and must have something to eat."

"But he's going to die tomorrow," I protested. "What's it matter whether he dies with a full stomach or an empty one?"

"For the time being he's alive," the child said sententiously." My father nodded in acquiescence, and all the others followed his example. "He's alive and hungry, and you refuse to give him anything to eat?"

All these heads, nodding like the tops of black trees, made me shudder. I wanted to close my eyes but I was ashamed. I couldn't close my eyes in the presence of my father.

"Very well," I said resignedly. "I accept. I'll take him something to eat." As if obeying the baton of an invisible conductor the nodding heads were still. "I'll take him something to eat," I repeated. "But first tell me something, little boy. Are the dead hungry too?"

He looked surprised.

"What—you don't know?" he exclaimed. "Of course they are."

"And should we give them something to eat?"

"How can you ask? Of course you should give them something to eat. Only it's difficult. . . ."

"Difficult . . . difficult . . . difficult . . . ," the ghosts echoed together.

The boy looked at me and smiled.

"I'll tell you a secret," he whispered. "You know that at midnight the dead leave their graves, don't you?"

I told him that I knew; I had been told.

"Have you been told that they go from the graveyard to the synagogue?"

Yes, I had been told that also.

"Well, it's true," said the little boy. Then, after a silence which accentuated what was to follow, he went on in a voice so still that if it had not been inside myself I could never have heard it: "Yes, it's true. They gather every night in the synagogue. But not for the purpose you imagine. They come not to pray but to eat——"

Everything in the room—walls, chairs, heads—began to whirl around me, dancing in a pre-established rhythm, without stirring the air or setting foot on the ground. I was the center of a multitude of circles. I wanted to close my eyes and stop up my ears, but my father was there, and my mother, and the master and the beggar and the boy. With all those who had formed me around me I had no right to stop up my ears and close my eyes.

"Give me those things," I said to Ilana. "I'll take them to him."

The dancers stopped in their tracks, as if I were the conductor and my words his baton. I stepped toward Ilana, still standing at the kitchen door. Suddenly Gad rushed forward and reached her side before me.

"I'll do it," he said.

Almost brutally he snatched the cup and plate from Ilana's hands and went precipitately down the stairs.

Joab looked at his watch. "It's after two."

"Is that all?" asked Ilana. "It's a long night, the longest I've ever lived through."

"Yes, it's long," Joab agreed.

Ilana bit her lips. "There are moments when I think it will never end, that it will last indefinitely. It's like the rain. Here the rain, like everything else, suggests permanence and eternity. I say to myself: It's raining today and it's going to rain tomorrow and the next day, the next week and the next century. Now I say to myself: There's night now and there will be night tomorrow, and the day, the week, the century after."

She paused abruptly, took a handkerchief from the cuff of her blouse and wiped her perspiring forehead.

"I wonder why it's so stuffy in here," she said, "particularly this late at night."

"It will be cooler early tomorrow," promised Joab.

"I hope so," said Ilana. "What time does the sun rise?"

"Around five o'clock."

"And what time is it now?"

"Twenty past two," said Joab, looking again at his watch.

"Aren't you hot, Elisha?" Ilana asked me.

"Yes, I am," I answered.

Ilana went back to her place at the table. I walked over to the window and looked out. The city seemed faraway and unreal. Deep in sleep, it spawned anxious dreams, hopeful dreams, dreams which would proliferate other dreams on the morrow. And these dreams in their turn would engender new heroes, who would live through the night and prepare to die at dawn, to die and to give death.

"Yes, I'm hot, Ilana," I said. "I'm stifling."

I don't know how long I stood, sweating, beside the open window, before a warm, vibrant, reassuring hand was laid on my shoulder. It was Ilana.

"What are you thinking?" she said.

"I'm thinking of the night," I told her. "Always the same thing——"

"And of John Dawson?"

"Yes, of John Dawson."

Somewhere in the city a light shone in a window and then went out. No doubt a man had looked at his watch or a mother had gone to find out whether her child was smiling in his sleep.

"You didn't want to see him, though," said Ilana.

"I don't want to see him."

One day, I was thinking, my son will say: "All of a sudden you look sad. What's wrong?" "It's because in my eyes there is a picture of an English captain called John Dawson, just as he appeared to me at the moment of his death. . . ." Perhaps I ought to put a mask on his face; a mask is more easily killed and forgotten.

"Are you afraid?" asked Ilana.

"Yes."

Being afraid, I ought to have told her, is nothing. Fear is only a color, a backdrop, a landscape. That isn't the problem. The fear of either the victim or the executioner is unimportant. What matters is the fact that each of them is playing a role which has been imposed upon him. The two roles are the extremities of the estate of man. The tragic thing is the imposition.

"You, Elisha, *you* are afraid?"

I knew why she had asked. You, Elisha, who lived through Auschwitz and Buchenwald? You who any number of times saw God die? You are afraid?"

"I *am* afraid, though, Ilana," I repeated.

She knew quite well that fear was not in fact the real theme. Like death, it is only a backdrop, a bit of local color.

"What makes you afraid?"

Her warm, living hand was still on my shoulder; her breasts brushed me and I could feel her breath on my neck. Her blouse was wet with perspiration and her face distraught. She doesn't understand, I thought to myself.

"I'm afraid he'll make me laugh," I said. "You see, Ilana, he's quite capable of swelling up his head and letting it burst into a thousand shreds, just in order to make me laugh. That's what makes me afraid."

But still she did not understand. She took the handkerchief from her cuff and wiped my neck and temples. Then she kissed my forehead lightly and said:

"You torture yourself too much, Elisha. Hostages aren't clowns. There's nothing so funny about them."

Poor Ilana! Her voice was as pure as truth, as sad as purity. But she did not understand. She was distracted by the externals and did not see what lay behind them.

"You may be right," I said in resignation. "We make *them* laugh. They laugh when they're dead."

She stroked my face and neck and hair, and I could still feel the pressure of her breasts against my body. Then she began to talk, in a sad but clear voice, as if she were talking to a sick child.

"You torture yourself too much, my dear," she said several times in succession. At least she no longer called me "poor boy," and I was grateful. "You mustn't do it.

You're young and intelligent, and you've suffered quite enough already. Soon it will all be over. The English will get out and we shall come back to the surface and lead a simple, normal life. You'll get married and have children. You'll tell them stories and make them laugh. You'll be happy because they're happy, and they *will* be happy, I promise you. How could they be otherwise with a father like you? You'll have forgotten this night, this room, me, and everything else———"

As she said "everything else" she traced a sweeping semicircle with her hand. I was reminded of my mother. She talked in the same moving voice and used almost the same words in the same places. I was very fond of my mother. Every evening, until I was nine or ten years old, she put me to sleep with lullabies or stories. There is a goat beside your bed, she used to tell me, a goat of gold. Everywhere you go in life the goat will guide and protect you. Even when you are grown up and very rich, when you know everything a man can know and possess all that he should possess, the goat will still be near you.

"You talk as if you were my mother, Ilana," I said.

My mother, too, had a harmonious voice, even more harmonious than Ilana's. Like the voice of God it had power to dispel chaos and to impart a vision of the future which might have been mine, with the goat to guide me, the goat I had lost on the way to Buchenwald.

"You're suffering," said Ilana. "That's what it means when a man speaks of his mother."

"No, Ilana," I said. "At this moment she's the one to suffer."

Ilana's caresses became lighter, more remote. She was beginning to understand. A shadow fell across her face. For some time she was silent, then she joined me in looking at the hand night held out to us through the window.

"War is like night," she said. "It covers everything."

Yes, she was beginning to understand. I hardly felt the pressure of her fingers on my neck.

"We say that ours is a holy war," she went on, "that we're struggling against something and for something, against the English and for an independent Palestine. That's what we say. But these are words; as such they serve only to give meaning to our actions. And our actions, seen in their true and primitive light, have the odor and color of blood. This is war, we say; we must kill. There are those, like you, who kill with their hands, and others— like me—who kill with their voices. Each to his own. And what else can we do? War has a code, and if you deny this you deny its whole purpose and hand the enemy victory on a silver platter. That we can't afford. We need victory, victory in war, in order to survive, in order to remain afloat on the surface of time."

She did not raise her voice. It seemed as if she were chanting a lullaby, telling a bedtime story. There was neither passion nor despair nor even concern in her intonation.

All things considered, she was quite right. We were at war; we had an ideal, a purpose—and also an enemy who stood between us and its attainment. The enemy must be eliminated. And how? By any and all means at our command. There were all sorts of means, but they were unimportant and soon forgotten. The purpose, the end, this was all that would last. Ilana was probably correct in saying that one day I should forget this night. But the dead never forget; they would remember. In their eyes I should be forever branded a killer. There are not a thousand ways of being a killer; either a man is one or he isn't. He can't say I'll kill only ten or only twenty-six men; I'll kill for only five minutes or a single day. He who has killed one man alone is a killer for life. He may choose another occupation, hide himself under another identity, but the executioner or at least the executioner's mask will be always with him. There lies the problem: in the influence of the backdrop of the play upon the actor. War had made me an executioner, and an executioner I would remain even after the backdrop had changed, when I was acting in another play upon a different stage.

"I don't want to be a killer," I said, sliding rapidly over the word as I ejected it.

"Who does?" said Ilana.

She was still stroking my neck, but somehow I had the impression that it was not really *my* neck, *my* hair her fingers were caressing. The noblest woman in the world would hesitate to touch the skin of a killer, of a man who would have the label of killer his whole life long.

I cast a rapid glance behind me to see if the others were still there. Gideon and Joab were dozing, with their heads pillowed on their arms, on the table. Gideon seemed, even in his sleep, to be praying. Gad was still in the cellar and I wondered why he had stayed there so long. As for the ghosts, they followed the conversation but, to my surprise, took no part in it. Ilana was silent.

"What are you thinking?" I murmured.

She did not reply and after a few minutes I posed the question again. Still there was no answer. We were both silent. And the crowd behind me, the crowd of petrified silences, whose shadows absorbed the light and turned it into something sad, funereal, hostile, was silent as well. The sum of these silences filled me with fear. Their silences were different from mine; they were hard, cold, immobile, lifeless, incapable of change.

As a child I had been afraid of the dead and of the graveyard, their shadowy kingdom. The silence with which they surrounded themselves provoked my terror. I knew that now, at my back, in serried ranks as if to protect themselves from the cold, they were sitting in judgment upon me. In their frozen world the dead have nothing to do but judge, and because they have no sense of past or future they judge without pity. They condemn not with words or gestures but with their very existence.

At my back they were sitting in judgment upon me; I felt their silences judging mine. I wanted to turn around but the mere idea filled me with fear. Soon Gad will come up from the cellar, I said to myself, and later it will be my turn to go down. Dawn will come, and this crowd will melt into the light of day. For the present I shall stay beside Ilana, at the window, with my back to them.

A minute later I changed my mind. My father and mother, the master and the beggar were all there. I could not insult them indefinitely by turning my back; I must look at them face to face. Cautiously I wheeled around. There were two sorts of light in the room: one white, around the sleeping Gideon and Joab, the other black, enveloping the ghosts.

I left Ilana lost in thought, perhaps in regret, at the window, and began to walk about the room, pausing every now and then before a familiar face, a familiar sorrow. I knew that these faces, these sorrows were sitting in judgment upon me. They were dead and they were hungry. When the dead are hungry they judge the living without pity. They do not wait until an action has been achieved, a crime committed. They judge in advance.

Only when I perceived the silence of the boy, a silence eloquent in his eyes, did I decide to speak. He had a look of anxiety which made him seem older, more mature. I shall speak up, I said to myself. They have no right to condemn the little boy.

179

As I approached my father I saw the sorrow on his face. My father had stolen away a minute before the Angel of Death came to take him; in cheating the Angel he had taken with him the human sorrow which he endured while he was alive.

"Father," I said, "don't judge me. Judge God. He created the universe and made justice stem from injustices. He brought it about that a people should attain happiness through tears, that the freedom of a nation, like that of a man, should be a monument built upon a pile, a foundation of dead bodies. . . ."

I stood in front of him, not knowing what to do with my head, my eyes, my hands. I wanted to transfer the lifeblood of my body into my voice. At moments I fancied I had done so. I talked for a long time, telling him things that doubtless he already knew, since he had taught them to me. If I repeated them it was only in order to prove to him that I had not forgotten.

"Don't judge me, Father," I implored him, trembling with despair. "You must judge God. He is the first cause, the prime mover; He conceived men and things the way they are. You are dead, father, and only the dead may judge God."

But he did not react. The sorrow written upon his emaciated, unshaven face became even more human than before. I left him and went over to my mother, who was standing at his right side. But my pain was too great for me to address her. I thought I heard her murmur: "Poor boy, poor boy!" and tears came to my eyes. Finally I said that I wasn't a murderer, that she had not given birth to a murderer but to a soldier, to a fighter for freedom, to an idealist who had sacrificed his peace of mind—a possession more precious than life itself—to his people, to his people's right to the light of day, to joy, to the laughter of children. In a halting, feverishly sobbing voice, this was all that I could find to say.

When she too failed to react I left her and went to my old master, of all those present the least changed by death. Alive, he had been very much the same as now; we used to say that he was not of this world, and now this was literally true.

"I haven't betrayed you," I said, as if the deed were already done. "If I were to refuse to obey orders I should betray my living friends. And the living have more rights over us than the dead. You told me that yourself. *Therefore choose life,* it is written in the Scriptures. I have espoused the cause of the living, and that is no betrayal."

Beside him stood Yerachmiel, my friend and comrade and brother. Yerachmiel was the son of a coachman, with the hands of a laborer and the soul of a saint. We two were the master's favorite pupils; every evening he studied with us the secrets of the Cabala. I did not know that Yerachmiel too was dead. I realized it only at the moment when I saw him in the crowd, at the master's side—or rather a respectful step behind him.

"Yerachmiel my brother," I said, ". . . remember . . . ?"

Together we had spun impossible dreams. According to the Cabala, if a man's soul is sufficiently pure and his love deep enough he can bring the Messiah to earth. Yerachmiel and I decided to try. Of course we were aware of the danger: No one can force God's hand with impunity. Men older, wiser, and more mature than ourselves had tried in vain to wrest the Messiah from the chains of the future; failing in their purpose they had lost their faith, their reason, and even their lives. Yerachmiel and I knew all this, but we were resolved to carry out our plan regardless of the obstacles that lay in wait along the way. We promised

181

to stick to each other, whatever might happen. If one of us were to die, the other would carry on. And so we made preparations for a voyage in depth. We purified our souls and bodies, fasting by day and praying by night. In order to cleanse our mouths and their utterances we spoke as little as possible and on the Sabbath we spoke not at all.

Perhaps our attempt might have been successful. But war broke out and we were driven away from our homes. The last time I had seen Yerachmiel he was one of a long column of marching Jews deported to Germany. A week later I was sent to Germany myself. Yerachmiel was in one camp, I in another. Often I wondered whether he had continued his efforts alone. Now I knew: he had continued, and he was dead.

"Yerachmiel," I said; "Yerachmiel my brother, remember. . . ."

Something about him had changed: his hands. Now they were the hands of a saint.

"We too," I said, "my comrades in the Movement and I, are trying to force God's hand. You who are dead should help us, not hinder. . . ."

But Yerachmiel and his hands were silent. And somewhere in the universe of time the Messiah was silent as well. I left him and went over to the little boy I used to be.

"Are you too judging me?" I asked. "You of all people have the least right to do that. You're lucky; you died young. If you'd gone on living you'd be in my place."

Then the boy spoke. His voice was filled with echoes of disquiet and longing.

"I'm not judging you," he said. "We're not here to sit in judgment. We're here simply because you're here. We're present wherever you go; we are what you do. When you raise your eyes to Heaven we share in their sight; when you pat the head of a hungry child a thousand hands are

182

laid on his head; when you give bread to a beggar we give him that taste of paradise which only the poor can savor. Why are we silent? Because silence is not only our dwelling-place but our very being as well. We *are* silence. And your silence is us. You carry us with you. Occasionally you may see us, but most of the time we are invisible to you. When you see us you imagine that we are sitting in judgment upon you. You are wrong. Your silence is your judge."

Suddenly the beggar's arm brushed against mine. I turned and saw him behind me. I knew that he was not the Angel of Death but the prophet Elijah.

"I hear Gad's footsteps," he said. "He's coming up the stairs."

"I hear Gad's footsteps," said Ilana, touching my arm. "He's coming up the stairs."

Slowly and with a blank look on his face Gad came into the room. Ilana ran toward him and kissed his lips, but gently he pushed her away.

"You stayed down there so long," she said. "What kept you?"

A cruel, sad smile crossed Gad's face.

"Nothing," he said. "I was watching him eat."

"He ate?" I asked in surprise. "You mean to say he was able to eat?"

"Yes, he ate," said Gad. "And with a good appetite, too."

I could not understand.

"What?" I exclaimed. "You mean to say he was hungry?"

"I didn't say he was hungry," Gad retorted. "I said he ate with a good appetite."

"So he wasn't hungry," I insisted.

Gad's face darkened.

"No, he wasn't hungry."

"Then why did he eat?"

"I don't know," said Gad nervously. "Probably to show me that he can eat even if he's not hungry."

Ilana scrutinized his face. She tried to catch his eye, but Gad was staring into space.

"What did you do after that?" she asked uneasily.

"After what?" said Gad brusquely.

"After he'd finished eating."

Gad shrugged his shoulders.

"Nothing," he said.

"What do you mean, *nothing?*"

"Nothing. He told me stories."

Ilana shook his arm.

"Stories? What kind of stories?"

Gad sighed in resignation.

"Just stories," he repeated, obviously tired of answering questions he considered grotesque.

I wanted to ask if he had laughed, if the hostage had got a laugh out of him. But I refrained. The answer could only have been absurd.

Gad's reappearance had roused Gideon and Joab from their sleep. With haggard faces they looked around the room, as if to assure themselves they weren't dreaming. Stifling a yawn, Joab asked Gad for the time.

"Four o'clock," said Gad, consulting his watch.

"So late? I'd never have thought it."

Gad beckoned to me to come closer.

"Soon it will be day," he observed.

"I know."

"You know what you have to do?"

"Yes, I know."

He took a revolver out of his pocket and handed it to me. I hesitated.

"Take it," said Gad.

The revolver was black and nearly new. I was afraid to even touch it, for in it lay all the whole difference between what I was and what I was going to be.

"What are you waiting for?" asked Gad impatiently. "Take it."

I held out my hand and took it. I examined it for a long time as if I did not know what purpose it could possibly serve. Finally I slipped it into my trouser pocket.

"I'd like to ask you a question," I said to Gad.

"Go ahead."

"Did he make you laugh?"

Gad stared at me coldly, as if he had not understood my question or the necessity for it. His brow was furrowed with preoccupation.

"John Dawson," I said. "Did he make you laugh?"

Gad's eyes stared through me; I felt them going through my head and coming out the other side. He must have been wondering what was going on in my mind, why I harped on this unimportant question, why I didn't seem to be suffering or to be masking my suffering or lack of suffering.

"No," he said at last; "he didn't make me laugh."

His own mask cracked imperceptibly. All his efforts were bent upon controlling the expression of his eyes, but he had neglected his mouth, and it was there that the crack showed. His upper lip betrayed bitterness and anger.

"How did you do it?" I asked in mock admiration. "Weren't his stories funny?"

Gad made a strange noise, not unlike a laugh. The silence that followed accentuated the sadness which an invisible hand had traced upon his lips.

"Oh, they were funny all right, very funny. But they didn't make me laugh."

He took a cigarette out of his shirt pocket, lit it, drew a few puffs and then, without waiting for me to ask anything more, went on:

"I was thinking of David, that's all."

I'll think of David too, I reflected. He'll protect me. John Dawson may try to make me laugh, but I won't do it. David will come to my rescue.

"It's getting late," said Joab, stifling another yawn.

The night was still looking in on us. But quite obviously it was getting ready to go away. I came to a sudden decision.

"I'm going down," I said.

"So soon?" said Gad, in a tone revealing either emotion or mere surprise. "You've got plenty of time. As much as an hour. . . . "

I said that I wanted to go down before the time was up, to see the fellow, and talk, and get to know him. It was cowardly, I said, to kill a complete stranger. It was like war, where you don't shoot at men but into the night, and the wounded night emits cries of pain which are almost human. You shoot into the darkness, and you never know whether any of the enemy was killed, or which one. To execute a stranger would be the same thing. If I were to see him only as he died I should feel as if I had shot at a dead man.

This was the reason I gave for my decision. I'm not sure it was exact. Looking back, it seems to me that I was moved by curiosity. I had never seen a hostage before. I wanted to see a hostage who was doomed to die and who told funny stories. Curiosity or bravado? Perhaps a little of both. . . .

"Do you want me to go with you?" asked Gad. A lock of hair had fallen over his forehead, but he did not push it back.

"No, Gad," I said. "I want to be alone with him."

Gad smiled. He was a commander, proud of his subaltern

186

and expressing his pride in a smile. He laid his hand affectionately on my shoulder.

"Do you want someone to go with you?" asked the beggar.

"No," I repeated. "I'd rather be alone."

His eyes were immeasurably kind.

"You can't do it without them," he said, nodding his head in the direction of the crowd behind us.

"They can come later," I conceded.

The beggar took my head in his hands and looked into my eyes. His look was so powerful that for a moment I doubted my identity. I am that look, I said to myself. What else could I be? The beggar has many looks, and I am one of them. But his expression radiated kindness, and I knew that he could not regard kindly his own look. That was how my identity came back to me.

"Very well," he said; "they'll come later."

Now the boy, looking over the shadowy heads and bodies between us, offered to go with me. "Later," I said. My answer made him sad, but I could only repeat: "Later. I want to be alone with him."

"Good," said the child. "We'll come later."

I let my look wander over the room, hoping to leave it there and pick it up when I returned.

Ilana was talking to Gad, but he did not listen. Joab was yawning. Gideon rubbed his forehead as if he had a headache.

In an hour everything will be different, I reflected. I shan't see it the same way. The table, the chairs, the walls, the window, they will all have changed. Only the dead— my father and mother, the master and Yerachmiel—will be the same, for we all of us change together, in the same way, doing the same things.

I patted my pocket to make sure the revolver was still

there. It was; indeed, I had the strange impression that it was alive, that its life was part of mine, that it had the same present and future destiny as myself. I was its destiny and it was mine. In an hour it too will have changed, I reflected.

"It's late," said Joab, stretching.

With my eyes I bade farewell to the room, to Ilana, to Gideon and his prayers, to Joab and his confused expression, to the table, the window, the walls, and the night. Then I went hurriedly into the kitchen as if I were going to my own execution. As I went down the stairs my steps slackened and became heavy.

$\mathbf{J}$ohn Dawson was a handsome man. In spite of his unshaven face, tousled hair, and rumpled shirt there was something distinguished about him.

He seemed to be in his forties—a professional soldier, no doubt—with penetrating eyes, a resolute chin, thin lips, a broad forehead, and slender hands.

When I pushed open the door I found him lying on a camp bed, staring up at the ceiling. The bed was the only piece of furniture in the narrow white cell. Thanks to an ingenious system of ventilation we had installed, the windowless cell was less stuffy than the open room above.

When he became aware of my presence John Dawson showed neither surprise nor fear. He did not get up but simply raised himself into a sitting position. He scrutinized me at length without saying a word, as if measuring the density of my silence. His stare enveloped my whole being and I wondered if he saw that I was a mass of eyes.

189

"What time is it?" he asked abruptly.

In an uncertain voice I answered that it was after four.
He frowned, as if in an effort to grasp the hidden meaning
of my words.

"When is sunrise?" he said.

"In an hour," I answered. And I added, without knowing
why: "Approximately."

We stared at each other for a long interval, and suddenly
I realized that time was not moving at its normal, regular
pace. In an hour I shall kill him, I thought. And yet I
didn't really believe it. This hour which separates me from
murder will be longer than a lifetime. It will belong,
always, to the distant future; it will never be one with the
past.

There was something age-old in our situation. We were
alone not only in the cell but in the world as well, he
seated, I standing, the victim and the executioner. We
were the first—or the last—men of creation; certainly we
were alone. And God? He was present, somewhere. Perhaps He was incarnate in the liking with which John Dawson inspired me. The lack of hate between executioner
and victim, perhaps this is God.

We were alone in the narrow white cell, he sitting on the
bed and I standing before him, staring at each other. I
wished I could see myself through his eyes. Perhaps he was
wishing he could see himself through mine. I felt neither
hate nor anger nor pity; I liked him, that was all. I liked
the way he scowled when he was thinking, the way he
looked down at his nails when he was trying to formulate
his thoughts. Under other circumstances he might have
been my friend.

"Are you the one?" he asked abruptly.

How had he guessed it? Perhaps by his sense of smell.
Death has an odor and I had brought it in with me. Or

perhaps as soon as I came through the door he had seen that I had neither arms nor legs nor shoulders, that I was all eyes.

"Yes," I said.

I felt quite calm. The step before the last is the hard one; the last step brings clearheadedness and assurance.

"What's your name?" he asked.

This question disturbed me. Is every condemned man bound to ask it? Why does he want to know the name of his executioner? In order to take it with him to the next world? For what purpose? Perhaps I shouldn't have told him, but I could refuse nothing to a man condemned to die.

"Elisha," I said.

"Very musical," he observed.

"It's the name of a prophet," I explained. "Elisha was a disciple of Elijah. He restored life to a little boy by lying upon him and breathing into his mouth."

"You're doing the opposite," he said with a smile.

There was no trace of anger or hate in his voice. Probably he too felt clearheaded and assured.

"How old are you?" he asked with aroused interest.

Eighteen, I told him. For some reason I added: "Nearly nineteen."

He raised his head and there was pity on his thin, suddenly sharpened face. He stared at me for several seconds, then sadly nodded his head.

"I'm sorry for you," he said.

I felt his pity go through me. I knew that it would permeate me completely, that the next day I should be sorry for myself.

"Tell me a story," I said. "A funny one, if you can."

I felt my body grow heavy. The next day it would be heavier still, I reflected. The next day it would be weighed down by my life and his death, "I'm the last man you'll see before you die," I went on. "Try to make him laugh."

Once more I was enveloped by his look of pity. I wondered if everyone condemned to die looked at the last man he saw in the same way, if every victim pitied his executioner.

"I'm sorry for you," John Dawson repeated.

By dint of an enormous effort I managed to smile.

"That's no funny story," I remarked.

He smiled at me in return. Which of our two smiles was the sadder?

"Are you sure it isn't funny?"

No, I wasn't so sure. Perhaps there *was* something funny about it. The seated victim, the standing executioner—smiling, and understanding each other better than if they were childhood friends. Such are the workings of time. The veneer of conventional attitudes was wiped off; every word and look and gesture was naked truth instead of just one of its facets. There was harmony between us; my smile answered his; his pity was mine. No human being would ever understand me as he understood me at this hour. Yet I knew that this was solely on account of the roles that were imposed upon us. This was what made it a funny story.

"Sit down," said John Dawson, making room for me to his left on the bed.

I sat down. Only then did I realize that he was a whole head taller than I. And his legs were longer than mine, which did not even touch the ground.

"I have a son your age," he began, "but he's not at all like you. He's fair-haired, strong, and healthy. He likes to eat, drink, go to the pictures, laugh, sing, and go out with the girls. He has none of your anxiety, your unhappiness."

And he went on to tell me more about this son who was

192

"studying at Cambridge." Every sentence was a tongue of flame which burned my body. With my right hand I patted the revolver in my pocket. The revolver too was incandescent, and burned my fingers.

I mustn't listen to him, I told myself. He's my enemy, and the enemy has no story. I must think of something else. That's why I wanted to see him, in order to think of something else while he was talking. Something else . . . but what? Of Ilana? Of Gad? Yes, I should think of Gad, who was thinking of David. I should think of our hero, David ben Moshe, who. . . .

I shut my eyes to see David better, but to no purpose, because I had never met him. A name isn't enough, I thought. One must have a face, a voice, a body, and pin the name of David ben Moshe upon them. Better think of a face, a voice, a body that I actually knew. Gad? No, it was difficult to imagine Gad as a man condemned to die. Condemned to die . . . that was it. Why hadn't I thought of it before? John Dawson was condemned to die; why shouldn't I baptize him David ben Moshe? For the next five minutes you are David ben Moshe . . . in the raw, cold, white light of the death cell of the prison at Acre. There is a knock at the door, and the rabbi comes in to read the Psalms with you and hear you say the *Vidui,* that terrible confession in which you admit your responsibility not only for the sins you have committed, whether by word, deed, or thought, but also for those you may have caused others to commit. The rabbi gives you the traditional blessing: "The Lord bless you and keep you . . ." and exhorts you to have no fear. You answer that you are unafraid, that if you had a chance you would do the same thing all over. The rabbi smiles and says that everyone on the outside is proud of you. He is so deeply moved that he has to make a visible effort to hold back his tears; finally the effort is too much for him and he sobs aloud. But you, David, do not cry. You have tender feelings for the rabbi because he is the last man (the executioner and his assistants don't count) you will see before you die. Because he is sobbing you try to comfort him. "Don't cry," you say; "I'm not afraid. You don't need to be sorry for me."

"I'm sorry for you," said John Dawson. "*You* worry me, not my son."

He put his feet down on the floor. He was so tall that when he stood up he had to bend over in order not to bump his head against the ceiling. He put his hands in the pockets of his rumpled khaki trousers and began to pace up and down the cell: five steps in one direction, five in the other.

"That I admit is funny," I observed.

He did not seem to hear, but went on pacing from wall to wall. I looked at my watch; it was twenty past four. Suddenly he stopped in front of me and asked for a cigarette. I had a package of Players in my pocket and wanted to give them to him. But he refused to take the whole package, saying quite calmly that obviously he didn't have time to smoke them all.

Then he said with sudden impatience:

"Have you a pencil and paper?"

I tore several pages out of my notebook and handed them to him, with a pencil.

"Just a short note which I'd like to have sent to my son," he declared. "I'll put down the address."

I handed him the notebook to use as a pad. He laid the notebook on the bed and leaned over to write from a standing position. For several minutes the silence was broken only by the sound of the pencil running over the paper.

I looked down in fascination at his smooth-skinned hands with their long, slender, aristocratic fingers. With hands like those, I thought, it's easy to get along. There's no need to bow, smile, talk, pay compliments, or bring flowers. A pair of such hands do the whole job. Rodin would have liked to sculpt them. . . .

The thought of Rodin made me think of Stefan, a German I had known at Buchenwald. He had been a sculptor before the war, but when I met him the Nazis had cut off his right hand.

In Berlin, during the first years after Hitler came to power, Stefan and some of his friends organized an embryonic resistance group which the Gestapo uncovered shortly after its founding. Stefan was arrested, questioned, and subjected to torture. Give us names, they told him, and we will set you free. They beat and starved him, but he would not talk. Day after day and night after night they prevented him from sleeping, but still he did not give in. Finally he was haled before the Berlin chief of the Gestapo, a timid, mild man, who in a soft-spoken, fatherly manner, advised him to stop being foolishly stubborn. The sculptor heard him out in stony silence. "Come on," said the chief. "Give us just one name, as a sign of good will." Still Stefan would not speak. "Too bad," said the chief. "You're obliging me to hurt you."

At a sign from the chief two SS men led the prisoner into what looked like an operating room, with a dentist's chair installed near the window. Beside it, on a table with a white oilcloth cover, was an orderly array of surgical instruments. They shut the window, tied Stefan onto the chair and lit cigarettes. The mild-mannered chief came into the room, wearing a white doctor's jacket.

"Don't be afraid," he said; "I used to be a surgeon."

He puttered around with the instruments and then sat down in front of the prisoner's chair.

"Give me your right hand," he said. Studying it at close

range, he added: "I'm told you're a sculptor. You have nothing to say? Well, I know it. I can tell from your hands. A man's hands tell a lot about him. Take mine, for instance. You'd never take them for a surgeon's hands, would you? The truth is that I never wanted to be a doctor. I wanted to be a painter or a musician. I never became one, but I still have the hands of an artist. Look at them."

"I looked at them, with fascination," Stefan told me. "He had the most beautiful, the most angelic hands I have ever seen. You would have sworn that they belonged to a sensitive, unworldly man."

"As a sculptor you need your hands," the Gestapo chief went on. "Unfortunately *we* don't need them," and so saying he cut off a finger.

The next day he cut off a second finger, and the day after that a third. Five days, five fingers. All five fingers of the right hand were gone.

"Don't worry," the chief assured him. "From a medical point of view, everything is in good order. There's no danger of infection."

"I saw him five times," Stefan told me. (For some inexplicable reason he was not killed but simply sent to a concentration camp.) "Every day for five days I saw him from very near by. And every time I could not take my eyes off those hands of his, the most beautifully shaped hands I had ever seen. . . ."

John Dawson finished his note and held it out to me, but I hardly saw it. My attention was taken by his proud smooth-skinned, frail hands.

"Are you an artist?" I asked him.

He shook his head.

"You've never painted or played a musical instrument, or at least wanted to do so?"

He scrutinized me in silence and then said dryly:

196

"No."

"Then perhaps you studied medicine."

"I never studied medicine," he said, almost angrily.

"Too bad."

"Too bad? Why?"

"Look at your hands. They're the hands of a surgeon. The kind of hands it takes to cut off fingers."

Deliberately he laid the sheets of paper on the bed.

"Is that a funny story?" he asked.

"Yes, very funny. The fellow who told it to me thought so. He used to laugh over it until he cried."

John Dawson shook his head and said in an infinitely sad voice:

"You hate me, don't you?"

I didn't hate him at all, but I wanted to hate him. That would have made it all very easy. Hate—like faith or love or war—justifies everything.

"Elisha, why did you kill John Dawson?"

"He was my enemy."

"John Dawson? Your enemy? You'll have to explain that better."

"Very well. John Dawson was an Englishman. The English were enemies of the Jews in Palestine. So he was my enemy."

"But Elisha, I still don't understand why you killed him. Were you his only enemy?"

"No, but I had orders. You know what that means."

"And did the orders make him your only enemy? Speak up, Elisha. Why did you kill John Dawson?"

If I had alleged hate, all these questions would have been spared me. Why did I kill John Dawson? Because I hated him, that's all. The absolute quality of hate explains any human action even if it throws something inhuman around it.

197

I certainly wanted to hate him. That was partly why I had come to engage him in conversation before I killed him. It was absurd reasoning on my part, but the fact is that while we were talking I hoped to find in him, or in myself, something that would give rise to hate.

A man hates his enemy because he hates his own hate. He says to himself: This fellow, my enemy, has made me capable of hate. I hate him not because he's my enemy, not because he hates me, but because he arouses me to hate.

John Dawson has made me a murderer, I said to myself. He has made me the murderer of John Dawson. He deserves my hate. Were it not for him, I might still be a murderer, but I wouldn't be the murderer of John Dawson.

Yes, I had come down to the cellar to feed my hate. It seemed easy enough. Armies and governments the world over have a definite technique for provoking hate. By speeches and films and other kinds of propaganda they create an image of the enemy in which he is the incarnation of evil, the symbol of suffering, the fountainhead of the cruelty and injustice of all times. The technique is infallible, I told myself, and I shall turn it upon my victim.

I did try to draw upon it. All enemies are equal, I said. Each one is responsible for the crimes committed by the others. They have different faces, but they all have the same hands, the hands that cut my friends' tongues and fingers.

As I went down the stairs I was sure that I would meet the man who had condemned David ben Moshe to death, the man who had killed my parents, the man who had come between me and the man I had wanted to become, and who was now ready to kill the man in me. I felt quite certain that I would hate him.

The sight of his uniform added fuel to my flames. There is nothing like a uniform for whipping up hate. When I saw his slender hands I said to myself: Stefan will carve out my hate for them. Again, when he bent his head to write the farewell note to his son, the son "studying at Cambridge," who liked to "laugh and go out with the girls," I thought: David is writing a last letter too, probably to the Old Man, before he puts his head in the hangman's noose. And when he talked, my heart went out to David, who had no one to talk to, except the rabbi. You can't talk to a rabbi, for he is too concerned with relaying your last words to God. You can confess your sins, recite the Psalms or the prayers for the dead, receive his consolation or console him, but you can't talk, not really.

I thought of David whom I had never met and would never know. Because he was not the first of us to be hanged we knew exactly when and how he would die. At about five o'clock in the morning the cell door would open and the prison director would say: Get ready, David ben Moshe; the time has come. "The time has come," this is the ritual phrase, as if this and no other time had any significance. David would cast a look around the cell and the rabbi would say: "Come, my son." They would go out, leaving the cell door open behind them (for some reason no one ever remembers to close it) and start down the long passageway leading to the execution chamber. As the man of the hour, conscious of the fact that the others were there solely on his account, David would walk in the center of the group. He would walk with his head held high—all our heroes held their heads high—and a strange smile on his lips. On either side of the passageway a hundred eyes and ears would wait for him to go by, and the first of the prisoners to perceive his approach would intone the *Hatikva*, the song of hope. As the group advanced the song would grow louder, more human, more powerful, until its sound rivaled that of the footsteps. . . .

When John Dawson spoke of his son I heard David's footsteps and the rising song. With his words John Dawson was trying to cover up the footsteps, to erase the sight of David walking down the passageway and the strange smile on his lips, to drown out the despairing sound of the *Hatikva*, the song of hope.

I wanted to hate him. Hate would have made everything so simple. . . . Why did you kill John Dawson? I killed him because I hated him. I hated him because David ben Moshe hated him, and David ben Moshe hated him because he talked while he David was going down the somber passageway at whose far end he must meet his death.

"You hate me, Elisha, don't you?" John Dawson asked. There was a look of overflowing tenderness in his eyes.

"I'm trying to hate you," I answered.

"Why must you try to hate me, Elisha?"

He spoke in a warm, slightly sad voice, remarkable for the absence of curiosity.

Why? I wondered. What a question! Without hate, everything that my comrades and I were doing would be done in vain. Without hate we could not hope to obtain victory. Why do I try to hate you, John Dawson? Because my people have never known how to hate. Their tragedy, throughout the centuries, has stemmed from their inability to hate those who have humiliated and from time to time exterminated them. Now our only chance lies in hating you, in learning the necessity and the art of hate. Otherwise, John Dawson, our future will only be an extension of the past, and the Messiah will wait indefinitely for his deliverance.

"Why must you try to hate me?" John Dawson asked again.

"In order to give my action a meaning which may somehow transcend it."

Once more he slowly shook his head.

"I'm sorry for you," he repeated.

I looked at my watch. Ten minutes to five. Ten minutes to go. In ten minutes I should commit the most important and conclusive act of my life. I got up from the bed.

"Get ready, John Dawson," I said.

"Has the time come?" he asked.

"Very nearly," I answered.

He rose and leaned his head against the wall, probably in order to collect his thoughts or to pray or something of the kind.

Eight minutes to five. Eight minutes to go. I took the revolver out of my pocket. What should I do if he tried to take it from me? There was no chance of his escaping. The house was well guarded and there was no way of getting out of the cellar except through the kitchen. Gad, Gideon, Joab, and Ilana were on guard upstairs, and John Dawson knew it.

Six minutes to five. Six minutes to go. Suddenly I felt quite clearheaded. There was an unexpected light in the cell; the boundaries were drawn, the roles well defined. The time of doubt and questioning and uncertainty was over. I was a hand holding a revolver; I was the revolver that held my hand.

Five minutes to five. Five minutes to go.

"Have no fear, my son," the rabbi said to David ben Moshe. "God is with you."

"Don't worry, I'm a surgeon," said the mild-mannered Gestapo chief to Stefan.

"The note," John Dawson said, turning around. "You'll send it to my boy, won't you?"

He was standing against the wall; he was the wall. Three minutes to five. Three minutes to go.

"God is with you," said the rabbi. He was crying, but now David did not see him.

"The note. You won't forget, will you?" John Dawson insisted.

"I'll send it," I promised, and for some reason I added: "I'll mail it today."

"Thank you," said John Dawson.

David is entering the chamber from which he will not come out alive. The hangman is waiting for him. He is all eyes. David mounts the scaffold. The hangman asks him whether he wants his eyes banded. Firmly David answers no. A Jewish fighter dies with his eyes open. He wants to look death in the face.

Two minutes to five. I took a handkerchief out of my pocket, but John Dawson ordered me to put it back. An Englishman dies with his eyes open. He wants to look death in the face.

Sixty seconds before five o'clock. One minute to go.

Noiselessly the cell door opened and the dead trooped in, filling us with their silence. The narrow cell had become almost unbearably stuffy.

The beggar touched my shoulder and said:

"Day is at hand."

And the boy who looked the way I used to look said, with an uneasy expression on his face:

"This is the first time——" His voice trailed off, and then, as if remembering that he had left the sentence suspended he picked it up: "the first time I've seen an execution."

My father and mother were there too, and the grizzled master, and Yerachmiel. Their silence stared at me.

David stiffened and began to sing the *Hatikva*.

John Dawson smiled, with his head against the wall and his body as erect as if he were saluting a general.

"Why are you smiling?" I asked.

"You must never ask a man who is looking at you the reason for his smile," said the beggar.

"I'm smiling," said John Dawson, "because all of a sudden it has occurred to me that I don't know why I am dying." And after a moment of silence he added: "Do you?"

"You see?" said the beggar. "I told you that was no question to ask a man who is about to die."

Twenty seconds. This minute was more than sixty seconds long.

"Don't smile," I said to John Dawson. What I meant was: "I can't shoot a man who is smiling."

Ten seconds.

"I want to tell you a story," he said, "a funny story."

I raised my right arm.

Five seconds.

"Elisha——"

Two seconds. He was still smiling.

"Too bad," said the little boy. "I'd like to have heard his story."

One second.

"Elisha—" said the hostage.

I fired. When he pronounced my name he was already dead; the bullet had gone through his heart. A dead man, whose lips were still warm, had pronounced my name: *Elisha*.

He sank very slowly to the ground, as if he had slipped from the top of the wall. His body remained in a sitting position, with the head bowed down between the knees, as if he were still waiting to be killed. I stayed for a few moments beside him. There was a pain in my head and my body was growing heavy. The shot had left me deaf and dumb. That's it, I said to myself. It's done. I've killed. I've killed Elisha.

The ghosts began to leave the cell, taking John Dawson with them. The little boy walked at his side as if to guide him. I seemed to hear my mother say: "Poor boy! Poor boy!"

Then with heavy footsteps I walked up the stairs leading to the kitchen. I walked into the room, but it was not the same. The ghosts were gone. Joab was no longer yawning. Gideon was looking down at his nails and praying for the repose of the dead. Ilana lifted a sad countenance upon me; Gad lit a cigarette. They were silent, but their silence was different from the silence which all night long had weighed upon mine. On the horizon the sun was rising.

I went to the window. The city was still asleep. Somewhere a child woke up and began to cry. I wished that a dog would bark, but there was no dog anywhere nearby.

The night lifted, leaving behind it a grayish light the color of stagnant water. Soon there was only a tattered fragment of darkness, hanging in midair, the other side of the window. Fear caught my throat. The tattered fragment of darkness had a face. Looking at it, I understood the reason for my fear. The face was my own.

The Accident

Translated from the French
by Anne Borchardt

For Paul Braunstein

"*I was once more struck by the truth of the ancient saying: Man's heart is a ditch full of blood. The loved ones who have died throw themselves down on the bank of this ditch to drink the blood and so come to life again; the dearer they are to you, the more of your blood they drink.*"

—NIKOS KAZANTZAKIS, *Zorba the Greek*

The accident occurred on an evening in July, right in the heart of New York, as Kathleen and I were crossing the street to go to see the movie *The Brothers Karamazov*.

The heat was heavy, suffocating: it penetrated your bones, your veins, your lungs. It was difficult to speak, even to breathe. Everything was covered with an enormous, wet sheet of air. The heat stuck to your skin, like a curse.

People walked clumsily, looking haggard, their mouths dry like the mouths of old men watching the decay of their existence; old men hoping to take leave of their own beings so as not to go mad. Their bodies filled them with disgust.

I was tired. I had just finished my work: a five-hundred word cable. Five hundred words to say nothing. To cover up another empty day. It was one of those quiet and monotonous Sundays that leave no mark on time. Washington: nothing. United Nations: nothing. New York:

nothing. Even Hollywood said: nothing. The movie stars had deserted the news.

It wasn't easy to use five hundred words to say that there was nothing to say. After two hours of hard work, I was exhausted.

"What shall we do now?" Kathleen asked.

"Whatever you like," I answered.

We were on the corner of Forty-fifth Street, right in front of the Sheraton-Astor. I felt stunned, heavy, a thick fog in my head. The slightest gesture was like trying to lift a planet. There was lead in my arms, in my legs.

To my right I could see the human whirlwind on Times Square. People go there as they go to the sea: neither to fight boredom nor the anguish of a room filled with blighted dreams, but to feel less alone, or more alone.

The world turned in slow motion under the weight of the heat. The picture seemed unreal. Beneath the colorful neon carnival, people went back and forth, laughing, singing, shouting, insulting one another, all of this with an exasperating slowness.

Three sailors had come out of the hotel. When they saw Kathleen they stopped short, and, in unison, gave a long admiring whistle.

"Let's go," Kathleen said, pulling me by the arm. She was obviously annoyed.

"What do you have against them?" I asked. "They think you're beautiful."

"I don't like them to whistle like that."

I said, in a professorial tone, "It's their way of looking at a woman: they see her with their mouths and not with their eyes. Sailors keep their eyes for the sea: when they are on land, they leave their eyes behind as tokens of love."

The three admirers had already been gone for quite some time.

"And you?" Kathleen asked. "How do you look at me?"

She liked to relate everything to us. We were always the center of her universe. For her, other mortals lived only to be used as comparisons.

"I? I don't look at you," I answered, slightly annoyed. There was a silence. I was biting my tongue. "But I love you. You know that."

"You love me, but you don't look at me?" she asked gloomily. "Thanks for the compliment."

"You don't understand," I went right on. "One doesn't necessarily exclude the other. You can love God, but you can't look at Him."

She seemed satisfied with this comparison. I would have to practice lying.

"Whom do you look at when you love God?" she asked after a moment of silence.

"Yourself. If man could contemplate the face of God, he would stop loving him. God needs love; he does not need understanding."

"And you?"

For Kathleen, even God was not so much a subject for discussion as a way to bring the conversation back to us.

"I too," I lied. "I too, I need your love."

We were still in the same spot. Why hadn't we moved? I don't know. Perhaps we were waiting for the accident.

I'll have to learn to lie, I kept thinking. Even for the short time I have left. To lie well. Without blushing. Until then I had been lying much too badly. I was awkward, my face would betray me and I would start blushing.

"What are we waiting for?" Kathleen was getting impatient.

"Nothing," I said.

I was lying without knowing it: we were waiting for the accident.

"You still aren't hungry?"

"No," I answered.

"But you haven't eaten anything all day," she said reproachfully.

"No."

Kathleen sighed.

"How long do you think you can hold out? You're slowly killing yourself. . . ."

There was a small restaurant nearby. We went in. All right, I told myself. I'll also have to learn to eat. And to love. You can learn anything.

Ten or twelve people, sitting on high red stools, were eating silently at the counter. Kathleen now found herself in the crossfire of their stares. She was beautiful. Her face, especially around the lips, showed the first signs of a fear that was waiting for a chance to turn into live suffering. I would have liked to tell her once more that I loved her.

We ordered two hamburgers and two glasses of grapefruit juice.

"Eat," Kathleen said, and she looked up at me pleadingly.

I cut off a piece and lifted it to my mouth. The smell of blood turned my stomach. I felt like throwing up. Once I had seen a man eating with great appetite a slice of meat without bread. Starving, I watched him for a long time. As if hypnotized, I followed the motion of his fingers and jaws. I was hoping that if he saw me there, in front of him, he would throw me a piece. He didn't look up. The next day he was hanged by those who shared his barracks: he had been eating human flesh. To defend himself he had

screamed, "I didn't do any harm: he was already dead. . . ."
When I saw his body swinging in the latrine, I wondered,
"What if he had seen me?"

"Eat," Kathleen said.

I swallowed some juice.

"I'm not hungry," I said with an effort.

A few hours later the doctors told Kathleen, "He's
lucky. He'll suffer less because his stomach is empty. He
won't vomit so much."

"Let's go," I told Kathleen as I turned to leave.

I could feel it: another minute there and I'd faint.

I paid for the hamburgers and we left. Times Square
hadn't changed. False lights, artificial shadows. The same
anonymous crowd twisting and untwisting. In the bars and
in the stores, the same rock-'n'-roll tunes hitting away at
your temples with thousands of invisible little hammers.
The neon signs still announced that to drink this or that
was good for your health, for happiness, for the peace of
the world, of the soul, and of I don't know what else.

"Where would you like to go?" Kathleen inquired.

She pretended not to have noticed how pale I was. Who
knows, I thought. She too perhaps will learn how to lie.

"Far," I answered. "Very far."

"I'll go with you," she declared.

The sadness and bitterness of her voice filled me with
pity. Kathleen has changed, I told myself. She, who believed in defiance, in fighting, in hatred, had now chosen
to submit. She, who refused to follow any call that didn't
come from herself, now recognized defeat. I knew that our
suffering changes us. But I didn't know that it could also
destroy others.

"Of course," I said. "I won't go without you."

I was thinking: to go far away, where the roads leading

to simplicity are known not merely to a select group, but to all; where love, laughter, songs, and prayers carry with them neither anger nor shame; where I can think about myself without anguish, without contempt; where the wine, Kathleen, is pure and not mixed with the spit of corpses; where the dead live in cemeteries and not in the hearts and memories of men.

"Well?" Kathleen asked, pursuing her idea. "Where shall we go? We can't stand here all night."

"Let's go to the movies," I said.

It was still the best place. We wouldn't be alone. We would think about something else. We would be somewhere else.

Kathleen agreed. She would have preferred to go back to my place or to hers, but she understood my objection: it would be too hot, while the movie would be air-conditioned. I came to the conclusion that it wasn't so hard to lie.

"What shall we see?"

Kathleen looked around her, at the theatres that surround Times Square. Then she exclaimed excitedly, *"The Brothers Karamazov!* Let's see *The Brothers Karamazov."*

It was playing on the other side of the square. We would have to cross two avenues. An ocean of cars and noises separated us from the movie.

"I'd rather see some other picture," I said. "I like Dostoevski too much."

Kathleen insisted: it was a good, great, extraordinary movie. Yul Brynner as Dmitri. It was a picture one had to see.

"I'd rather see an ordinary mystery," I said. "Something without philosophy, without metaphysics. It's too hot for intellectual exercises. Look, *Murder in Rio* is playing on this side. Let's go to that. I'd love to know how they commit murders in Brazil."

Kathleen was stubborn. Once again, she wanted to test our love. If Dostoevski won, I loved her; otherwise I didn't. I glanced at her. Still the fear around her lips, the fear that was going to become suffering. Kathleen was beautiful when she suffered; her eyes were deeper, her voice warmer, fuller; her dark beauty was simpler and more human. Her suffering had a quality of saintliness. It was her way of offering herself. I couldn't see Kathleen suffer without telling her I loved her, as if love was the negation of evil. I had to stop her suffering.

"You really care that much?" I asked her. "You're really that anxious to see the good brothers Karamazov mistreated?"

Apparently she was. It was Yul Brynner or our love.

"In that case, let's go."

A triumphant smile, that lasted only a second, lit up her face. Her fingers gripped my arm as if to say: now I believe in what is happening to us.

We took three or four steps, to the edge of the sidewalk. We had to wait a little. Wait for the red light to become green, for the flow of cars to stop, for the policeman who was directing traffic to raise his hand, for the cab driver, unaware of the role he was going to play in a moment, to reach the appointed spot. We had to wait for the director's cue.

I turned around. The clock in the TWA window said 10:25.

"Come on," Kathleen decided, pulling me by the arm. "It's green."

We started to cross the street. Kathleen was walking faster than I. She was on my right, a few inches ahead of me at most. The Brothers Karamazov weren't very far away any more, but I didn't see them that night.

What did I hear first? The grotesque screeching of brakes or the shrill scream of a woman? I no longer remember.

When I came to, for a fraction of a second, I was lying on my back in the middle of the street. In a tarnished mirror a multitude of heads were bending over me. There were heads everywhere. Right, left, above, and even underneath. All of them alike. The same wide-open eyes reflecting fright and curiosity. The same lips whispering the same incomprehensible words.

An elderly man seemed to be saying something to me. I think it was not to move. He had close-cropped hair and a mustache. Kathleen no longer had the beautiful black hair that she was so proud of. Disfigured, her face had lost its youth. Her eyes, as if in the presence of death, had grown larger, and, incredibly enough, she had grown a mustache.

A dream, I told myself. Just a dream that I'll forget when I wake up. Otherwise, why should I be here, on the pavement? Why would these people be around me as if I were going to die? And why would Kathleen suddenly have a mustache?

Noises, coming from all directions, bounced against a curtain of fog they weren't able to penetrate. I couldn't make out anything that was being said. I would have liked to tell them not to talk, because I couldn't hear them. I was dreaming, while they were not. But I was unable to utter the slightest sound. The dream had made me deaf and mute.

A poem by Dylan Thomas—always the same one—kept coming back to me, about not going gently into the night, but to "rage, rage, against the dying of the light."

Scream? Deaf-mutes don't scream. They go gently into the night, lightly, timidly. They don't scream against the dying of the light. They can't: their mouths are full of blood.

It's useless to scream when your mouth is filled with blood: people see the blood but cannot hear you scream. That's why I was silent. And also because I was dreaming of a summer night when my body was frozen. The heat was sickening, the faces bent over me streaming with sweat— sweat falling in rhythmical drops—and yet I was dreaming that I was so cold I was dying. How can one cry out against a dream? How can one scream against the dying of the light, against life that grows cold, against blood flowing out?

It was only later, much later, when I was already out of danger, that Kathleen told me about the circumstances surrounding the accident.

A speeding cab approaching from the left had caught me, dragging me several yards. Kathleen had suddenly heard the screeching of brakes and a woman's shrill scream.

She barely had time to turn around before a crowd was already surrounding me. She didn't know at first that I was the man lying at the spectators' feet.

Then, having a strong feeling that it was I, she pushed her way through and saw me: crushed with pain, curled up, my head between my knees.

And the people were talking, talking endlessly. . . .

"He's dead," one of them said.

"No, he's not. Look, he's moving."

Preceded by the sound of sirens, the ambulance arrived within twenty minutes. During that time I showed few signs of life. I didn't cry, I didn't moan, I didn't say anything.

In the ambulance I came to several times for a few seconds. During these brief moments I gave Kathleen astonishingly precise instructions about things I wanted her to do for me: inform the paper; call one of my friends and ask him to replace me temporarily; cancel various appointments; pay the rent, the phone bill, the laundry. Having handed her the last of these immediate problems, I closed my eyes and didn't open them again for five days.

Kathleen also told me this: the first hospital to which the ambulance took me refused to let me in. There wasn't any room. All the beds were taken. At least that's what they said. But Kathleen thought it was just a pretext. The doctors, after one glance at me, had decided there was no hope. It was better to be rid of a dying man as fast as possible.

The ambulance drove on to New York Hospital. Here, it seemed, they weren't afraid of the dying. The doctor on duty, a composed and sympathetic-looking young resident, immediately took care of me while trying to make a diagnosis.

"Well, Doctor?" Kathleen had asked.

Through some miracle she hadn't been sent out of the emergency room while Dr. Paul Russel was taking care of me.

"At first sight it looks rather bad," the young doctor answered.

And he explained in a professional tone, "All the bones on the left side of his body are broken; internal hemorrhage; brain concussion; I can't tell about his eyes yet; whether they'll be affected or not. The same for his brain: let's hope it hasn't been damaged."

216

Kathleen tried not to cry.

"What can be done, Doctor?"

"Pray."

"Is it that serious?"

"Very serious."

The young doctor, whose voice was as restrained as an old man's, looked at her for a moment, then asked, "Who are you? His wife?"

On the verge of hysteria, Kathleen just shook her head to say no.

"His fiancée?"

"No," she whispered.

"His girl friend?"

"Yes."

After hesitating a moment, he had asked her softly, "Do you love him?"

"Yes," Kathleen whispered.

"In that case, there are good reasons not to lose hope. Love is worth as much as prayer. Sometimes more."

Then Kathleen burst into tears.

After three days of consulting and waiting, the doctors decided that it was worth trying surgery after all. In any case I didn't have much to lose. On the other hand, with luck, if all went well . . .

The operation lasted a long time. More than five hours. Two surgeons had to take turns. My pulse fell dangerously low, I was almost given up for dead. With blood transfusions, shots, and oxygen, they brought me back to life.

Finally the surgeons decided to limit the operation to the hip. The ankle, the ribs, and the other small fractures could wait. The vital thing for the time being was to stop the bleeding, sew together the torn arteries, and close the incision.

I was brought back to my room and for two days swung between life and death. Dr. Russel, who was devotedly taking care of me, was still pessimistic about the final result. My fever was too high and I was losing too much blood.

On the fifth day I at last regained consciousness.

I'll always remember: I opened my eyes and had to close them right away because I was blinded by the whiteness of the room. A few minutes went by before I could open them again and locate myself in time and space.

On both sides of my bed there were bottles of plasma hanging from the wall. I couldn't move my arms: two big needles were fastened to them with surgical tape. Everything was ready for an emergency transfusion.

I tried to move my legs: my body no longer obeyed me. I felt a sudden fear of being paralyzed. I made a superhuman effort to shout, to call a nurse, a doctor, a human being, to ask for the truth. But I was too weak. The sounds stuck in my throat. Maybe I've lost my voice too, I thought.

I felt alone, abandoned. Deep inside I discovered a regret: I would have preferred to die.

An hour later, Dr. Russel came into the room and told me I was going to live. My legs were not going to be amputated. I couldn't move them because they were in a cast that covered my whole body. Only my head, my arms, my toes, were visible.

"You've come back from very far," the young doctor said.

I didn't answer. I still felt regret at having come back from so far.

"You must thank God," he went on.

I looked at him more carefully. Sitting on the edge of my bed, his fingers intertwined, his eyes were filled with an intense curiosity.

"How does one thank God?" I asked him.

My voice was only a whisper. But I was able to speak. This filled me with such joy that tears came to my eyes. That I was still alive had left me indifferent, or nearly so. But the knowledge that I could still speak filled me with an emotion that I couldn't hide.

The doctor had a wrinkled baby face. He was blond. His light blue eyes showed a great deal of goodness. He was looking at me very attentively. But this didn't bother me. I was too weak.

"How does one thank God?" I repeated.

I would have liked to add: why thank him? I had not been able to understand for a long time what in the world God had done to deserve man.

The doctor continued to look at me closely, very closely. A strange gleam—perhaps a strange shadow—was in his eyes.

Suddenly my heart jumped. Frightened, I thought: he knows something.

"Are you cold?" he asked, still looking at me.

"Yes," I answered, worried. "I'm cold."

My body was trembling.

"It's your fever," he explained.

Usually they take your pulse. Or else they touch your forehead with the back of their hand. He did nothing. He knew.

"We'll try to fight the fever," he went on sententiously. "We'll give you shots. Many shots. Penicillin. Every hour. Day and night. The enemy now is fever."

He stopped talking and looked at me for a long time before going on. He seemed to be looking for a sign, an indication, a solution to a problem whose particulars I couldn't guess.

"We're afraid of infection," he continued. "If the fever goes up, you're lost."

"And the enemy will be victorious," I said in a tone of voice that intended irony. "You see, Doctor, what people say is true: man carries his fiercest enemy within himself. Hell isn't others. It's ourselves. Hell is the burning fever that makes you feel cold."

An indefinable bond had grown between us. We were speaking the mature language of men who are in direct contact with death. I tried to put on a smile but, being too cold, I could only manage a grin. That's one reason why I don't like winter: smiles become abstract.

Dr. Russel got up.

"I'll send the nurse. It's time for a shot."

He was touching his lips with his fingers, as if to think better, and then added, "When you feel better, we'll have a lot to talk about."

Again I had the uncomfortable impression that he knew —or at least that he suspected—something.

I closed my eyes. Suddenly I became conscious of the pain that was torturing me. I had not realized it before. And yet the suffering was there. It was the air I was breathing, the words forming in my brain, the cast that covered my body like a flaming skin. How had I managed to remain unaware of it until then? Perhaps I had been too absorbed in the conversation with the doctor. Did he know I was suffering, suffering horribly? Did he know I was cold? Did he know that the suffering was burning my flesh and that at the same time I was shaking with an unbearable cold, as if I were being plunged first into a furnace and then into an icy tub? Apparently he did. He knew. Paul Russel was a perceptive doctor. He could see me biting my lips furiously.

"You're in pain," he stated.

He was standing motionless at the foot of my bed. I was ashamed that my teeth were chattering in his presence.

"It's normal," he went on without waiting for an answer. "You're covered with wounds. Your body is rebelling. Pain is your body's way of protesting. But I told you: suffering is not the enemy, the fever is. If it goes up you are lost."

Death. I was thinking: He thinks that death is my enemy. He's mistaken. Death is not my enemy. If he doesn't know that, he knows nothing. Or at least he doesn't know everything. He has seen me come back to life, but he doesn't know what I think of life and death. Or could he possibly know and not show it? Doubt, like the insistent buzz of a bee inside me, was putting my nerves on edge.

I could feel the fever, as it spread, seize me by the hair, which seemed like a burning torch. The fever was throwing me from one world into another, up and down, very high up and very far down, as if it meant to teach me the cold of high places and the heat of abysses.

"Would you like a sedative?" the doctor inquired.

I shook my head. No, I didn't want any. I didn't need any. I wasn't afraid.

I heard his steps moving toward the door, which must have been somewhere behind me. Let him go, I thought. I'm not afraid of being alone, of walking the distance between life and death. No, I don't need him. I'm not afraid. Let him go!

He opened the door, hesitated before closing it. He stopped. Was he going to come back?

"Incidentally," he said softly, so softly I could hardly hear him. "Incidentally, I nearly forgot to tell you . . . Kathleen . . . she's an extremely charming young woman. Extremely charming . . ."

With that he quietly left the room. Now I was alone. Alone as only a paralyzed and suffering man can be. Soon the nurse would come, with her penicillin, to fight the enemy. It was maddening: to fight the enemy with an injection, with the help of a nurse. It was laughable. But I didn't laugh. The muscles in my face were motionless, frozen.

The nurse was going to come soon. That's what the young doctor had said, the doctor whose calm voice was like an old man's, having just discovered that human goodness carries its own reward. What else had he told me? Something about Kathleen. Yes: he had mentioned her name. Charming young woman. No. Not that. He had said something else: extremely charming. Yes: that's it. That's what he had said: Kathleen is a charming young woman. I remembered perfectly: extremely charming.

Kathleen . . . Where could she be now? In what world? In the one above or the one below? I hope she won't come. I hope she won't appear in this room. I don't want her to see me like this. I hope she won't come with the nurse. I hope she won't become a nurse. And that she won't give me penicillin. I don't want her help in my fight against the enemy. She's a charming girl, extremely charming, but she doesn't understand. She doesn't understand that death is not the enemy. That would be too easy. She doesn't understand. She has too much faith in the power, in the omnipotence of love. Love me and you'll be protected. Love each other and all will be well: suffering will leave man's earth forever. Who said that? Christ probably. He also believed too much in love. As for me, love or death. I didn't care. I was able to laugh when I thought about either. Now too, I could burst out laughing. Yes, but the muscles in my face didn't obey me. I was too cold.

It had been cold on the day—no, the evening—that evening when I met Kathleen for the first time.

A winter evening. Outside, a wind sharp enough to cut through walls and trees.

"Come along," Shimon Yanai told me. "I'd like you to meet Halina."

"Let me listen to the wind," I answered (I wasn't in a talkative mood). "The wind has more to say than your Halina. The sound of the wind carries the regrets and prayers of dead souls. Dead souls have more to say than living ones."

Shimon Yanai—the most beautiful mustache in Palestine, not to say in the whole Middle East—wasn't paying any attention to what I was saying.

"Come," he said, his hands in his pockets. "Halina is waiting for us."

I gave in. I thought: perhaps Halina is a dead soul too.

We were standing in the lobby during an intermission.

at the ballet in Paris, the Roland Petit Company or the Marquis de Cuevas, I no longer remember.

"Halina must be an attractive woman," I said as we crossed the lobby to get to the bar.

"What makes you think that?" asked Shimon Yanai, who seemed amused.

"The way you're dressed tonight. You look like a bum."

I liked to tease him. Shimon was in his forties, tall, bushy hair, blue and dreamy eyes. He never wanted to be taken seriously. "You spend hours in front of the mirror mussing your hair, spoiling the knot in your tie, rumpling your trousers," I would often tell him, ironically but with affection. There was something pathetic about his love for the Bohemian.

I knew him well because he came to Paris often and gave me tips for the newspaper. He liked to be with journalists. He needed them. He was the Paris representative of the Hebrew Resistance Movement—the state of Israel hadn't been born yet—and he didn't hesitate to admit that the press could be helpful to him.

Halina was waiting for us at the bar, a glass in her hand. She was thirtyish. Thin, narrow face, pale, with the eternally frightened look of a woman fighting with her past.

We shook hands.

"I thought you'd be older." She was smiling awkwardly.

"I am," I said. "At times I am as old as the wind."

Halina laughed. She didn't really know how to laugh. When she laughed, she could break your heart. Her laughter was as haunting as a dead soul.

"I'm serious," she said. "I read your articles. They are written by a man who has come to the end of his life, to the end of his hopes."

"That is a sign of youth," I answered. "The young to-

225

day don't believe that some day they'll be old: they are convinced they'll die young. Old men are the real youngsters of our generation. They at least can brag about having had what we do not have: a slice of life called youth."

The young woman's face became still paler. "What you are saying is dreadful."

I burst out laughing, but my laughter must have sounded forced: I didn't feel like laughing. Not any more than like talking.

"Don't listen to me," I said. "Shimon will tell you: my words are never serious. I am playing, that's all. Playing at frightening you. But you mustn't pay any attention. What I'm saying is just wind."

I was going to leave them—on the usual pretext of an urgent phone call to make—when I noticed a worried look in Halina's eyes.

"Shimon!" she exclaimed without raising her voice. "Look who is here: Kathleen!"

Shimon looked where she was pointing and for a second —only a second—his face clouded over. His cheeks darkened, as if from a painful memory.

"Go and ask her to join us," Halina said.

"But she's not alone. . . ."

"Just for a minute! She'll come."

She did come. And that's when it all started.

Actually I could easily have left while Shimon was talking to her at the other end of the lobby. My phone call was just as urgent then as it had been before. I didn't at all feel like staying. At first glance it looked like the classic situation. Three characters: Shimon, Halina, Kathleen. Halina loves Shimon who doesn't love her; Shimon loves Kathleen who does not love him; Kathleen loves . . . I didn't know whom she loved and cared less. I was thinking: they make one another suffer, in a tightly closed circle. Better not to have anything to do with it, not even as a witness. I'd never been interested in sterile suffering. Other people's suffering only attracts me to the extent that it allows man to become conscious of his strength and of his weakness, in a climate that favors rebellion. The loves of Halina and Shimon allowed nothing of the kind.

"I have to go," I told Halina.

She looked at me but didn't hear; she was watching Shimon and Kathleen at the end of the lobby.

"I have to go," I said again.

She seemed to come out of a dream, surprised to see me next to her. "Please stay," she asked in a humble, almost humiliated tone of voice. Then she added, either to convince me or to stress her indifference. "You're going to meet Kathleen. She is an extraordinary girl. You'll see."

It had become useless to resist: Kathleen and Shimon were there.

"Hello, Halina," Kathleen said in French with a strong American accent.

"Hello, Kathleen," Halina answered, barely hiding a certain nervousness. "Let me introduce a friend. . . ."

Without a gesture, without a move, without saying a word, Kathleen and I looked at each other for a long time, as if to establish a direct contact. She had a long, symmetrical face, uncommonly beautiful and touching. Her nose turned up slightly, accentuating her sensuous lips. Her almond-shaped eyes were filled with a dark, secret fire: an inactive volcano. With her, there could be real communication. All of a sudden I understood why Halina's laughter wasn't more carefree.

"You already know each other?" Halina asked with her awkward smile. "You look at each other as if you knew each other."

Shimon was silent. He was looking at Kathleen.

"Yes," I answered.

"What?" Halina exclaimed, not quite believing it. "You've already met?"

"No," I answered. "But we already know each other."

An imperceptible quiver went through Shimon's mustache. The situation was becoming unpleasantly tense when a warning bell suddenly rang. The intermission was over. The lobby began to empty.

"Shall we see you after the show?" Halina asked.

"I'm afraid not," Kathleen answered. "Someone is waiting for me."

"And you?" Halina looked at me, her big eyes filled with a cold sadness.

"No," I answered. "I have to make a phone call. It's urgent."

Halina and Shimon went off. We were alone, Kathleen and I.

"Do you speak English?" she asked me in English, as if in a hurry.

"I do."

"Wait for me," she said.

She walked quickly to the man who was waiting at the other end of the lobby, said a few words to him. I still had a chance to leave. But why run away? And where to? The desert is the same everywhere. Souls die in it. And sometimes they play at killing the souls that are not yet dead.

When Kathleen came back a few seconds later, I saw a fleeting expression of defiance and decision on her face, as if she had just completed the most important act in her life. The man she had just left and humiliated remained completely motionless and stiff, as if struck by a curse.

Inside, the curtain had gone up.

"Let's leave," Kathleen said in English.

I felt like asking endless questions, but decided to keep them for later.

"All right," I said. "Let's leave."

We left the lobby hurriedly. The man stayed behind alone. For a long time after I was afraid to go back to that theatre. I was afraid of finding him there, on the very spot where we had left him.

We went down the stairs, got our coats, and went out into the street where the wind whipped us angrily. The air was clear and pure, as it is on the peaks of snowy mountains.

We began to walk. It was cold. We were advancing slowly, as if to prove that we were strong and that the cold had no power over us.

Kathleen hadn't taken my arm and I hadn't taken hers. She didn't look at me and I didn't look at her. Either of us would have gone on walking at the same pace if the other had stopped suddenly to think, or to pray.

After walking silently along the Seine for an hour or two, we crossed the Pont du Châtelet, and then, when we reached the middle of the Pont Saint-Michel, I stopped to look at the river. Kathleen took two more steps and stopped too.

The Seine, reflecting the sky and the lampposts, now showed us its mysterious winter face, its quiet cloudiness, where any life is extinguished, where any light dies. I looked down and thought that someday I too would die.

Kathleen came closer and was about to say something. With a motion of my head, I stopped her.

229

"Don't talk," I told her after a while.

I was still thinking about death and didn't want her to talk to me. It is only in silence, leaning over a river in winter, that one can really think about death.

One day I had asked my grandmother, "How should one keep from being cold in a grave in the winter?"

My grandmother was a simple, pious woman who saw God everywhere, even in evil, even in punishment, even in injustice. No event would ever find her short of prayers. Her skin was like white desert sand. On her head she wore an enormous black shawl which she never seemed able to part with.

"He who doesn't forget God isn't cold in his grave," she said.

"What keeps him warm?" I insisted.

Her thin voice had become like a whisper: it was a secret. "God himself." A kind smile lit up her face all the way to the shawl that covered half her forehead. She smiled like that every time I asked her a question with an obvious answer.

"Does that mean that God is in the grave, with the men and the women that are buried?"

"Yes," my grandmother assured me. "It is he who keeps them warm."

I remember that then a strange sadness came upon me. I felt pity for God. I thought: he is more unhappy than man, who dies only once, who is buried in only one grave.

"Grandma, tell me, does God die too?"

"No, God is immortal."

Her answer came as a blow. I felt like crying. God was buried alive! I would have preferred to reverse the roles, to think that God is mortal and man not. To think that,

230

when man acts as if he were dying, it is God who is covered with earth.

Kathleen touched my arm. I jumped.

"Don't touch me," I told her. I was thinking of my grandmother and you cannot truly remember a dead grandmother if you aren't alone, if a girl with black hair—black like my grandmother's shawl—touches your arm.

Suddenly it occurred to me that my grandmother's smile had a meaning that the future was to reveal: she knew that my question did not concern her, that she would not know the cold of a grave. Her body had not been buried, but entrusted to the wind that had blown it in all directions. And it was her body—my grandmother's white and black body—that whipped my face, as if to punish me for having forgotten. No, Grandmother! No! I haven't forgotten. Every time I'm cold, I think of you, I think only of you.

"Come on," Kathleen said. "Let's go. I'm getting cold."

We started walking again. The wind cut our faces, but we went on. We didn't walk faster. Finally we stopped on Boulevard Saint-Germain, opposite the Deux-Magots.

"Here we are," she said.

"This is where you live?"

"Yes. Do you want to come up?"

I had to fight against myself not to say no. I wanted to stay with her too much, to talk to her, to touch her hair, to see her fall asleep. But I was afraid of being disappointed.

"Come," Kathleen insisted.

She opened the heavy door and we walked up one flight to her apartment.

I was cold. And I was thinking of my grandmother whose face was white like the transparent desert sand, and whose shawl was as black as the dense night of cemeteries.

231

Who are you?"

I could hardly hear my own voice. Thousands of needles were injecting fire into my blood. I was thirsty. I felt hot. My throat was dry. My veins were about to burst. And yet the cold hadn't left me. My body, shaken by convulsions, trembled like a tree in a storm, like leaves in the wind, like the wind in the sea, like the sea in the head of a madman, of a drunkard, of a dying man.

"Who are you?" I asked again, while my teeth chattered. I could feel there was someone in the room.

"The nurse," said an unknown voice.

"Water," I said. "I'm thirsty. I'm burning. Please give me some water."

"You mustn't drink," the voice said. "You'll feel bad. If you drink, you'll throw up."

Against my will, I began to cry silently.

"There, now," the nurse said. "I'm going to moisten your face."

She wiped my forehead and then my lips with a wet towel which caught fire as it touched my skin.

"What time is it?" I asked.

"Six o'clock."

"At night?"

"Yes."

I thought: when Dr. Russel came to see me, it was well before noon. Six penicillin shots, I hadn't even noticed.

"Are you in pain?" the nurse asked.

"I'm thirsty."

"It's the fever that's making you thirsty."

"Do I still have a high fever?"

"Yes."

"How high?"

"High."

"I want to know."

"I'm not allowed to tell you. That's the rule."

The door opened. Someone came in. Whispers.

"Well, my friend? What have you got to say?"

Dr. Russel was trying to be casual.

"I'm thirsty, Doctor."

"The enemy refuses to retreat," he said. "It's up to you to hold out."

"He'll win, Doctor. He doesn't suffer from thirst."

I thought: Grandmother would have understood. It was hot in the airless, waterless chambers. It was hot in the room where her livid body was crushed by other livid bodies. Like me, she must have opened her mouth to drink air, to drink water. But there was no water where she was, there was no air. She was only drinking death, as you drink water or air, mouth open, eyes closed, fingers clenched.

Suddenly I felt a strange need to speak out loud. To tell the story of Grandmother's life and death, to describe her black shawl that used to frighten me until I was reassured by her kind, simple expression. Grandmother was my refuge. Every time my father scolded me, she would intervene: fathers are like that, she'd explain smilingly. They get angry over nothing.

One day my father slapped me. I had stolen some money from the store cash register in order to give it to a classmate. A sickly, poor little boy. They called him Haïm the orphan. I always felt ill at ease in his presence. I knew I was happier than he was and this made me feel guilty. Guilty that my parents were alive. That's why I stole the money. But when my father asked me, trying to find out what I had done with it, I didn't tell him. After all, I couldn't tell my father that I felt guilty because he was alive! He slapped my face and I ran to Grandmother. I could tell her the whole truth. She didn't scold me. Sitting in the middle of the room, she lifted me onto her lap and began to sob. Her tears fell on my head, which she was holding against her bosom, and I discovered to my surprise that a grandmother's tears are so hot that they burn everything in their path.

"She's there," the doctor said. "She's outside. In the hallway. Do you want her to come in?"

With the strength that came from my fear, I screamed, "No! I don't, I don't."

I thought he was talking about my grandmother. I didn't want to see her. I knew she had died—of thirst, maybe— and I was afraid she wouldn't be as I remembered her. I was afraid she wouldn't have the black shawl on her head, nor those burning tears in her eyes, nor that clear, calm expression that could make you forget you were cold.

"You should see her," the doctor said softly.

"No! Not now!"

My tears left scars on my cheeks, on my lips, on my chin. From time to time, they even managed to slip under the cast. Why was I crying? I had no idea. I think it was because of Grandmother. She used to cry very often. She would cry when she was happy and also when she was unhappy. When she was neither happy nor unhappy, she would cry because she could no longer feel the things that bring about happiness and unhappiness. I wanted to prove to her that I had inherited her tears, which, as it is written, open all doors.

"It's up to you," the doctor said. "Kathleen can come back tomorrow."

Kathleen! What did she have to do with this? How did she meet Grandmother? Had she also died?

"Kathleen?" I said, letting my head fall back. "Where is she?"

"Outside," the doctor said somewhat surprised. "In the hallway."

"Bring her in."

The door opened and light footsteps came toward my bed. Again I made a desperate effort to open my eyes, but my eyelids felt sewn together.

"How are you, Kathleen?" I asked in a barely audible voice.

"Fine."

"You see: I am Dmitri Karamazov's most recent victim."

Kathleen forced a little laugh.

"You were right. It's a bad movie."

"Better to die than to see it."

Kathleen's laugh sounded false.

"You're exaggerating. . . ."

Whispers. The doctor was speaking to her very softly.

"I have to leave you," Kathleen said, sounding very sorry.

"Be careful crossing the street."

She leaned over to kiss me. An old fear took hold of me. "You mustn't kiss me, Kathleen!"

She pulled back her head abruptly. For a moment there was silence in the room. Then I felt her hand on my forehead. I was going to tell her to take it away quickly and not to run the risk of catching fire, but she had already taken it away.

Kathleen tiptoed out of the room, followed by the doctor. The nurse stayed with me. I would really have liked to know what she looked like: old or young, beautiful or sullen, blond or brunette. . . . But I still couldn't move my eyelids. All my efforts to open them came to nothing. At one point I told myself that will power wasn't enough, that I had to use both my hands. But they were tied to the sides of the bed and the big needles were still there.

"I'm going to give you two shots," the nurse announced in a voice from which I could guess nothing.

"Two? Why two?"

"First penicillin. And the second to help you fall asleep."

"You don't have a third one against thirst?" I had a hard time breathing. My lungs were going to burst: empty kettles forgotten on the fire.

"You'll sleep. You won't be thirsty."

"I won't dream that I'm thirsty?"

The nurse lifted the covers. "I'll give you a shot against dreams."

She's nice, I thought. Her heart is made of gold. She suffers when I suffer. She's quiet when I'm thirsty. She's quiet when I sleep. She's quiet when I dream. She is probably young, beautiful, beaming, attractive. She has a serious face, laughing eyes. She has a sensual mouth, made for kissing, not for talking. Just like Grandmother's eyes, which she used not for looking, not for wondering, but simply for crying.

First shot. Nothing. I didn't feel it. Second shot, this one in the arm. Still nothing. I had so much pain that I couldn't even feel the injection.

The nurse fixed the covers, put the needles in a metal box, moved a chair, and turned a switch.

"I'm putting out the light," she said. "You'll go to sleep soon."

All at once I got the idea that she too would want to kiss me before leaving. Just a little meaningless kiss on the forehead or on the cheek and maybe even on the eyelids. They do that in hospitals. A good nurse kisses her patients when she says good night. Not on the mouth. On the forehead, on the cheeks. It reassures them. A patient thinks he is less ill if a woman wants to kiss him. He doesn't know that a nurse's mouth isn't made for speaking, or even for crying, but for keeping quiet and for kissing patients so they can fall asleep without fear, without fear of the dark.

Again, I was completely covered with perspiration.

"You mustn't kiss me," I whispered.

The nurse laughed in a friendly way.

"Of course not. It makes you thirsty."

Then she left the room. And I waited to fall asleep.

Tell me a little about yourself," Kathleen said.

We were sitting in her room where it was pleasantly warm. We were listening to a Gregorian chant, which swelled inside us. The words and the music contained a peace that no storm could have disturbed.

On a small table, our two cups were still half full. The coffee had become cold. The semidarkness made me keep my eyes closed. The feeling of exhaustion that had been weighing me down at the beginning of the evening had completely disappeared. My nerves tense, I was conscious that time, as it passed through me, was carrying a part of me along with it.

"Tell me," Kathleen said. "I want to know you."

Her legs folded under her, she was sitting on my right on the beige couch. A dream was floating in the air, looking for a place on which to settle.

238

"I don't feel like it," I answered. "I don't feel like talking about myself."

To talk about myself, really talk about myself, I would have had to tell the story of my grandmother. I didn't feel like expressing it in words: Grandmother could only be expressed in prayers.

After the war, when I arrived in Paris, I had often, very often, been urged to tell. I refused. I told myself that the dead didn't need us to be heard. They are less bashful than I. Shame has no hold on them, while I was bashful and ashamed. That's the way it is: shame tortures not the executioners but their victims. The greatest shame is to have been chosen by destiny. Man prefers to blame himself for all possible sins and crimes rather than come to the conclusion that God is capable of the most flagrant injustice. I still blush every time I think of the way God makes fun of human beings, his favorite toys.

Once I asked my teacher, Kalman the cabalist, the following question: For what purpose did God create man? I understand that man needs God. But what need of man has God?

My teacher closed his eyes and a thousand wounds, petrified arteries traveled by terror-stricken truths, drew a tangled labyrinth on his forehead. After a few minutes of contemplation, his lips formed a delicate, very distant smile.

"The Holy Books teach us," he said, "that if man were conscious of his power, he would lose his faith or his reason. For man carries within him a role which transcends him. God needs him to be ONE. The Messiah, called to liberate man, can only be liberated by him. We know that not only man and the universe will be freed, but also the one who established their laws and their relations. It

239

follows that man—who is nothing but a handful of earth —is capable of reuniting time and its source, and of giving back to God his own image."

At the time I was too young to understand the meaning of my teacher's words. The idea that God's existence could be bound to mine had filled me with a miserable pride as well as a deep pity.

A few years later I saw just, pious men walking to their death, singing, "We are going to break, with our fire, the chains of the Messiah in exile." That's when the symbolic implication of what my teacher had said struck me. Yes, God needs man. Condemned to eternal solitude, he made man only to use him as a toy, to amuse himself. That's what philosophers and poets have refused to admit: in the beginning there was neither the Word, nor Love, but laughter, the roaring, eternal laughter whose echoes are more deceitful than the mirages of the desert.

"I want to know you," Kathleen said.

Her face had darkened. The dream, finding no place to settle, had dissolved. I thought: it could have entered her wide-open eyes. But dreams never enter from outside.

"You might end up hating me," I told her.

She drew her legs under her still more. Her whole body contracted, became smaller, as if it had wanted to follow the dream and disappear altogether.

"I'll take a chance," she answered.

She'll hate me, I thought. It is unavoidable. What happened will happen again. The same causes bring about the same effects, the same hatreds. Repetition is a decisive factor in the tragic aspect of our condition.

I don't know the name of the first man who openly cried out his hatred to me, nor who he was. He represented all the nameless and faceless people who live in the universe of dead souls.

I was on a French ship sailing to South America. It was my first encounter with the sea. Most of the time I was on deck, studying the waves which, untiringly, dug graves only to fill them again. As a child I had searched for God because I imagined him great and powerful, immense and infinite. The sea gave me such an image. Now I understood Narcissus: he hadn't fallen into the fountain. He had jumped into it. At one point my desire to be one with the sea became so strong that I nearly jumped overboard.

I had nothing to lose, nothing to regret. I wasn't bound to the world of men. All I had cared for had been dispersed by smoke. The little house with its cracked walls, where children and old men came humming to pray or study in the melancholy light of candles, was nothing but ruins. My teacher, who had been the first to teach me that life is a mystery, that beyond words there is silence, my teacher, whose head was always hanging as if he didn't dare face heaven—my teacher had long since been reduced to ashes. And my little sister, who made fun of me because I never played with her, because I was too serious, much too serious, my little sister no longer played.

It was a stranger who, unknowingly, unwittingly, had prevented me from giving up that night. As I stood at the rail he had come up behind me, I don't know from where, and had started talking to me. He was an Englishman.

"Beautiful night," he said, leaning against the railing on my right, nearly touching me.

"Very beautiful," I answered coldly.

I thought: beautiful night for saying good-bye to cheaters, to the constants that become uncertainties, to ideals which imply treason, to the world where there is no longer room for what is human, to history that leads to the destruction of the soul instead of broadening its powers!

The stranger wasn't intimidated by my ill-humor. He continued. "The sky is so close to the sea that it is difficult to tell which is reflected in the other, which one needs the other, which one is dominating the other."

"That's true," I again answered coldly.

He stopped for a moment. I could see his profile: thin, sharp, noble.

"If the two were at war," he went on, "I'd be on the side of the sea. The sky only inspires painters. Not musicians. While the sea . . . Don't you feel that the sea comes close to man through its music?"

"Perhaps," I answered with hostility.

Again he stopped, as if wondering if he shouldn't leave me alone. He decided to stay.

"Cigarette?" he asked, holding out his pack.

"No thanks. I don't feel like smoking."

He lit his cigarette and threw the match overboard: a shooting star swallowed up by darkness.

"They're dancing inside," he said. "Why don't you join them?"

"I don't feel like dancing."

"You prefer to be alone with the sea, don't you?"

His voice had suddenly changed. It had become more personal, less anonymous. I wasn't aware that a man could change his voice, as he would change a mask.

"Yes, I prefer to remain alone with the sea," I answered nastily, stressing the word "alone."

He took a few puffs on his cigarette.

"The sea. What does it make you think of?"

I hesitated. The fact that he was shrouded in darkness, that I didn't know him, that I probably wouldn't even recognize him the next day in the dining room, worked in his favor. To talk to a stranger is like talking to stars: it doesn't commit you.

"The sea," I said, "makes me think of death."

I had the impression that he smiled.

"I knew it."

"How did you know?" I asked, disconcerted.

"The sea has a power of attraction. I am fifty and have been traveling for thirty years. I know all the seas in the world. I know. One mustn't look at the waves for too long. Especially at night. Especially alone."

He told me about his first trip. His wife was with him. They had just gotten married. One night he left his wife, who was sleeping, and went up on deck to get some air. There he became aware of the terrible power of the sea over those who see in it their transformed silhouette. He was happy and young; and yet he felt a nearly irresistible need to jump, to be carried away by the living waves whose roar, more than anything else, evokes eternity, peace, the infinite.

"I'm telling you," he repeated very softly. "One mustn't look at the sea for too long. Not alone, and not at night."

Then I too started telling him things about myself. Knowing that he had thought about death and was attracted by its secret, I felt closer to him. I told him what I had never told anyone. My childhood, my mystic dreams, my religious passions, my memories of German concentration camps, my belief that I was now just a messenger of the dead among the living. . . .

243

I talked for hours. He listened, leaning heavily on the railing, without interrupting me, without moving, without taking his eyes off a shadow that followed the ship. From time to time he would light a cigarette and, even when I stopped in the middle of a thought or a sentence, he said nothing.

Sometimes I left a sentence unfinished, jumped from one episode to another, or described a character in a word without mentioning the event with which he was connected. The stranger didn't ask for explanations. At times I spoke very softly, so softly that it was impossible that he heard a word of what I was saying; but he remained motionless and silent. He seemed not to dare exist outside of silence.

Only toward the end of the night did he recover his speech. His voice, a streak of shade, was hoarse. The voice of a man who, alone in the night, looks at the sea, looks at his own death.

"You must know this," he finally said. "I think I'm going to hate you."

Emotion made me gasp. I felt like shaking his hand to thank him. Few people would have had the courage to accompany me lucidly to the end.

The stranger threw his head back as if to make sure that the sky was still there. Suddenly he started hammering the railing with his clenched fist. And in a restrained, deep voice he repeated the same words over and over, "I'm going to hate you . . . I'm going to hate you. . . ."

Then he turned his back to me and walked off.

A fringe of white light was brightening the horizon. The sea was quiet, the ship was dozing. The stars had started to disappear. It was daybreak.

I stayed on deck all day. I came back to the same place the following night. The stranger never joined me again.

"I'll take a chance," Kathleen said.

I got up and took a few steps around the room to stretch my legs. I stopped at the window and looked out. The sidewalk across the street was covered with snow. A strange anguish came over me. Cold sweat covered my forehead. Once again the night would lift its burden and it would be day. I was afraid of the day. At night, I find all faces familiar, every noise sounds like something already heard. During the day, I only run into strangers.

"Do you know what Shimon Yanai told me about you?" Kathleen asked.

"I have no idea."

What could he have told her? What does he know about me? Nothing. He doesn't know that when I get carried away by a sunset, my heart fills with such nostalgia for Sighet, the little town of my childhood, it begins to pound so hard, so fast, that a week later I still haven't caught my breath; he doesn't know that I'm more moved by a Hassidic melody, which brings men back to his origins, than by Bach, Beethoven, and Mozart together; he couldn't know that when I look at a woman, it is always the image of my grandmother that I see.

"Shimon Yanai thinks you're a saint," Kathleen said.

My answer was a loud, unrestrained laugh.

"Shimon Yanai says that you suffered a lot. Only saints suffer a lot."

I couldn't stop laughing. I turned toward Kathleen, toward her eyes, not made for seeing, nor for crying, but for speaking and perhaps for making people laugh. She was hiding her chin in the neck of her sweater, concealing her lips which were trembling.

"Me, a saint? What a joke. . . ."

"Why are you laughing?"

"I'm laughing," I answered still shaking, "I'm laughing because I'm not a saint. Saints don't laugh. Saints are dead. My grandmother was a saint: she's dead. My teacher was a saint: he's dead. But me, look at me, I'm alive. And I'm laughing. I'm alive and I'm laughing because I'm not a saint. . . ."

At first I had had a hard time getting used to the idea that I was alive. I thought of myself as dead. I couldn't eat, read, cry: I saw myself dead. I thought I was dead and that in a dream I imagined myself alive. I knew I no longer existed, that my real self had stayed *there,* that my present self had nothing in common with the other, the real one. I was like the skin shed by a snake.

Then one day, in the street, an old woman asked me to come up to her room. She was so old, so dried out, that I couldn't hold back my laughter. The old woman grew pale and I thought she was going to collapse at my feet.

"Haven't you any pity?" she said in a choked voice.

Then, all of a sudden, reality struck me: I was alive, laughing, making fun of unhappy old women, I was able to humiliate and hurt old women who, like saints, spit on their own bodies.

"Where does suffering lead to?" Kathleen asked tensely. "Not to saintliness?"

"No!" I shouted.

That stopped my laughter. I was getting angry. I walked away from the window and stood in front of her; she was sitting on the floor now, her arms around her knees and her head resting on her arms.

"Those who say that are false prophets," I said.

I had to make an effort not to scream, not to wake up the whole house, and the dead who were waiting outside in the wind and the snow flurries. I went on:

"Suffering brings out the lowest, the most cowardly in man. There is a phase of suffering you reach beyond which you become a brute: beyond it you sell your soul—and worse, the souls of your friends—for a piece of bread, for some warmth, for a moment of oblivion, of sleep. Saints are those who die before the end of the story. The others, those who live out their destiny, no longer dare look at themselves in the mirror, afraid they may see their inner image: a monster laughing at unhappy women and at saints who are dead. . . ."

Kathleen listened, in a daze, her eyes wide open. As I spoke, her back bent over even more. Her pale lips whispered the same sentence tirelessly, "Go on! I want to know more. Go on!"

Then I fell on my knees, took her head in my hands, and, looking straight into her eyes, I told her the story of my grandmother, then the story of my little sister, and of my father, and of my mother; in very simple words, I described to her how man can become a grave for the unburied dead.

I kept talking. In every detail, I described the screams and the nightmares that haunt me at night. And Kathleen, very pale, her eyes, red, continued to beg:

"More! Go on! More!"

She was saying "more" in the eager voice of a woman who wants her pleasure to last, who asks the man she loves not to stop, not to leave her, not to disappoint her, not to abandon her halfway between ecstasy and nothing. "More. . . . More. . . ."

I kept looking at her and holding her. I wanted to get rid of all the filth that was in me and graft it onto her pupils and her lips which were so pure, so innocent, so beautiful.

I bared my soul. My most contemptible thoughts and desires, my most painful betrayals, my vaguest lies, I tore them from inside me and placed them in front of her, like an impure offering, so she could see them and smell their stench.

But Kathleen was drinking in every one of my words as if she wanted to punish herself for not having suffered before. From time to time she insisted in the same eager voice that sounded so much like the old prostitute's, "More. . . . More. . . ."

Finally I stopped, exhausted. I stretched out on the carpet and closed my eyes.

We didn't talk for a long time: an hour, perhaps two. I was out of breath. I was wet with perspiration, my shirt stuck to my body. Kathleen didn't stir. Outside, the night softly moved on.

Suddenly we heard the noise of the milkman's truck, coming from the street. The truck stopped near the door.

Kathleen took a deep breath and said, "I feel like going down and kissing the milkman."

I didn't answer. I didn't have the strength.

"I would like to kiss him," Kathleen said, "just to thank him. To thank him for being alive."

I was silent.

"You're not saying anything." She sounded surprised. "You're not laughing?"

And as I still didn't say anything, she began to stroke my hair, then her fingers explored the outlines of my face. I liked the way she caressed me.

"I like you to touch me," I told her, my eyes still closed. After hesitating, I added, "You see, it's the best proof that I'm not a saint. Saints in that respect are like the dead: they don't know desire."

Kathleen's voice became lighter and sounded more provocative. "And you desire me?"

"Yes."

I again felt like laughing: a saint, me? What a wonderful joke! Me, a saint! Does a saint feel this desire for a woman's body? Does he feel this need to take her into his arms, cover her with kisses, to bite her flesh, to possess her breath, her life, her breasts? No, a saint would not be willing to make love to a woman, with his dead grandmother watching, wearing her black shawl that seems to hold the nights and days of the universe.

I sat down. And I said angrily, "I'm not a saint!"

"No?" Kathleen asked without being able to smile.

"No," I repeated.

I opened my eyes and noticed that she was really suffering. She was biting her lips; there was despair in her face.

"I'll prove to you that I'm not a saint," I muttered angrily.

Without a word I started to undress her. She didn't resist. When she was naked, she sat down again as before. Her head resting on her knees, she looked at me in anguish as I too undressed. Now there were two lines around her mouth. I could see fear in her eyes. I was pleased; she was afraid of me, and that was good. Those who, like me, have left their souls in hell, are here only to frighten others by being their mirrors.

"I am going to take you," I told her in a harsh, almost hostile voice. "But I don't love you."

I thought: she must know. I'm not a saint at all. I'll

make love without any commitments. A saint commits his whole being with every act.

She undid her hair, which fell to her shoulders. Her breast rose and fell irregularly.

"What if I fall in love with you?" she asked with studied naïveté.

"Small chance! You'll hate me rather."

Her face became a little sadder, a little more distressed. "I'm afraid you're right."

Somewhere, above the city, there was a hint of dawn in the foggy world.

"Look at me," I said.

"I'm looking at you."

"What do you see?"

"A saint," she answered.

I laughed again. There we were, both naked, and one of us was a saint? It was grotesque! I took her brutally, trying to hurt her. She bit her lips and didn't cry out. We stayed together until late that afternoon.

Without saying another word.

Without exchanging a kiss.

Suddenly, the fever vanished. My name was taken off the critical list. I still had pain, but my life was no longer in danger. I was still given antibiotics, but less frequently. Four shots a day. Then three, then two. Then none.

When I was allowed visitors, I had been in the hospital for nearly a week and in a cast for three days.

"Your friends may come to see you today," the nurse said as she washed me.

"Fine," I said.

"That's your only reaction? Aren't you pleased to be able to see your friends?"

"I am. Very pleased."

"You've come a long way," she said.

"A very long way."

"You're not talkative."

"No."

I had discovered one advantage in being ill: you can remain silent without having to apologize.

"After breakfast, I'll come and shave you," the nurse said.

"It won't be necessary," I answered.

"Not necessary?"

She seemed not to believe me: nothing that's done in a hospital is unnecessary!

"That's right. Unnecessary. I want to grow a beard."

She stared at me a moment, then gave her verdict.

"No. You need a shave. You look too ill this way."

"But I am ill."

"You are. But if I shave you you'll feel better."

And without giving me time to answer, she continued, "You'll feel like new."

She was young, dark, obstinate. Tall, buttoned up in her white uniform, she towered over me and not merely because she was standing up.

"All right," I said, to put an end to the discussion. "In that case, fine."

"Good! That's the boy!"

She was happy with her victory, her mouth wide open showing her white teeth. Laughingly, she began to tell me all kinds of stories which seemed to have the following moral: death is afraid to attack those who make themselves look nice in the morning. The secret of immortality may well be to find the right shaving cream.

After helping me wash, she brought my breakfast.

"I'll feed you as if you were a baby. Aren't you ashamed to be a baby? At your age?"

She left and immediately returned with an electric razor.

"We want you to look nice. I want my baby to be nice!"

The razor made a tremendous noise. The nurse went on chattering. I wasn't listening to her. I was thinking about the night of the accident. The cab was speeding. I had no idea it would send me to the hospital.

"There you are," the nurse said beaming. "Now you're nice."

"I know," I said. "Now I'm like a newborn baby!"

"Wait and I'll bring you a mirror!"

She had very large eyes, with black pupils, and the white around them was very white.

"I don't want it," I said.

"I'll bring it, you'll see."

"Listen," I said threateningly, "if you hand me a mirror I'll break it. A broken mirror brings seven years of unhappiness! Is that what you want? Seven years of unhappiness?"

For a second her eyes were still, wondering if I wasn't joking.

"It's true. Anybody will tell you: one should never break a mirror."

She was still laughing, but now her voice sounded more worried than before. She was wiping her hands on her white uniform.

"You're a bad boy," she said. "I don't like you."

"Too bad!" I answered. "I adore you!"

She muttered something to herself and left the room.

I was facing the window and could see the East River from my bed. A small boat was going by: a grayish spot on a blue background. A mirage.

Someone knocked at the door.

"Come in!"

Dr. Paul Russel, hands in his pockets, was back to resume our conversation where we had left off.

"Feeling better this morning?"

"Yes, Doctor. Much better."

"No more fever. The enemy is beaten."

"A beaten enemy, that's dangerous," I remarked. "He'll only think of vengeance."

The doctor became more serious. He took out a cigarette and offered it to me. I refused. He lit it for himself.

"Do you still have pain?"

"Yes."

"It will last a few weeks more. You're not afraid?"

"Of what?"

"Of suffering."

"No. I'm not afraid of suffering."

He looked me straight in the eye. "What are you afraid of, then?"

Again I had the impression that he was keeping something from me. Could he actually know? Had I talked in my sleep, during the operation?

"I'm not afraid of anything," I answered, staring back at him.

There was a silence.

He went to the window and stayed there a few moments. There, I thought: the back of a man and the river no longer exists. Paradise is when nothing comes between the eye and the tree.

"You have a beautiful view," he said without turning.

"Very beautiful. The river is like me: it hardly moves."

"Sheer illusion! It is calm only on the surface. Go beneath the surface, you'll see how restless it is. . . ." He turned suddenly. ". . . Just like you, as a matter of fact."

What does he know exactly, I wondered, somewhat worried. He speaks as if he knows. Is it possible that I betrayed myself?

"Every man is like the river," I said to shift the conversation toward abstractions. "Rivers flow toward the sea, which is never full. Men are swallowed up by death which is never satiated."

He made a gesture of discouragement, as if to say, All right, you don't want to talk, you're dodging, it doesn't matter. I'll wait.

Slowly he moved toward the door, then stopped.

"I have a message for you. From Kathleen. She's coming to see you in the late afternoon."

"You saw her?"

"Yes. She's been coming every day. She's an extremely nice girl."

"Ex-treme-ly."

He was standing in the opening of the door. His voice seemed very close. The door must have been right next to my bed.

"She loves you," he said. His voice became hard, insistent. "And you? Do you love her?"

He stressed the "you." I was breathing faster. What does he know, I asked myself, tormented.

"Of course," I answered, trying to look calm. "Of course I love her."

Nothing stirred. There was complete silence. In the hallway, the foggy loud speaker announced: "Dr. Braunstein, telephone . . . Dr. Braunstein, telephone . . ." Echoes from another world. In the room there was utter silence.

"Fine," Dr. Russel said. "I have to go. I'll see you tonight, or tomorrow."

Another boat was gliding by the window. Outside the air was sharp, alive. I thought: at this very moment, men are walking in the streets, without ties, in their shirt sleeves. They are reading, arguing, eating, drinking, stopping to avoid a car, to admire a woman, to look at windows. Outside, at this very moment, men are walking.

Toward the beginning of the afternoon, some of my colleagues showed up. They came together, gay and trying to make me feel equally gay.

They told me some gossip: who was doing what, who was saying what, who was unfaithful to whom. The latest word, the latest indiscretion, the latest story.

Then the conversation came back to the accident.

"You must admit you've been lucky: this could have been it," one of them said.

And another: "Or you could have lost a leg."

"Or even your mind."

"You're going to be rich," Sandor, a Hungarian, said. "I was hit by a car once myself. I got a thousand dollars from the insurance company. You were lucky it was a cab. Cabs always have a lot of insurance. You'll be rich, you'll see, you lucky bastard!"

I hurt everywhere. I couldn't move. I was practically paralyzed. But I was very lucky. I was going to be rich. I'd be able to travel, go to night clubs, keep mistresses, be on top of the world: what luck! They just about said they envied me.

"I'd always been told that in America you find dollars in the street," I said. "So it's true: you just have to fall down to pick them up."

They laughed still more and I laughed with them. Once or twice the nurse came in to bring me something to drink and she also laughed with them.

"And you know this morning he didn't even want to shave!" she told them.

"He's rich," Sandor said. "Rich men can afford to be unshaven."

"You're funny," the nurse exclaimed, clapping her hands. "And did he tell you about the mirror?"

"No!" they all shouted together. "Tell us about the mirror!"

She told them that I had refused to look at myself in the mirror that morning.

"Rich men are afraid of mirrors," I said. "Mirrors have no respect for that which glitters. They're too familiar with it."

It was warm in the room, even warmer than in the cast. My friends were perspiring. The nurse was wiping her forehead with the back of her hand. When she left, Sandor winked.

"Not bad, hum?"

"She must be something!" another added.

"Well, you won't get bored here, you can be sure of that much!"

"No, I won't get bored," I said.

We had been together for quite some time, when Sandor remembered that there was a press conference at four.

"That's true, we'd forgotten."

They left in a hurry, taking their laughter with them into the hallway, into the street, and finally, where it assumes an historic function, into the United Nations Building.

It was nearly seven when Kathleen arrived. She seemed paler than usual, and gayer, also more exuberant. It was as if she were living the happiest moments of her life. What a beautiful view! Look, the river! And such a nice room! So big, so clean! You're looking great!

It's weird, I thought. A hospital room is the gayest place on earth. Everybody turns into an actor. Even the patients. You put on new attitudes, new make-up, new joys.

Kathleen kept talking. Even though she didn't like people who talk without saying anything, she was doing precisely that now. Why is she afraid of silence? I wondered, as I grew more tense. Is it possible she knows something too? She is in a position to know. She was there at the time of the accident. A little ahead. She may have turned around.

I would have liked to steer the conversation to that subject, but I couldn't stop the flow of her words. She kept talking and talking. Isak is replacing you on the paper. In the office, the phone keeps ringing: all kinds of people asking how you are. And you know, even the one—what's his name?—you know the one I mean, the fat one, the one who looks pregnant, you know, the one who's angry at you, even he called. Isak told me. And——

There was a knock on the door. A nurse—a new one, not the morning nurse—brought in my dinner. She was an old woman with glasses, haughtily indifferent. She offered to help me eat.

"Don't bother," Kathleen said. "I'll do it."

"Very well," the old nurse said. "As you wish."

I wasn't hungry. Kathleen kept insisting: some soup? Yes, yes. You have to. You've lost a lot of strength. Come on. Just one spoonful. Just one. One more. Do it for me. And one more. Fine. And now the rest. Let's see: a piece of meat. Ah! Does that look good!

I closed my eyes and tried not to hear. That was the only way. I suddenly felt like shouting. But I knew I shouldn't. Anyway what would have been the use?

Kathleen talked on and on.

". . . I also retained a lawyer. A very good one. He's going to sue the cab company. He'll be here tomorrow. He is very hopeful. He says you'll get a lot of money. . . ."

When I was through eating, she took the tray and put it on the table. I could see as she busied herself how tired she was. Now I understood why she was talking so much: she was at the end of her strength. Behind her forced good-humor was exhaustion. Seven days. It had been a week since the accident.

"Kathleen?" I called.

"Yes?"

"Come here. Sit down."

She obeyed and sat on the bed.

"What is it?" she asked worried.

"I want to ask you something."

She frowned. "Yes?"

"I don't recognize you. You've changed. You talk a lot. Why?"

A shudder went through her eyelids, through her shoulders.

"So many things have happened in a week," she said blushing slightly. "I want to tell you about them. Everything. Don't forget that I haven't talked to you in a week. . . ."

She looked at me as if she had been beaten, and lowered her head. Then slowly, mechanically, she repeated several times in a low, tired, toneless voice, "I don't want to cry, I don't want to cry, I don't want to. . . ."

Poor Kathleen, I thought. Poor Kathleen. I have changed her. Kathleen so proud, Kathleen whose will was stronger than others', Kathleen whose strength was pure and who

259

was truly tough, Kathleen against whom men with character, strong-minded men, liked to pit themselves; now Kathleen didn't even have the strength to hold back her tears, her words.

I had transformed her. And she had wanted to change me! "You can't change a human being," I had told her in the beginning, once, a thousand times. "You can change someone's thoughts, someone's attitudes, someone's ties. You might even change someone's desires, but that's all." "That's enough for me," she had answered.

And the battle had started. She wanted to make me happy no matter what. To make me taste the pleasures of life. To make me forget the past. "Your past is dead. Dead and buried," she would say. And I would answer, "I am my past. If it's buried, I'm buried with it."

She was fighting stubbornly. "I'm strong," she would say. "I'll win." And I would answer, "You are strong. You are beautiful. You have all the qualities to conquer the living. But here you are fighting the dead. You cannot conquer the dead!" "We shall see."

"I don't want to cry," she said, her head down, as if under the weight of all the dead since creation.

I had said human beings don't change? I was wrong. They do. The dead are all-powerful. That's what she refused to understand: that the dead are invincible. That through me she was fighting them.

The only child of very rich parents, she was determined and obstinate. Her arrogance was almost naïve. She wasn't accustomed to losing battles. She thought she could take the place of my fate.

Once I had asked her if she loved me. "No," she had answered heatedly. And it was true. She hadn't lied. The truly proud don't lie.

260

Our understanding had nothing to do with love. Not at first. Later, yes. But not at the beginning. What united us was exactly what kept us apart. She liked life and love; I only thought of life and love with a strong feeling of shame. We stayed together. She needed to fight and I was watching her. I watched her knocking against the cold, unchanging reality she had discovered first in my words, then in my silence.

We traveled a lot. The days were full, the hours dense. Time was once more an adventure. Whenever Kathleen watched a beautiful dawn, she knew how to make me share her enthusiasm; in the street she was the one to point out beautiful women; at home she taught me that the body is also a source of joy.

At first, at the very beginning, I avoided her kisses. We were living together but our mouths had never met. Something in me shrank from the touch of her lips. It was as if I were afraid that she would become different if I kissed her. Several times she had nearly asked me why but she had been too proud. Then, little by little, I let myself go. Every kiss reopened an old wound. And I was aware that I was still capable of suffering. That I was still answering the calls of the past.

Our affair lasted a whole year. When we celebrated the first anniversary of our meeting—that's what we liked to call our affair—we both decided to separate. Since the experiment had foundered, there was no reason to draw it out.

That night neither one of us slept. Stretched out next to each other, frightened, in silence, we waited for daybreak. Just before dawn, she pulled me toward her and in the dark our bodies made love for the last time. An hour later, still silent, I got up, dressed, and left the room without saying good-bye, without even turning around.

Outside, the biting morning wind whipped the houses. The streets were still deserted. Somewhere a door creaked. A window lit up, lonely and pale. It was cold. My legs would have liked me to run. I managed to walk slowly, very slowly: I didn't want to give in to any weakness. My eyes were crying, probably because of the cold.

"I don't want to cry," Kathleen said.

She was shaking her lowered head.

Poor Kathleen, I thought. You too have been changed by the dead.

The lawyer came the next day. He wore glasses, was of medium height, and had the self-satisfied air of someone who knows the answer before he has even asked you the question.

He introduced himself: Mark Brown. "Call me Mark."

He sat down as if he were at home and took a large yellow pad out of his brief case.

"I talked to your doctors," he said. "You were in very bad shape. That's very good."

"You're right, that's very good."

He understood the irony. "Of course I'm only speaking from the point of view of the lawsuit," he said, winking at me.

"So am I," I answered. "I hear you're going to make me rich."

"I have high hopes."

"Be careful. My enemies will never forgive me: I'm about to become a rich journalist!"

He laughed: "For once the law will be on the side of literature!"

He started asking me detailed questions: what exactly had happened on the night of the accident? Had I been alone? No. Who was with me? Kathleen. Yes, the young woman who had called him. Had we quarreled? No. Had we waited for the light to turn green before crossing the street? Yes. The cab had come from the left. Had I seen it approaching?

I took a little more time to answer this last question. Mark took off his glasses and as he wiped them he repeated, "Did you see it approaching?"

"No," I said.

He looked at me more sharply. "You seem to hesitate."

"I'm trying to relive the incident, to see it again."

Mark was intelligent, perceptive. To prepare a good case, he was determined to get lots of details which, on the surface, seemed to have no direct relation to the accident. Before working out his strategy he wanted to know everything. His questioning lasted several hours. He seemed satisfied.

"Not the shadow of a doubt," he decided. "The driver is guilty of negligence."

"I hope he won't have to suffer because of this!" I said. "I wouldn't want him to be punished. After all he didn't do it on purpose. . . ."

"Don't worry," he reassured me, "he won't have to pay; it will be the insurance company. We have nothing against him, poor chap."

"You're sure, absolutely sure, that nothing will happen to him?"

Poor devil, I thought. It wasn't his fault. The day before, his wife had called and asked me to forgive him. She was calling on behalf of her husband. He was afraid. He was even afraid to ask me to forgive him.

"Absolutely sure," the lawyer said with a little, dry laugh. "You'll be richer and he won't be any poorer. So, there's nothing to worry about."

I couldn't hide a sigh of relief.

Every morning Dr. Russel came to chat. He had made it a habit to end his daily rounds with me. Often he would remain an hour or more. He would walk in without knocking, sit on the window sill, his hands in the pockets of his white coat, his legs crossed, his eyes reflecting the changing colors of the river.

He spoke a lot about himself, his life in the army—he had been in the Korean War—his work, the pleasures and disappointments that came with it. Each prey torn away from death made him as happy as if he had won a universal victory. A defeat left dark rings under his eyes. I only had to look at him carefully to know whether the night before he had won or lost the battle. He considered death his personal enemy.

"What makes me despair," he often told me bitterly, "is that our weapons aren't equal. My victories can only be temporary. My defeats are final. Always."

One morning he seemed happier than usual. He gave up his favorite spot near the window and started walking up and down the room like a drunkard, talking to himself.

"You have been drinking, Doctor!" I teased him.

"Drinking!" he exclaimed. "Of course I haven't been drinking. I don't drink. Today I'm simply happy. Awfully happy. I won! Yes, this time I won. . . ."

His victory tasted like wine. He couldn't stand still. To split up his happiness he would have liked to be simultaneously himself and someone else: witness and hero. He wanted to sing and to hear himself singing, to dance and to see himself dancing, to climb to the top of the highest mountain and to shout, to scream with all his strength, "I won! I conquered Death!"

The operation had been difficult, dangerous: a little twelve-year-old boy who had a very slim chance of surviving. Three doctors had given up hope. But he, Paul Russel, had decided to try the impossible.

"The kid will make it!" he thundered, his face glowing as if lit up by a sun inside him. "Do you understand? He's going to live! And yet all seemed lost! The infection had reached his leg and was poisoning his blood. I amputated the leg. The others were saying that it wouldn't do any good. That it was too late. That the game was lost. But I didn't hesitate. I started to act. For each breath, I had to fight with every weapon I had. But you see: I won! This time I really won!"

The joy of saving a human life, I thought. I have never experienced it. I didn't even know that it existed. To hold in your hands a boy's life is to take God's place. I had never dreamt of rising above the level of man. Man is not defined by what denies him, but by that which affirms him. This is found within, not across from him or next to him.

"You see," Paul Russel said in a different tone of voice, "the difference between you and me is this. Your relation with what surrounds you and with what marks the limits of your horizon develops in an indirect way. You only know the words, the skin, the appearances, the ideas, of life. There'll always be a curtain between you and your neighbor's life. You're not content to know man is alive; you also want to know what he is doing with his life. For me this is different. I am less severe with my fellow men. We have the same enemy and it has only one name: Death. Before it we are all equal. In its eyes no life has more weight than another. From that point of view, I am just like Death. What fascinates me in man is his capacity for living. Acts are just repetitions. If you had ever held a man's life in the palm of your hand, you too would come to prefer the immediate to the future, the concrete to the ideal, and life to the problems which it brings with it."

He stood at the window for a moment and stopped talking, just long enough to smile, before continuing an octave lower.

"Your life, my friend, I had it right there. In the palm of my hand."

He turned slowly, his hand held out. Little by little his face became as it usually was and his gestures became less abrupt.

"Do you believe in God, Doctor?"

My question took him by surprise. He stopped suddenly, wrinkling his forehead.

"Yes," he answered. "But not in the operating room. There I only count on myself."

His eyes looked deeper. He added, "On myself and on the patient. Or, if you prefer, on the life in the diseased flesh. Life wants to live. Life wants to go on. It is opposed to death. It fights. The patient is my ally. He fights on my side. Together we are stronger than the enemy. Take the boy last night. He didn't accept death. He helped me to win the battle. He was holding on, clinging. He was asleep, anesthetized, and yet he was taking part in the fight. . . ."

Still motionless, he again stared at me intensely. There was an awkward silence. Once more I had the impression he knew, that he was speaking only to penetrate my secret. Now, I decided. Now or never. I had to put an end to any uncertainty.

"Doctor, I would like to ask you a question."

266

He nodded.

"What did I say during the operation?"

He thought a moment. "Nothing. You didn't say anything."

"Are you sure? Not even a word?"

"Not even a word."

I was relieved and couldn't help smiling.

"My turn now," the doctor said seriously. "I also have a question."

My smile froze. "Go ahead," I said.

I had to fight an urge to close my eyes. All of a sudden the room seemed too light. Anxiety took hold of my voice, my breath, my eyes.

The doctor lowered his head slightly, almost imperceptibly.

"Why don't you care about living?" he asked very softly.

For a moment everything shook. Even the light flickered and changed color. It was white, red, black. The blood was beating in my temples. My head was no longer my own.

"Don't deny it," the doctor went on, speaking still more softly. "Don't deny it. I know."

He knows. He knows. He knows. My throat was in an invisible vise. I was going to choke any moment.

Weakly I asked him who had told him: Kathleen?

"No. Not Kathleen. Nobody. Nobody told me. But I know it anyway. I guessed. During the operation. You never helped me. Not once. You abandoned me. I had to wage the fight alone, all alone. Worse. You were on the other side, against me, on the side of the enemy."

His voice became hard, painfully hard. "Answer me! Why don't you want to live? Why?"

I was calm again. He doesn't know, I thought. The little he is guessing is nothing. An impression. That's all. Nothing definite. Nothing worked out. And yet he is moving in the right direction. Only he's not going all the way.

"Answer me," he repeated. "Why? Why?"

He was becoming more and more insistent. His lower lip was shaking nervously. Was he aware of it? I thought: he's angry at me because I left him alone, because even now I escape him and have neither gratitude nor admiration for him. That's why he's angry. He guessed that I don't care about living, that deep inside me there is no desire left to go on. And that undermines the foundation of his philosophy and his system of values. Man, according to his book, must live and must fight for his life. He must help doctors and not fight them. I had fought him. He brought me back to life against my will. I had nearly joined my grandmother. I was actually on the threshold. Paul Russel stood behind me and prevented me from crossing. He was pulling me toward him. Alone against Grandmother and the others. And he had won. Another victory for him. A human life. I should shout with happiness and make the walls of the universe tremble. But instead I disturb him. That's what is distressing him.

Dr. Russel was making an obvious effort to restrain himself. He was still looking at me with anger, his cheeks purple, his lips trembling.

"I order you to answer me!"

A pitiless inquisitor, he had raised his voice. A cold anger made his hands rigid.

I thought: he is going to shout, to hit me. Who knows? He might be capable of strangling me, of sending me back to the battlefield. Dr. Russel is a human being, therefore capable of hatred, capable of losing control. He could easily put his hands around my neck and squeeze. That would be normal, logical on his part. I represent a danger to him. Anyone who rejects life is a threat to him and to everything he stands for in this world where life already counts for so little. In his eyes I am a cancer to be eliminated. What would become of humanity and of the laws of equilibrium if all men began to desire death?

I felt very calm, completely controlled. If I had searched further I might have discovered that my calm also hid the satisfaction, the strange joy—or was it simply humor?— that comes from the knowledge of one's own strength, of one's own solitude. I was telling myself: he doesn't know. And I alone can decide to tell him, to transform his future. At this very moment, I am his fate.

"Did I tell you the dream I had during the first operation I ever had?" I asked him smilingly in an amused tone of voice. "No? Shall I tell you? I was twelve. My mother had taken me to a clinic that belonged to my cousin, the surgeon Oscar Sreter, to have my tonsils removed. He had put me to sleep with ether. When I woke up, Oscar Sreter asked me, 'Are you crying because it hurts?' 'No,' I answered. 'I'm crying because I just saw God.' Strange dream. I had gone to heaven. God, sitting on his throne, was presiding over an assembly of angels. The distance which separated Him from me was infinite but I could see Him as clearly as if He had been right next to me. God motioned to me and I started to walk forward. I walked several lifetimes but the distance grew no shorter. Then two angels picked me up, and suddenly I found myself face to face with God. At last! I thought. Now I can ask Him the question that haunts all the wise men of Israel: What is the meaning of suffering? But, awed, I couldn't utter a sound. In the meantime other questions kept moving through my head: When will the hour of deliverance come? When will Good conquer Evil, thus allowing chaos to be forever dispelled? But my lips could only tremble and the words stuck in my throat. Then God talked to me. The silence had become so total, so pure, that my heart was ashamed of its beating. The silence was still as absolute, when I heard the words of God. With Him the word and the silence were not contradictory. God answered all my questions and many others. Then two angels took me by the arm again and brought me back. One of them told the other, 'He has become heavier,' and the other replied, 'He is carrying an important answer.' That is when I woke up. Dr. Sreter was leaning over me with a smile. I wanted to tell him that I had just heard the words of God, when I realized to my horror that I had forgotten them. I no longer knew what God had told me. My tears began to flow. 'Are you crying because it hurts?' the good Dr. Sreter asked me. 'It doesn't hurt,' I answered. 'I'm crying because I just saw God. He talked to me and I forgot what He said.' The doctor burst into a friendly laugh: 'If you want I can put you back to sleep; and you can ask Him to repeat. . . .' I was crying and my cousin was laughing heartily. . . . And you see, Doctor, this time, stretched out on your operating table, fast asleep, I didn't see God in my dream. He was no longer there."

Paul Russel had been listening attentively. Leaning forward he seemed to be looking for a hidden meaning in every word. His face had changed.

"You haven't answered my question!" he remarked, still tense.

So he hadn't understood. An answer to his question? But this was an answer! Couldn't he see how the second operation was different from the first? It wasn't his fault. He couldn't understand. We were so different, so far from each other. His fingers touched life. Mine death. Without

270

an intermediary, without partitions. Life, death, each as bare, as true as the other. The problem went beyond us. It was in an invisible sphere, on a faraway screen, between two powers for whom we were only ambassadors.

Standing in front of my bed, he filled the room with his presence. He was waiting. He suspected a secret that made him angry. That's what was throwing him off. We were both young, and above all we were alive. He looked at me steadily, stubbornly, to catch in me that which eluded him. In the same way primitive man must have watched the day disappear behind the mountain.

I felt like telling him: go. Paul Russel, you are a straightforward and courageous man. Your duty is to leave me. Don't ask me to talk. Don't try to know. Neither who I am, nor who you are. I am a storyteller. My legends can only be told at dusk. Whoever listens questions his life. Go, Paul Russel. Go. The heroes of my legends are cruel and without pity. They are capable of strangling you. You want to know who I am, truly? I don't know myself. Sometimes I am Shmuel, the slaughterer. Look at me carefully. No, not at my face. At my hands.

They were about ten in the bunker. Night after night they could hear the German police dogs looking through the ruins for Jews hiding out in their underground shelters. Shmuel and the others were living on practically no water or bread, on hardly any air. They were holding out. They knew that there, down below in their narrow jail, they were free; above, death was waiting for them. One night a disaster nearly occurred. It was Golda's fault. She had taken her child with her. A baby, a few months old. He began to cry, thus endangering the lives of all. Golda was trying to quiet him, to make him sleep. To no avail.

271

That's when the others, including Golda herself, turned to Shmuel and told him: "Make him shut up. Take care of him, you whose job it is to slaughter chickens. You will be able to do it without making him suffer too much." And Shmuel gave in to reason: the baby's life in exchange for the lives of all. He had taken the child. In the dark his groping fingers felt for the neck. And there had been silence on earth and in heaven. There was only the sound of dogs barking in the distance.

A slight smile came to my lips. Shmuel too had been a doctor, I thought.

Motionless, Paul Russel was still waiting.

Moishe is a smuggler. He too comes from Sighet. We were friends. Every morning at six, ever since we were eight years old, we met in the street and, lantern in hand, we walked to the *cheder* where we found books bigger than we. Moishe wanted to become a rabbi. Today he is a smuggler and he is wanted by every police force in Europe. In the concentration camp he had seen a pious man exchange his whole week's bread rations for a prayer book. The pious man passed away less than a month later. Before dying he had kissed his precious book and murmured, "Book, how many human beings have you destroyed?" That day Moishe had decided to change the course of his existence. And that's how the human race gained a smuggler and lost a rabbi. And it isn't any the worse off for it.

You want to know who I am, Doctor? I am also Moishe the smuggler. But above all I am the one who saw his grandmother go to heaven. Like a flame, she chased away the sun and took its place. And this new sun which blinds instead of giving light forces me to walk with my head down. It weighs upon the future of man. It casts a gloom over the hearts and vision of generations to come.

If I had spoken to him out loud, he would have understood the tragic fate of those who came back, left over, living-dead. You must look at them carefully. Their appearance is deceptive. They are smugglers. They look like the others. They eat, they laugh, they love. They seek money, fame, love. Like the others. But it isn't true: they are playing, sometimes without even knowing it. Anyone who has seen what they have seen cannot be like the others, cannot laugh, love, pray, bargain, suffer, have fun, or forget. Like the others. You have to watch them carefully when they pass by an innocent looking smokestack, or when they lift a piece of bread to their mouths. Something in them shudders and makes you turn your eyes away. These people have been amputated; they haven't lost their legs or eyes but their will and their taste for life. The things they have seen will come to the surface again sooner or later. And then the world will be frightened and won't dare look these spiritual cripples in the eye.

If I had spoken out loud, Paul Russel would have understood why one shouldn't ask those who came back too many questions: they aren't normal human beings. A spring snapped inside them from the shock. Sooner or later the results must appear. But I didn't want him to understand. I didn't want him to lose his equilibrium; I didn't want him to see a truth which threatened to reveal itself at any moment.

I began to persuade him he was wrong so he would go away, so he would leave me alone. Of course I wanted to live. Obviously I wanted to live, create, do lasting things, help man make a step forward, contribute to the progress of humanity, its happiness, its fulfillment! I talked a long time, passionately, using complicated, grandiloquent words and abstract expressions on purpose. And since he still wasn't completely convinced, I threw in the argument to which he couldn't remain deaf: love. I love Kathleen. I love her with all my heart. And how can one love if at the same time one doesn't care about life, if one doesn't believe in life or in love?

The young doctor's face gradually assumed its usual expression. He had heard the words he wanted to hear. His philosophy wasn't threatened. Everything was in order again. Nothing like friendship between patients and doctors! Nothing is more sacred than life, or healthier, or greater, or more noble. To refuse life is a sin; it's stupid and mad. You have to accept life, cherish it, love it, fight for it as if it were a treasure, a woman, a secret happiness.

Now he was becoming friendly again. He offered me a cigarette, encouraging me to accept it. He was no longer tense. His lips had their normal color again. There was no more anger in his eyes.

"I'm glad," he said finally. "At the beginning I was afraid. . . . I admit my mistake. I'm glad. Really."

I too. I was glad to have convinced him. Really.

Nothing easier. He only wanted to be deceived and I had played his game. I had recited a text he knew by heart. Love is a question mark, not an exclamation point. It can explain everything without calling on arguments whose strength as well as whose weakness is based on logic. A boy who is in love knows more about the universe and about creation than a scholar. Why do we have to die? Because I love you, my love. And why do parallel lines meet at infinity? What a question! It's only because I love you, my love.

And it works. For them, for the boy and for the girl, prisoners of a magic circle, the answer seems completely valid. In their eyes there is a direct relation between their adventure and the mysteries of the universe.

Yes, it was easy. I love Kathleen. Therefore life has a meaning, man isn't alone. Love is the very proof of God's existence.

Kathleen. In the end I managed to convince her also. True, this was more difficult. She knew me better and was on her guard. Unlike the young doctor, who was running away from uncertainties, she had a feeling for nuances. For her, Hamlet was just romantic and the question he asked himself was too simplistic. The problem is not: to be or not to be. But rather: to be and not to be. What it comes down to is that man lives while dying, that he represents death to the living, and that's where tragedy begins.

Why had she come back? She shouldn't have. I had even told her so. No. I hadn't told her. She was unhappy. This had surprised me so much that I had felt incapable of telling her not to reopen the parentheses.

She was suffering. Even on the telephone, her voice had betrayed her weariness. Five years had gone by since my silent departure. It had been bitingly cold that morning. Now it was fall. Five years! I had heard from Shimon Yanai that Kathleen had gone back to Boston and had married a man much older than she, and quite rich.

One afternoon, in the office. Up to my neck in work: the General Assembly of the United Nations was holding its annual session. Speeches, statements, accusations and counteraccusations, resolutions and counterresolutions.

Judging from what was said on the speaker's platform, our planet was extremely ill.

The phone rang.

At the other end, in a whisper, a voice murmured, "It's Kathleen."

That's all she said and there was a long silence. I looked at the receiver I was holding in my hand and I had the impression it was alive. I thought: years ago, winter; now, fall.

"I would like to see you," Kathleen added.

Her voice had the sound of despair. Of nothingness.

"Where are you?" I asked her.

She mentioned a hotel.

"Wait for me," I said.

We hung up at the same time.

She was staying at one of the most expensive and most elegant places in New York. Her apartment was on the fifteenth floor. Quietly I pushed the half-open door. Kathleen was framed by the window. Her beautiful black hair fell to her shoulders. She was wearing a dark gray dress with a low-cut back. I was moved.

"Hello, Kathleen," I said as I walked in.

"Hello," she answered without turning.

I walked toward the open window. It looked on Central Park, the no man's land which at night, in this enormous city, shelters with equal kindness criminals and lovers. The trees were turning orange. It was humid and hot: the last heat wave before winter. Far below, thousands of cars drove into the foliage and disappeared. The sun grafted its golden rays onto the skyscrapers' windows.

"Help me," Kathleen said, her eyes fixed on the dead leaves that covered the park.

Furtively I looked at her left profile. From the curve of

276

her neck I could see that she was still sensitive.

"You will help me, won't you?" she said.

"Of course," I answered.

Only then did she turn her face toward me, with a look of gratitude. She was still beautiful, but her beauty had lost its pride.

"I've suffered a lot," she said.

"Don't say anything," I answered. "Let me look at you."

I sat down in an armchair and she began to walk about the room. When she talked, a line of sadness appeared near her upper lip. From time to time her eyes had the hard expression that comes from humiliation. She was smoking more than she used to. I thought: Kathleen the proud, Kathleen the untamable, Kathleen the queen— here she is. A beaten woman. A drowning woman.

She sat in the armchair opposite me. She was breathing heavily.

"I want to talk," she said.

"Go ahead," I told her.

"I'm not ashamed to tell you that I want to talk."

"Go ahead," I told her.

"I am no longer ashamed to tell you that I suffered a lot."

"Go ahead, talk."

She was trying to live up to the image she still had of herself. She used to speak firmly and with harsh words. She never used to speak of her own suffering. Now she did. You just had to listen to her and look at her closely to realize that her beauty had lost its power and its mystery.

She spoke for a long time. Sometimes her eyes would cloud over. But she managed not to cry, and I was grateful.

She had gotten married. He loved her. She didn't love him. She did not even love the feeling she had inspired in him. She had agreed to marry him precisely because she did not care about him. What she wanted was to suffer, to pay. Finally her husband understood: Kathleen saw in him not a companion but a kind of judge. She didn't expect happiness from him, however limited, but punishment. That's why he also began to suffer. Their life became a torture chamber. Each was the tormentor and victim of the other. This went on for three years. Then, one day, her husband had had enough. He asked for a divorce. She came to New York. To rest, to find herself again, to see me.

"You'll help me, won't you?"

"Of course," I answered.

All she asked was to stay beside me. Her life was empty. She was hoping to climb up again. To start living again, intensely, as before. To be moved to tears by a transparent dusk, to laugh aloud in the theatre, to protest against ugliness. All she wanted was to become once more what she had been.

I should have refused. I know. Kathleen—the one I had known—deserved more than my consent. To help her was to insult her, to humiliate her. But I accepted. She was unhappy and I was too weak, perhaps too cowardly, to say no to a woman who was hitting her head against a wall, even if this woman was Kathleen.

"Of course," I repeated. "I'll help you."

She moved forward, as if to throw herself into my arms, but held herself back. We looked at each other in silence for a long time.

Who is Sarah?"

I was speechless. Sitting on the edge of the bed, Kathleen watched me with a smile. Her eyes didn't accuse me, they just looked curious.

"You spoke her name the first day, when you were in a coma. You said nothing else. Sarah."

"Why did you wait until today to ask me?"

I had been in the hospital for four weeks.

"I was too curious. I wanted to prove to myself that I was able to wait."

"That's all I said?"

"That's all."

"You're sure?"

"I'm sure. The first few days I was never very far away. You said nothing else. You didn't unclench your teeth. But once or twice you spoke that name: Sarah."

An old suffering stirred somewhere. I didn't know exactly where.

"Sarah," I said distractedly.

Kathleen kept smiling. Her eyes showed no worry. But anguish was there, around her swollen mouth, waiting for a chance to invade her whole face, her whole being.

"Who is she?" she asked again.

"Sarah was my mother's name," I said.

The smile disappeared. Naked suffering was now mixed with the anguish. Kathleen was hardly breathing.

I told her: as a child I lived with the perpetual fear of forgetting my mother's name after I died. In school my teacher had told me: three days after your funeral, an angel will come and knock three times on your grave. He'll ask you your name. You will answer. "I am Eliezer, the son of Sarah." Woe if you forget! A dead soul, you will remain buried for all eternity. You won't be able to come before the tribunal to know if your place is in paradise or in hell with those who waited too long before repenting. You will be condemned to wander in the sphere of chaos where nothing exists, neither punishment nor pain, neither justice nor injustice, neither past nor future, neither hope nor despair. It is a serious thing to forget your mother's name. It is like forgetting your own origin. Remember: "Eliezer, the son of Sarah, the son of Sarah, Sarah, Sarah. . . ."

"Sarah was my mother's name," I said. "I didn't forget it."

Kathleen's body twisted as if she were tied to an invisible stake. She was afraid not to suffer enough. But then she shouldn't have used the state I was in to interpret my silences, to gather names that I had kept secret. My mother's name was Sarah. I never talked about it. I loved her but I had never told her. I loved her with such violence that I had to seem hard toward her so she wouldn't

280

guess. Yes. She is dead. She went to heaven at the side of my grandmother.

"Sarah," Kathleen said in a broken voice. "I like that name. It sounds like Biblical times."

"My mother's name was Sarah," I said again. "She is dead."

Kathleen's face was twisted with pain. She looked like a sorceress who has lost her true face from having put on too many masks. A great fire burned around her. Suddenly she cried out and began to sob. My mother, I had never seen my mother cry.

Sarah.

It was also the name of a girl with blue eyes and golden hair whom I had met in Paris long before I knew Kathleen.

I was reading a newspaper in front of a café near Montparnasse. She was drinking lemonade at the table next to mine. She was trying to attract my attention and this made me blush. She noticed it and smiled.

Embarrassed, I didn't know what attitude to adopt. Where to hide my head, my hands, where to hide my confusion. Finally, unable to stand it any more, I spoke to her.

"You know me?"

"No," she said shaking her head.

"Do I know you?"

"I don't think so," she said teasingly.

I couldn't help stuttering, "Then . . . why? Why . . . why are you staring at me like that?"

She seemed about to shudder, to laugh, or to sigh. "Just like that," she answered.

While cursing my own bashfulness, I buried myself in the newspaper, trying to forget the blond girl and to avoid her straightforward, innocent eyes and the sadness of her smile. The print danced before my eyes. The words didn't stay still long enough for me to catch them. I was going to call the waiter in order to pay and leave, when the girl with the strange smile began to talk to me.

"You're waiting for someone?"

"No," I said.

"I'm not either."

And as she said this, she came over to my table with her glass of lemonade.

"You're alone?" she asked me.

"No," I said blushing still more.

"You don't feel alone?"

"Not at all."

"Really?"

She did not seem to believe me. And her smile was there, like a third presence, somewhere on her face. In her eyes? No. Her eyes were cold, frightened. On her lips? Not there either. They were sensuous, bitter, tired. Where was it then? There, between her forehead and her chin, but I couldn't tell exactly where.

"Really?" she repeated. "You don't feel alone?"

"No."

"How do you manage?"

I was losing face.

"I don't know," I blurted out. "I don't know. I read a lot."

She took a sip, raised her head, and began to laugh at me

openly. I had noticed that in the meantime her real smile had vanished. Maybe she had swallowed it.

"Do you want to make love?" she asked in the same tone of voice.

"Now?" I exclaimed with surprise. "In the afternoon?"

In my mind, love-making was a thing of the night. To make love during the day seemed to me like getting undressed in the middle of the street.

"Right away," she answered. "Do you want to?"

"No," I said quickly.

"Why not?"

"I . . . I don't have any money."

She stared at me a minute with the mocking and forgiving attitude of someone who knows and forgives all.

"That doesn't matter," she said after a pause. "You'll pay me some other time."

I was ashamed. I was afraid. I was young, without any experience. I was afraid not to know what to do. And mostly, I was afraid of afterwards: I would never be the same any more.

"Well? You want to?"

A lock of hair was falling on her forehead. Again the smile appeared. Now I no longer knew if it was the first smile or the one it replaced, the true or the false one.

"Yes," I answered. "I want to."

I thought: this girl has, without knowing it, perhaps the most elusive smile I have ever seen. I might be able to capture it while making love to her.

"Call the waiter," she said.

I called him. I paid for my coffee; she paid for her lemonade. We got up and began to walk. I felt awkward, ill at ease. Smaller than I, she walked on my right; her head only came a little above my shoulders. I didn't dare look at her.

She lived not far away. The hotel doorman seemed to be sleeping. The girl took her key and told me it was on the third floor. I followed her. From the back she looked less young.

When we got to the third floor, we turned right and went into her room. She told me to close the door. I closed it softly; I didn't want it to make any noise.

"Not like that," the girl said. "Lock it."

I turned the key. I was filled with a new kind of anxiety. I didn't talk as I was sure my voice would tremble. Alone with a woman. Alone in a hotel room with a woman. With a prostitute. And soon we would make love. For I was sure of it: she was a prostitute. Otherwise she would have acted differently.

I was alone with her in her neat and clean room, most of which was painted gray. My first woman would be a prostitute. A prostitute whose strange smile was the smile of a saint.

She had drawn the shades, taken off her shoes, and was waiting. Standing near the bed, she was waiting. I felt very stupid, not knowing what to do. Get undressed? Just like that? I thought: first I should kiss her. In the movies the man always kisses the woman before making love to her. I stepped toward her, looked at her intensely, then harshly pulled her toward me and kissed her on the mouth for a long time. Instinctively I had closed my eyes. When I opened them I saw hers, and in them an animal-like terror. This made me draw back a step.

"What's the matter?" I asked her, my heart beating.

"Nothing," she answered; her voice came from another world. "Nothing. Come. Let's make love."

All of a sudden she brought her hand to her mouth. Her face became white as if all life had left it.

"What's the matter with you? Say something!"

She didn't answer. Her hand on her mouth, she was looking through me as if I were transparent. Her eyes were dry, like a blind child's.

"Have I offended you?" I asked.

She didn't hear me.

"Do you want me to leave you?"

She was far away, taking refuge where no stranger was allowed. I could only be present outside. I understood that by kissing her I had set in motion an unknown mechanism.

"Say something," I begged her.

My plea didn't reach her. She looked mad, possessed. Maybe I had only lived for this meeting, I thought. For this meeting with a prostitute who preserved within her a trace of innocence, like madmen who in the midst of their madness hold on to a trace of lucidity.

This lasted a few minutes. Then she seemed to wake up; her hand fell from her face. A tired and infinitely sad smile lit up her features.

"You must forgive me," she said softly. "I spoiled everything. Excuse me. It was stupid of me."

She began to undress, but I no longer felt like making love to her. Now I only wanted to understand.

"Wait," I told her. "Let's talk a little."

"You no longer want to make love?" she asked worried.

"Later," I reassured her. "First let's talk a little."

"What would you like to talk about?"

"About you."

"What do you want to know?"

Mechanically she unhooked her skirt.

"Who are you?"

"A girl. A girl like many others."

"No," I protested. "You're not like the others."

She let her skirt fall to the floor. Now she was unbuttoning her blouse.

"How do you know?" she asked.

"Intuition probably," I answered awkwardly.

Now she was only wearing a black bra and pants. Slowly she stretched out on the bed. I sat down next to her.

"Who are you?" I asked again.

"I told you. A girl, a girl like many others."

Unconsciously I was stroking her hair.

"What is your name?"

"It doesn't matter."

"What is your name?"

"Sarah."

A familiar sadness took hold of me.

"Sarah," I said. "A beautiful name."

"I don't like it."

"Why not?"

"Sometimes it frightens me."

"I like it," I said. "It was my mother's name."

"Where is she?"

I was still stroking her hair. My heart felt heavy. Should I tell her? I couldn't pronounce such simple, such very simple words: "My mother is dead."

"My mother is dead," I said finally.

"Mine too."

Silence. I was thinking of my mother. If she saw me now . . . She would ask me:

Who is this girl?

My wife, I would say.

And what is her name?

Sarah, Mother.

Sarah?

Yes, Mother. Sarah.

Have you gone mad? Have you forgotten that I too am called Sarah?

No, Mother. I haven't forgotten.

Then, have you forgotten that a man has no right to marry a woman who bears his own mother's name? Have you forgotten that this brings bad luck? That a mother dies from this?

No, Mother. I haven't forgotten. But you can no longer die. You are already dead.

That's true. . . . I am dead. . . .

"Do you really want to know?"

Sarah's voice brought me back to earth. She was looking straight ahead, as if she were looking through walls, years, and memories, in order to reach the source, where the sky touches the earth, where life calls for love. Sarah put this question to me as if I, by myself, had created the universe.

"You really want to know who I am?"

Her voice had become hard, pitiless.

"Of course," I answered, hiding my fear.

"In that case . . ."

There are times when I curse myself. I shouldn't have listened. I should have fled. To listen to a story under such circumstances is to play a part in it, to take sides, to say yes or no, to move one way or the other. From then on there is a before and an after. And even to forget becomes a cowardly acceptance.

I should have run away. Or put my hands over my ears. Or thought about something else. I should have screamed, or sung, or kissed her, kissed her on the mouth so she would have stopped talking. Made love to her. Told her that I loved her. Anything, just so she would have stopped talking. So she would have stopped talking.

I did nothing. I listened. Attentively. I was sitting on the edge of the bed, next to her half-undressed body, listening to her story. My clenched fingers were like a vise around my throat.

Now, every time I think of her, I curse myself, as I curse those who do not think of her, who did not think of her at the time of her undoing. Her inscrutable face was like a sick child's. She looked straight ahead without fear, piercing the walls as if she could see the chaos that preceded the creation of the world.

I think of her and I curse myself, as I curse history which has made us what we are: a source of malediction. History which deserves death, destruction. Whoever listens to Sarah and doesn't change, whoever enters Sarah's world and doesn't invent new gods and new religions, deserves death and destruction. Sarah alone had the right to decide what is good and what is evil, the right to differentiate what is true from what usurps the appearance of truth.

And I was sitting next to her half-naked body, and listening. Each word tightened the vise. I was going to strangle myself.

I should have left. Fast. Fast. I should have fled when she opened her mouth, as soon as I noticed the first sign.

I stayed. Something was holding me back. I wanted to suffer with her. To suffer the way she was suffering. I also felt that she was going to humiliate herself. Maybe that prevented me from leaving. I wanted to take part in her humiliation. I was hoping her humiliation would fall back on me too.

She spoke and I listened in silence. Sometimes I felt like screaming like an animal.

Sarah spoke in an even, monotonous voice, stopping only to let silence comment upon an image that words would have been too weak to evoke. Her story opened a secret floodgate within me.

I knew there had been Sarahs in the concentration camps. I had never met any, but I had heard of them. I didn't know their faces were those of sick children. I had no idea that some day I would kiss one of them on the mouth.

Twelve years old. She was twelve years old when, separated from her parents, she had been sent to a special barracks for the camp officers' pleasure. Her life had been spared because there are German officers who like little girls her age. Who like to make love to little girls her age.

Suddenly she turned her darkened eyes toward me: God was still in them. The God of chaos and impotence. The God who tortures twelve-year-old children.

"Did you ever sleep with a twelve-year-old woman?" she asked me.

Her voice was calm, composed, naked. I tried not to scream. I couldn't justify myself. It would have been too easy.

"But you have felt like it, haven't you?" she asked when she noticed I kept quiet. "All men feel like it."

My eyes burned from her stare. I was afraid to scream. I couldn't justify myself. Not to her. Especially not to her. She deserved better.

"Tell me," she went on in a somewhat softer voice. "Is that why you're not making love to me? Because I'm no longer twelve?"

The God of impotence made her eyes flame. Mine too. I thought: I am going to die. Whoever sees God must die. It is written in the Bible. I had never quite understood that: why should God be allied with death? Why should He want to kill a man who succeeded in seeing Him? Now, everything became clear. God was ashamed. God likes to sleep with twelve-year-old girls. And He doesn't want us to know. Whoever sees it or guesses it must die so as not to divulge the secret. Death is only the guard who protects God, the doorkeeper of the immense brothel that we call the universe. I am going to die, I thought. And my fingers, clenched around my throat, kept pressing harder and harder, against my will.

Sarah decided to let me breathe a moment. She again looked straight ahead and went on talking as if I didn't exist or as if I alone existed, everywhere and always.

"He was drunk. A drunken pig. He was laughing. He stank of obscenity. Especially his laugh. 'It's my birthday today,' he said. 'I want a present. A special present!' He examined me from head to toe and snickered, 'You'll be my birthday present.' I didn't understand the meaning of his words. I was twelve. At that age you don't know yet that girls can be offered as birthday presents. . . . I wasn't alone in the barracks. A dozen women stood around us. Bertha was white. So were the others. White. Like corpses. He alone, the drunkard, was red. His hands too, like the butcher's. And his laughter went from his mouth to his eyes. 'You'll be my birthday present, you!' he said. Bertha was biting her lips. She was my friend."

She was a beautiful and sad-looking woman. She carried her head like an Oriental princess. The night she arrived in the camp, she had lost her daughter who was about Sarah's age.

"She's too young, sir," she interceded. "She's only a child."

"If she's here it means she is no longer a child," he had

answered, winking. "Otherwise, she would be you know where. Up there. . . ."

His fat finger pointed to the ceiling.

"Bertha was my friend," Sarah said. "She didn't give up. She fought to the end. To save me she was ready to take my place. The others too for that matter."

Sarah was silent for a moment.

In the half-darkness of the barracks, Bertha tried to divert him. Without saying a word, she began to undress. The other women—brunettes, blondes, redheads—without consulting one another did the same. In a flash they were all naked like silent, motionless statues. Sarah thought it was a bad dream, a sick nightmare. Or that she had gone mad. An inhuman silence had come over the barracks, contrasting vividly with the tenseness on the women's faces. Outside, the sun was moving behind the horizon spilling its rusty blood over the moving shadows. It seemed that if the scene went on something terrible would happen at any moment; something that would shatter the universe, change the course of time, unmask destiny, and allow man to see at last what awaits him beyond truth, beyond death.

That's when the drunkard caught the child by the arm and brutally pulled her outside the barracks. It was already dark. A reddish glow rose from the earth filling the sky with the deep color of blood.

"The officer was intelligent," Sarah said. "Among all the naked women who were in the barracks he had chosen me, although I was dressed. Because I was twelve. Men like to make love to women who are twelve."

Again she turned her head toward me and the vise tightened around my throat with renewed vigor.

"You too," she said. "If I were twelve, you would have made love to me."

I couldn't listen to her any more. I had reached the end of my strength, and I thought: one more word and I'll die. I'll die here, on this bed, where men come to sleep with a golden-haired girl and in fact don't know that they are making love to a twelve-year-old child.

For a brief moment I had the idea that perhaps I should take her right away. Abruptly. Without gestures, without useless words. To show her that one could fall still lower. That mud is everywhere and has no bottom. I got up slowly, took her hand, and kissed it gently. I wanted her to see. I wanted her to realize that I wanted her. That I desired her. That I too did not transcend the limits of my body. I placed my lips on her cold hand.

"That's all?" she asked me. "You don't want to do anything else?"

She laughed. She was trying to laugh like the other one, like the drunkard in the barracks. But she didn't succeed. She wasn't drunk. There was nothing obscene in her hands, or in her voice. She was as pure as one could be.

"I do," I answered shaken.

Bending over her, I kissed her on the mouth again. She didn't return my kiss. My lips were sealed on hers, my tongue was looking for hers. She remained passive, absent.

I straightened up and after a short hesitation I said very slowly, "I'll tell you what you are. . . ."

She tried to talk but I didn't give her a chance.

". . . You are a saint. A saint: that's what you are."

A flash of surprise crossed her sick and childlike face. Her eyes looked clearer. More cruel.

"You are mad!" she said violently. "You are really mad!"

And, letting loose, she laughed again. She imitated someone laughing. But her eyes didn't laugh. Nor did her mouth.

"Me, a saint!" she said. "You are out of your mind. Didn't I tell you how old I was when I had my first man? How old I was when I embarked on my career?"

She stressed the word "career," looking defiant as she asked her question.

"Yes," I said. "You did tell me. Twelve. You were twelve."

She was laughing more and more. It's the drunkard, I thought. He hasn't left her yet.

"And in your opinion," she went on, "a woman who starts her career at twelve is a saint? Right?"

"Right," I said. "A saint."

I thought: let her cry. Let her scream. Let her insult me. Anything would be better than this laugh which belongs to someone else, to a body without a soul, to a head without eyes. Anything would be better than this foreign and harmful laugh which turns her into a possessed soul.

"You're mad," Sarah said in a voice that tried to be gay and joyous. "The drunkard was only the first. After him came the others. All the others. I became the 'special present' of the barracks. The 'special present' that they all wanted to give themselves. I was more popular than all the other women combined. All the men loved me: the happy and the unhappy, the good and the bad, the old and the young, the gay and the taciturn. The timid and the depraved, the wolves and the pigs, the intellectuals and the butchers, all of them, do you hear? All came to me. And you think I am a saint. You are out of your mind, you poor man."

And she laughed even more. But the laugh had nothing to do with her. Her whole being brought to mind an ageless, nameless suffering. Her laugh sounded dry, inhuman: it wasn't hers, but God's or the drunkard's.

"You poor man!" she said. "I pity you! I would like to do something for you. Tell me, when is your birthday? I'll have a present for you. A special present. . . ."

And her laugh settled in me. Someday I too will be possessed. Sarah, in her black underwear, one leg slightly bent, suddenly stopped laughing. I felt the final blow was coming. Instinctively I started moving back toward the door. That's where I heard her scream.

"You're mad!"

"Be quiet! For heaven's sake, be quiet!" I shouted.

I knew she would talk, that she would tell me something terrible, abominable, words that I would always hear whenever I tried to find happiness in a woman's body.

"Be still!" I begged.

"A saint, me?" she screamed like a madwoman. "I want you to know this and remember it: sometimes I felt pleasure with them. . . . I hated myself afterwards and even while it lasted, but my body sometimes loved them. . . . And my body is me. . . . Me, a saint? Do you know what I really am? I was telling you. I am——"

I had reached the limit. I couldn't take it any more. I was going to throw up. Quickly I unlocked the door and opened it as fast as I could. I had to get out of that house at once. Second floor. First floor. Doorman. The street. Run. Fast. Run.

Only later, while running, did I notice that my fingers were still clutching my throat.

"Sarah," I said in a choked voice.

"Yes," Kathleen said. "It's your mother's name. I know."

"It's the name of a saint."

I spent days and weeks looking for Sarah. I went back to the café where I had met her. I asked in every hotel in the neighborhood. To no avail. Nobody seemed to have seen or known the golden-haired girl who bore my mother's name. The waiter who had served us did not remember. The hotel doormen all said they had never seen her. And yet I didn't give up hope. Sometimes I think I'm still looking for her. I would like to meet her, if only once. To do what I should have done that afternoon: make love to her.

"Your mother is dead," Kathleen said.

She wanted to hurt herself. Suffer openly. So I would see. So I would know that she was suffering with me, that we were bound together by suffering. She was able to hurt me just to show me that she too was unhappy.

"I know she is dead," I said. "But sometimes I refuse to admit it. Sometimes I think that mothers can't die."

It's true. I can't believe my mother is dead. Perhaps because I didn't see her dead. I saw her walking away with hundreds of people who were swallowed up by the night. If she had told me, "Good-bye, my son. I'm going to die," perhaps I could believe it more now.

Father is dead. I know that. I saw him pass away. I don't look for him among the people in the street. But sometimes I look for my mother. She's not dead. Not really. Here and there I see one of her features in some woman on the subway, on a bus, in a café. And these women, I love and hate them at the same time.

Kathleen. Tears were coming to her eyes. My mother didn't cry. At least not when other people were there. She only offered her tears to God.

Kathleen looked a little like my mother; she had her high forehead, and her chin had the same pure lines. But Kathleen wasn't dead. And she was crying.

In the beginning she didn't cry. We were on the same level. We dealt with each other like equals. We were free. Each one free from himself and free from the other. When I didn't feel like keeping a date, I didn't. She did the same. And neither of us was angry or even hurt. When I didn't talk for a whole night, she didn't try to make me explain. The familiar question asked by lovers, "What are you thinking about?" didn't enter our conversations. Hardness had become our religion. Nothing was said that wasn't essential. We tried to convince each other that we could live, hope, and despair, alone. Each kiss could have been the last. At any moment the temple could have collapsed. The future didn't exist since it was useless. At night we made love silently, almost like our own witnesses. A stranger watching us in the street could easily have taken us for enemies. Rightly so, perhaps. True enemies aren't always the ones who hate each other.

I shouldn't have said I'd see her again in New York. I should have told her that it wasn't worthy of us to reopen the parentheses: air moving into it would make everything rot.

She had changed. Kathleen was no longer free. She only imitated the other. Her marriage had destroyed her inside. She had lost all interest in life. The days were all alike. People all said the same thing. Instead of listening to them, you could follow TV programs. Her husband's friends and colleagues bored her. Their wives got on her nerves; she saw herself sentenced to become one of them. Very soon.

In New York, we met every day. She came to my place. I went to her place. We went out a lot, to the theatre, to concerts. We discussed literature, music, poetry. I tried to be nice. I was patient, kind, understanding. I treated her as if she were ill. The fight had been over for a long time. Now I was trying to help her get back on her feet.

We seldom evoked the past and only with caution, so as not to tarnish it. Sometimes as we listened to a passage from Bach, or noticed the shape of a cloud playing with the sun, we were seized by the same emotion. She would touch my hand and ask me, "Do you remember?"

And I would answer, "Yes, Kathleen. Of course. I remember."

Before, she would never have felt like proving to me that she remembered. On the contrary, we both would have felt ashamed to have fallen prey to the past, to an emotion from the past. I would have turned my head away. I would have talked about something else. Now we no longer struggled.

Then one day, she confessed. . . .

We were drinking coffee in her room. On the radio Isaac Stern was playing the Beethoven violin concerto. We had heard it in Paris at the Salle Pleyel. I remembered that she had taken my hand and that I had pushed her away brusquely. If she would take my hand now, I thought, I wouldn't pull it away.

"Look at me," Kathleen said.

I looked at her. She had a tormented smile. She had the face of a woman who has been abandoned and is conscious of it. She was tapping on the cup with her long fingers.

"Yes," I told her. "I remember."

She put down the cup, got up, and knelt before me. There, without lowering her head, without blushing, in a firm voice—almost as she used to be—she told me, "I think I love you."

She was going to continue but I interrupted her. "Be quiet!" I told her harshly.

I didn't want to hear her say: I have loved you since the first time we met.

My harshness was not reflected on her face. But her smile had become a little deeper, a little more sickly.

"It isn't my fault," she apologized. "I tried. I struggled."

Beethoven, the Salle Pleyel, Stern, love. Love that makes everything complicated. While hate simplifies everything. Hatred puts accents on things and beings, and on what separates them. Love erases accents. I thought: here's another minute that will punctuate my existence.

"Are you sad?" Kathleen asked, distressed.

"No."

Poor Kathleen! She was no longer trying to imitate her other self. Her face was covered with anguish. Her eyes had become strangely small.

"You're going to leave me?"

Love and despair. They go together. One contains some trace of the other. I thought: she must have suffered a lot.

It is my turn to try to repair the damage. I have to treat her as if she were ill. I know. To do this is to insult her other self. But the other self doesn't exist. No longer exists. And this one is broken.

"I'm not going to leave you," I answered in the voice of a faithful friend.

A tear slid down her cheek. "You pity me," Kathleen said.

"I don't pity you," I said eagerly.

I was lying. I would have to lie. A lot. She was ill. It is all right to lie to sick people. To her other self I would not have lied.

During the following weeks and months, Kathleen wasted away.

Having nothing to do—she neither felt like working nor needed to work—she spent her days in her room, at her window, or in front of a mirror, alone and unhappy, conscious of her solitude, of her unhappiness.

As before, we went on seeing each other every evening. Dinners, shows, concerts. Once I tried to reason with her: she was wrong to feel sorry for herself. It wasn't worthy of her or of me. She should find some work, be busy, fill up her days. She had to find an aim in life.

"An aim," she said, shrugging her shoulders. "An aim. What aim? The Salvation Army? Be a patron of starving artists? Go to India to help the lepers? An aim? Where would I look for it?"

That's when I had an idea. I told her that I loved her too.

She refused to believe it. She demanded proof. I proved it to her. All the incidents that in the past had shown that there was no love between us, now, all of a sudden, showed the contrary. "Why did you pull away your hand at the concert?" "I didn't want to betray myself." "Why didn't you ever tell me that you loved me?" "Because I loved you." "Why did you always look me right in the eyes?" "To discover my love mirrored in them."

For weeks she was on her guard. And so was I. I considered myself her nurse. Sometimes I toyed with the thought that perhaps she too was treating me like a sick person. Someday we would take off our masks. One of us would say: I was only playing. So was I, the other would answer. And there would be a bitter taste in our mouths. But then it was a pity this was only a game.

However, she wasn't playing. If you play you do not suffer. The part of us which observes us, which watches us play, does not suffer. Kathleen had suffered. In spite of my arguments, she wasn't convinced. She often cried while I was away. When we were together her good spirits were too forced.

I was no longer free. My freedom would have humiliated Kathleen, who had been without freedom for so long. I had invented an attitude toward her which I could no longer get rid of.

If only this had done some good! If only it had helped Kathleen! But she was still unhappy and her laugh was still without sincerity.

Kathleen was getting worse and worse. She began to drink. She was letting herself go.

I discussed this with her. "You have no right to act this way."

"Why not?" she would say, her eyes wide open with an expression of false innocence.

"Because I love you. Your life matters to me, Kathleen."

"Come on! You don't love me. You just say so. If it were true you wouldn't say it."

"I'm saying it because it is true."

"You're saying it out of pity. You don't need me. I don't make you feel good or happy."

These arguments had none of the results I hoped for. On the contrary, after each one, Kathleen let herself go still further.

Then one evening—the day before the accident—she explained to me at last why she couldn't believe in the integrity of my love.

"You claim you love me but you keep suffering. You say you love me in the present but you're still living in the past. You tell me you love me but you refuse to forget. At night you have bad dreams. Sometimes you moan in your sleep. The truth is that I am nothing to you. I don't count. What counts is the past. Not ours: yours. I try to make you happy: an image strikes your memory and it is all over. You are no longer there. The image is stronger than I. You think I don't know? You think your silence is capable of hiding the hell you carry within you? Maybe you also think that it is easy to live beside someone who suffers and who won't accept any help?"

She wasn't crying. That night she hadn't been drinking. We were in bed. Her head was resting on my outstretched arm. A warm wind was blowing through the open windows. We had just gone to bed. This was one of our rituals: never to make love right away; to talk first.

I could feel how heavy my heart had become, as if it were unable to contain itself. She had guessed correctly. You cannot hide suffering and remorse for long. They come out. It was true: I was living in the past. Grandmother, with her black shawl on her head, wasn't giving me up.

"It isn't my fault," I answered.

I explained to her: a man who tells a woman he thinks

he loves, "I love you and shall love you forever; may I die if I stop loving you," believes it. And yet one day he sounds his heart and finds it empty. And he stays alive. With us—those who have known the time of death—it's different. There, we said we would never forget. It still holds true. We cannot forget. The images are there in front of our eyes. Even if our eyes were no longer there, the images would remain. I think if I were able to forget I would hate myself. Our stay there planted time bombs within us. From time to time one of them explodes. And then we are nothing but suffering, shame, and guilt. We feel ashamed and guilty to be alive, to eat as much bread as we want, to wear good, warm socks in the winter. One of these bombs, Kathleen, will undoubtedly bring about madness. It's inevitable. Anyone who has been there has brought back some of humanity's madness. One day or another, it will come to the surface.

Kathleen was sober and lucid that evening. I had the impression her old self had come to visit her. But I knew that it would leave again. That the visit would be short and that only the self that was trying to imitate it would remain. And someday even that one would stop searching. Then the divorce would be final.

That night I understood that sooner or later I would have to leave Kathleen. To stay with her had become meaningless.

I told myself: suffering pulls us farther away from other human beings. It builds a wall made of cries and contempt to separate us. Men cast aside the one who has known pure suffering, if they cannot make a god out of him; the one who tells them: I suffered not because I was God, nor because I was a saint trying to imitate Him, but only because I am a man, a man like you, with your weaknesses, your cowardice, your sins, your rebellions, and your ridiculous ambitions; such a man frightens men, because he makes them feel ashamed. They pull away from him as if he were guilty. As if he were usurping God's place to illuminate the great vacuum that we find at the end of all adventures.

Actually it is good that this should be so. A man who has suffered more than others, and differently, should live apart. Alone. Outside of any organized existence. He poisons the air. He makes it unfit for breathing. He takes away from joy its spontaneity and its justification. He kills hope and the will to live. He is the incarnation of time that negates present and future, only recognizing the harsh law of memory. He suffers and his contagious suffering calls forth echoes around him.

One day or another I shall have to leave Kathleen, I decided. It will be better for her. If I could forget, I would stay. I cannot. There are times when man has no right to suffer.

"I suggest an agreement," Kathleen said. "I'll let you help me, provided you let me help you. All right?"

Poor Kathleen! I thought. It's too late. To change, we would have to change the past. But the past is beyond our power. Its structure is solid, immutable. The past is Grandmother's shawl, as black as the cloud above the cemetery. Forget the cloud? The black cloud which is Grandmother, her son, my mother. What a stupid time we live in! Everything is upside down. The cemeteries are up above, hanging from the sky, instead of being dug in the moist earth. We are lying in bed, my naked body against your naked body, and we are thinking about black clouds, about floating cemeteries, about the snickering of death and fate which are one and the same. You speak of happiness, Kathleen, as if happiness were possible. It isn't even a dream. It too is dead. It too is up above. Everything has taken refuge above. And what emptiness here below! Real life is there. Here, we have nothing. Nothing, Kathleen. Here, we have an arid desert. A desert without even a mirage. It's a station where the child left on the platform sees his parents carried off by the train. And there is only black smoke where they stood. They are the smoke. Happiness? Happiness for the child would be for the train to move backward. But you know how trains are, they always go forward. Only the smoke moves backward. Yes, ours is a horrible station! Men like me who are in it should stay there alone, Kathleen. Not let the suffering in us come in contact with other men. We must not give them the sour taste, the smoke-cloud taste, that we have in our mouth. We must not, Kathleen. You say "love." And you don't know that love too has taken the train which went straight to heaven. Now everything has been transferred there. Love, happiness, truth, purity, children with happy smiles, women with mysterious eyes, old people who walk slowly, and little orphans whose prayers are filled with anguish. That's the true exodus. The exodus from one world to the other. Ancient peoples had a limited imagination. Our dead take with them to the hereafter not only clothes and food, but also the future of their descendants. Nothing remains below. And you speak of love, Kathleen? And you speak of happiness? Others speak of justice, universal or not, of freedom, of brotherhood, of progress. They don't know that the planet is drained and that an enormous train has carried everything off to heaven.

"So, you accept?" Kathleen asked.

"I accept what?" I wondered.

"The agreement I suggested."

"Of course," I answered absent-mindedly. "I accept."

"And you'll let me make you happy?"

"I'll let you make me happy."

"And you promise to forget the past?"

"I promise to forget the past."

"And you'll think only about our love?"

"Yes."

She had gone through her questionnaire. She stopped to catch her breath and asked in a different tone of voice, "Where were you before?"

"At the station," I said.

"I don't understand."

"At the station," I said. "I was at the station. It was very small. The station of a small provincial town. The train had just left. I was left alone on the platform. My parents were in the train. They had forgotten me."

Kathleen didn't say anything.

"At first I was resentful. They shouldn't have left me behind, alone on the platform. But a little later, I suddenly saw a strange thing: the train was leaving the tracks and climbing toward the smoke-gray sky. Stunned, I couldn't even shout out to my parents: What are you doing? Come back! Perhaps if I had shouted, they would have come back."

I was beginning to feel tired. I was perspiring. It was warm in the bed. A car had just screeched to a stop under the window.

"You promised not to think about it any more," Kathleen said in despair.

"Forgive me. I won't think about it any more. In any case, these days trains are an outmoded way to travel. The world has progressed."

"Sure?"

"Sure."

She pressed her body against mine.

"Every time your thoughts take you to the little station, tell me. We'll fight it together?"

"Yes."

"I love you."

The accident occurred the next day.

The ten weeks I spent in a world of plaster had made me richer.

I learned that man lives differently, depending on whether he is in a horizontal or vertical position. The shadows on the walls, on the faces, are not the same.

Three people came to see me every day. Paul Russel came in the morning; Kathleen in the evening; Gyula in the afternoon. He alone had guessed. Gyula was my friend.

A painter, of Hungarian origin, Gyula was a living rock. A giant in every sense of the word. Tall, robust, gray and rebellious hair, mocking and burning eyes; he pushed aside everything around him: altars, ideas, mountains. Everything trembled, vibrated, at his touch, at the sight of him.

In spite of our difference in age, we had a lot in common. Every week we would meet for lunch in a Hungarian restaurant on the East Side. We encouraged each other to stick it out, not to make compromises, not to come to terms with life, not to accept easy victories. Our conversation always sounded like banter. We detested sentimentality. We avoided people who took themselves seriously and particularly those who asked others to do so. We didn't spare each other. Thus our friendship was healthy, simple, and mature.

I was still half dead when he burst into my room, pushed the nurse aside with his shoulder (she was getting ready to give me an injection), and, without asking me anything, announced in a firm and decided voice that he was going to do my portrait.

The nurse, needle in hand, stared at him aghast.

"What are you doing here? Who let you in? Get out immediately!"

Gyula looked at her with compassion, as if her mind were not all there.

"You're beautiful," he told her. "But mad!"

He studied her with interest.

"Beautiful women nowadays aren't mad enough," he went on nostalgically. "But you are. I like you."

The poor nurse—a young student—was on the verge of tears. She was stuttering.

"The injection— Get out— I have to———"

"Later!" Gyula ordered.

And taking her by the arm, he pushed her toward the door. There, she whispered something in his ear.

"Hey! You!" Gyula said after closing the door. "She says you are seriously ill. That you're dying! Aren't you ashamed to be dying?"

"Yes," I answered weakly. "I'm ashamed."

Gyula walked about to familiarize himself with the view, the walls, the smell of the room. Then he stopped near the bed and challenged me.

"Don't die before I've finished your portrait, do you

309

hear? Afterwards, I don't give a darn! But not before! Understood?"

"You're a monster, Gyula," I told him, moved.

"You didn't know?" he wondered. "Artists are the worst monsters: they live on the lives and deaths of others."

I thought he would ask how the accident had happened. He didn't. And yet, I wanted him to know.

"Do you want me to tell you about it?" I asked him.

"You don't have to," he answered disdainfully. "I don't need your explanations."

There was a circle of fondness around his eyes.

"I want you to know," I said.

"I'll know."

"It's a secret," I said. "No one knows it. I'd like to tell you."

"You don't have to," he answered contemptuously. "I like to discover everything for myself."

I tried to laugh. "I might die before you have a chance."

He was flaming with threatening anger. "Not before I'm through with your portrait, I told you. Afterwards you can die whenever and as often as you like!"

I was proud. Proud of him, of myself, of our friendship. Of the tough laws we had made for it. They protected us against the successes and the certainties of the weak. True exchanges take place where simple words are called for, where we set out to state the problem of the immortality of the soul in shockingly banal sentences.

Gyula turned up every afternoon. The nurses knew they weren't to disturb us when he was there. For them he was an animal whose insults, in Hungarian, would have reddened even the cheeks of a black girl.

While he was sketching, Gyula told me stories. He was an excellent storyteller. His life was filled with innumerable adventures and hallucinatory experiences. He had died of hunger in Paris, handed out fortunes in Hollywood, taught magic and alchemy nearly everywhere. He had known all the great men of contemporary literature and the arts; he liked their weaknesses and forgave them their successes. Gyula too had an obsession: to pit himself against fate, to force it to give human meaning to its cruelty. But of course he only spoke of that mockingly.

One day he came as usual toward the beginning of the afternoon, and, framed by the window, began to work. He was silent. He hadn't even said hello when he came in. He seemed preoccupied. Half an hour, an hour. He suddenly stopped moving, remained motionless, and looked me straight in the eyes, as if he had just torn asunder an invisible veil that covered them. For a few seconds we stared at each other. His thick eyebrows arched as he frowned: he was beginning to understand.

"Do you want me to tell you?" I was upset.

"No," he answered coldly. "I have no use for your stories!"

And again he was absorbed by his work in which he found answers to all questions and questions for all answers.

A week later he told me something that didn't seem to have any relation to the subject we were then discussing. We were speaking of the international situation, the danger of a third world war, the important part that China would soon be playing. Suddenly Gyula changed the subject.

"Incidentally," he said, "have I told you the story of my unsuccessful drowning?"

"No," I answered mockingly. "Where did it happen: in China?"

"Spare me your comments," he said. "You'd do better to listen."

Good old Gyula! I thought. How do you tell a woman that you love her? You probably insult her, and if she doesn't understand that kind of love-talk, you simply stop loving her. Good old Gyula!

One summer he had gone to the French Riviera for his vacation, to get away from the heat. He often went to the seashore. That morning he swam out too far. Suddenly a sharp cramp paralyzed his body. Unable to use either his arms or his legs, he let himself sink.

"I began to drink the salt water of the sea," he said. "There was no fear in me. I knew that I was dying, but I remained calm. A strangely sweet serenity came over me. I thought: at last I'll know what a drowning man thinks about. That was my last thought. I lost consciousness."

He was saved. Someone had seen him sink and rescued him.

While watching the lines his brush drew on the canvas, Gyula went on, smiling imperceptibly.

"When I came to, I looked all around me. I was lying on the sand, in the midst of a group of curious people. A bald old man, a doctor, was leaning over me and taking my pulse. In the first row, a terrified young woman was looking at me. She put on a vague smile for me, but the expression of terror remained. How distressing: a horrified woman who smiles. I thought: I'm alive. I have outwitted death. One more time death didn't get me. Here is the proof: I'm looking at a woman who is looking at me and smiling. The horror on her face is there for death which must still be very near, right behind me. The smile is for me, for me alone. I told myself: I could have been here, in the same spot, and not have seen this woman, who, right now, is more graceful and beautiful than any other. I could have been looked at by a woman who didn't smile. I must consider myself happy, I told myself. I'm alive. Victory over death should give birth to happiness. Happiness to be free. Free to provoke death again. Free to accept freedom or to reject it. This reprieve should give me a feeling of well-being. And yet, I didn't have it. I was searching conscientiously within myself: not a trace of joy to be found. The doctor was examining me, the people gave me mute expressions of sympathy like alms, and the young woman's smile was becoming more open—that's how one smiles at life. In spite of that, I wasn't happy. On the contrary, I was terribly sad and disappointed. Later, this unsuccessful drowning made me sing and dance. But there, on the sand, under the burning, purple sun, under the eyes of this unknown woman, I felt disappointed, disappointed at having come back."

Gyula worked silently for a long time. I think he was painting with his eyes closed. I was wondering if he was still disappointed. And if later on he had seen the young woman again. But I said nothing. Paul Russel came back to my mind. He is wrong, I thought. Life doesn't necessarily want to live. Life is really fascinated only by death. It vibrates only when it comes in contact with death.

"Will you listen to me? Gyula, will you?" I implored.

He jumped up as if I had just forced him to reopen his eyes. There was a little sardonic laugh.

"No, I won't," he said.

"But I'd like you to know."

"To know what?" he asked harshly.

"Everything."

"I don't need your stories in order to know."

Good old Gyula! I thought. What happened to the young

313

woman on the beach? Did you insult her? Did you tell her, "You are a little bitch, a dirty little bitch?" Did she understand that these were words of love?

"Gyula," I asked him, "what happened to the unknown woman?"

"What unknown woman?"

"The one on the beach. The one who smiled at you?"

He was overcome by a loud laugh that must have been hiding a wave of tenderness surging up in him from the distant past.

"Oh, that one?" he said in a voice that tried to sound vulgar. "She was a little bitch, a dirty little bitch!"

I couldn't help smiling. "Did you tell her that?"

"Of course I told her!" He realized I was smiling. "You monster," he shouted at me in disgust. "Let me work. Otherwise I'll beat you up!"

The day before I was supposed to leave the hospital, Gyula came in surrounded by an aura of arrogance. He stood like a victorious general at the foot of my bed, between the river and me, and announced the good news: the portrait was finished.

"And now, you can die," he said.

Gyula placed it on a chair. He hesitated for a second. Then, turning his back to me, he stepped aside. My heart was beating violently. I was there, facing me. My whole past was there, facing me. It was a painting in which black, interspersed with a few red spots, dominated. The sky was a thick black. The sun, a dark gray. My eyes were a beating red, like Soutine's. They belonged to a man who had seen God commit the most unforgivable crime: to kill without a reason.

"You see," Gyula said. "You don't know how to speak; you are yourself only when you are silent."

He quivered slightly, unable to hide his emotion.

"Don't talk," he added. "That's all I'm asking you."

And to hide, he went to the window and looked at the playful waves of the East River moving elegantly toward their date with infinity.

He had guessed. It was enough to look at the painting to realize. The accident had been an accident only in the most limited sense of the word. The cab, I had seen it coming. It had only been a flash, but I had seen it, I could have avoided it.

A silent dialogue now took place between Gyula and me.

"You see? Maybe God is dead, but man is alive. The proof: he is capable of friendship."

"But what about the others? The others, Gyula? Those who died? What about them? Besides me, they have no friends."

"You must forget them. You must chase them from your memory. With a whip if necessary."

"Chase them, Gyula? With a whip, you said? To chase my father with a whip? And Grandmother? Grandmother too, chase her with a whip?"

"Yes, yes, and yes. The dead have no place down here. They must leave us in peace. If they refuse, use a whip."

"And this painting, Gyula? They are there. In the eyes of the portrait. Why did you put them there if you ask me to chase them away?"

"I put them there to assign them a place. So you would know where to hit."

"I can't, Gyula. I can't."

Gyula turned and all of a sudden I saw that he had grown older. His hair had become white, his face thinner, more hollow.

"Suffering is given to the living, not to the dead," he

315

said looking right through me. "It is man's duty to make it cease, not to increase it. One hour of suffering less is already a victory over fate."

Yes, he had grown older. It was now an old man talking to me and handing over to me the ageless knowledge that explains why the earth is still revolving and why man is still looking forward to tomorrow. Without catching his breath, he went on as if he had saved these words for me for a long time.

"If your suffering splashes others, those around you, those for whom you represent a reason to live, then you must kill it, choke it. If the dead are its source, kill them again, as often as you must to cut out their tongues."

A boundless sadness came over me. I had the impression I was losing my friend: he was judging me.

"What if it cannot be done?" I asked him, feeling very dejected. "What should one do? Lie? I prefer lucidity."

He shook his head slowly.

"Lucidity is fate's victory, not man's. It is an act of freedom that carries within itself the negation of freedom. Man must keep moving, searching, weighing, holding out his hand, offering himself, inventing himself."

All of a sudden I had the impression that it was my teacher, Kalman the cabalist, who was talking to me. His voice had the same kind, understanding accent. But Kalman was my teacher, not my friend.

"You should know this," Gyula went on without changing his tone of voice, without even blinking an eye, "you should know that the dead, because they are no longer free, are no longer able to suffer. Only the living can. Kathleen is alive. I am alive. You must think of us. Not of them."

He stopped to fill his pipe, or perhaps he had nothing

else to add. Everything had been said. The pros and the cons. I would choose the living or the dead. Day or night. Him or Kalman.

I looked at the portrait and hidden in its eyes I saw Grandmother with her black shawl. On her emaciated face she wore an expression of peaceful suffering. She was telling me: *Fear nothing. I'll be wherever you are. Never again shall I leave you alone on a station platform. Or alone on a street corner of a foreign town. I'll take you with me. In the train that goes to heaven. And you won't see the earth any more. I'll hide it from you. With my black shawl.*

"You're leaving the hospital tomorrow?" Gyula asked in a voice that sounded normal again.

"Yes, tomorrow."

"Kathleen will take care of you?"

"Yes."

"She loves you."

"I know."

Silence.

"You'll be able to walk?"

"With crutches." I answered. "They took off the cast. But I can't put any weight on my leg. I have to walk with crutches."

"You can lean on Kathleen. She'll be happy if you lean on her. Receiving is a superior form of generosity. Make her happy. A little happiness justifies the effort of a whole life."

Kathleen will be happy, I decided. I'll learn to lie well and she'll be happy. It's absurd: lies can give birth to true happiness. Happiness will, as long as it lasts, seem real. The living like lies, the way they like to acquire friendships. The dead don't like them. Grandmother would not accept being told less than the truth. Next time, I promise you Grandmother, I'll be careful. I won't miss the train again.

I must have been staring at the portrait too intensely because all of a sudden Gyula started gritting his teeth. With an angry, enraged motion, he took a match and put it against the canvas.

"No!" I exclaimed in despair. "Don't do that! Gyula, don't do it! Don't burn Grandmother a second time! Stop, Gyula, stop!"

Gyula, unmoved, didn't react. His face closed and withdrawn, he was holding the canvas with his finger tips, turning it in all directions, and waiting for it to be reduced to ashes. I wanted to throw myself on him, but I was too weak to get out of the bed. I couldn't hold back my tears. I cried a long time after Gyula had closed the door behind him.

He had forgotten to take along the ashes.